GRIDIRON CAPITAL

Gri
Capit

DUKE UNIVERSITY PRESS DURHAM AND LONDON 2022

diron
al

HOW AMERICAN FOOTBALL
BECAME A SAMOAN GAME **LISA UPERESA**

© 2022 DUKE UNIVERSITY PRESS *All rights reserved*
Printed in the United States of America on acid-free paper ∞
Designed by Aimee C. Harrison
Typeset in Minion Pro and Helvetica Neue LT Std
by Westchester Publishing Services

Library of Congress Cataloging-in-Publication Data
Names: Uperesa, Lisa, [date] author.
Title: Gridiron capital : how American football became a Samoan
game / Lisa Uperesa.
Description: Durham : Duke University Press, 2022. | Includes
bibliographical references and index.
Identifiers: LCCN 2021046445 (print) | LCCN 2021046446 (ebook)
ISBN 9781478015468 (hardcover)
ISBN 9781478018094 (paperback)
ISBN 9781478022701 (ebook)
Subjects: LCSH: Football—Social aspects—American Samoa. |
Football—Economic aspects—American Samoa. | Football players—
American Samoa. | BISAC: SOCIAL SCIENCE / Anthropology /
Cultural & Social | SPORTS & RECREATION / Cultural & Social
Aspects
Classification: LCC GV959.54.A46 U647 2022 (print) |
LCC GV959.54.A46 (ebook) | DDC 796.3309961/3—dc23/eng/20220104
LC record available at https://lccn.loc.gov/2021046445
LC ebook record available at https://lccn.loc.gov/2021046446

Cover art: Malik Alatasi Haynes. Photograph by John Hook.

Publication of this book is supported by Duke University Press's Scholars
of Color First Book Fund.

FOR DAD

Contents

Preface ix
Acknowledgments xv

Introduction. Fabled Futures and Gridiron Dreams 1

1 Malaga: Forging New Pathways in Sport and Beyond 23
2 Football, Tautua, and Faʻasāmoa 48
3 Producing the Gridiron Warrior 71
4 Gridiron Capital 103
5 "Faʻamālosi!": Strength, Injury, and Sacrifice 123

Conclusion. Niu Futures 151

Glossary 155
Notes 159
Bibliography 185
Index 211

Preface

In the picture we stand smiling at the camera and bundled in jackets, with me in a yellow beanie cap and scarf and my brother Derek in uniform, shivering in the cold after the game. The stadium lights are still on in the background, and it is long past sunset in autumn on the US East Coast. It was October 2004 and we had just finished watching his school team, St. Francis University (PA), play Stony Brook on Long Island, New York. From the bleachers of the small stadium our small group had cheered for him and the other players from Sāmoa, who gave all they had on the field. Our brief reunion far outshined the incidental outcome of the game. It was my second year of graduate school in New York City, and with no family on the East Coast, I was overjoyed to see one of my siblings there. The picture captures the excitement of our short visit, crossing paths on an island far from the one we called home.

We were both part of the legacy of Samoan migration and mobility in the United States, even if our paths were different. Both wound through the educational institutions and networks that connect the islands with Hawai'i and the continental United States through an elaborate K–12 and college system headed by the US Department of Education and underpinned by longstanding political agreements and structures of US empire. Like many young women, my path stayed firmly on the academic route, but his intersected with the burgeoning football industry that was drawing student-athletes from the islands, thousands of miles away, as part of a growing network of sport migration. In that moment, smiling into the flash of the camera, our only concern was the excitement of reunion, far from family and "the rock." At that point I could not have predicted the path this research would take; this was long before the questions about sport in Sāmoa emerged during research at the National Archives and gave me new direction. The photo, however, captures a snapshot in time in which shifting pathways of movement, infrastructures, and mobilities are woven together, and so is an apt point of departure for unraveling this larger story of Samoan pasts, presents, and futures.

This book is about Samoan involvement in American football—its history, its appeal, its economies, and its social impact. I chose this focus not just because it is a major phenomenon (as the numbers of NFL players and the quotes from US media indicate) or because it is linked to so many aspects of Samoan social, economic, and imaginative life, as well as my own, but because as someone for whom American Sāmoa will always be home, how it is represented matters. It is important that these narratives reflect its complexity: as a multifaceted society with a proud history and distinct culture, as a site of American colonial intervention, as transformed by transnational migration and networks and contending with the pressures of underdevelopment, and as a society in which new forms of labor and new symbolic economies have become linked with local institutions and cultural values. As a critical Pacific scholar trained in anthropology, this also allows me to address the exotic representations of Sāmoa that have been central to the anthropological literature beginning with Margaret Mead but which persist in the sensational media coverage of contemporary football.

Wayfinding and Navigating Research

Ancient and contemporary navigators in Polynesia use their knowledge of the sun, stars, ocean swells, and bird sightings to find their way between and among the islands and across the globe. While navigation implies a concise process of moving from one place to another (such as through detailed measurement, maps, and directions), wayfinding signals a more organic unfolding of one's journey in a way that draws on a variety of conceptions and understandings of space, place, and relationships. It builds embodied knowledge through all the senses, relations, and ongoing experiences. Research is often conceptualized as a process of charting and navigating, from research design to human subject reviews, to interview schedules and/or set surveys, to collation of data and analysis of findings. While this project has drawn on those methodologies, they were insufficient to the task at hand. As a researcher working in and with communities to whom I am connected, I have found my way by trying, and sometimes failing, to locate and navigate my position in different spaces, in place and in relation to others.

Shifting from the larger context of sport and empire to focus on the history and evolution of gridiron football in American Sāmoa as part of an examination of "development" and local transformation in the islands, this project became shaped by my own family history with the sport, the network of contacts accessible to me, its importance in contemporary local public culture, and my study of gender in the Pacific (and elsewhere). Finding my way through this process reinforced the reality that research is always embodied and enmeshed in particular sets of relationships. Football has been part of my family life since before I was born, and no doubt some supported my work in recognition of my extended family's long-standing involvement. I am grateful for the many ways, big and small, that a variety of people supported this work, and especially to all who shared their stories with me.

Over a two-year period (2007–2008), I spent seven months doing focused research ("homework") on the island of Tutuila (K. M. Teaiwa 2005, Uperesa 2010a). During that time I carried out archival research in the Territorial Archives and at the Feleti Barstow Library while living in my family home in the village of Fagatogo; I also attended practices at the local high schools and attended weekly games during the football season. While I was on island I attended and observed three football clinic/camps run by US-based coaches and conducted formal and informal interviews with coaches and player participants at each; I attended meetings of the Samoa Bowl Committee; and I collected basic survey information on recruitment trends for players. As part of the research more broadly, I carried out formal and informal interviews with players (former and current), coaches (local and US college), players' family members, sport administrators and other key stakeholders, matai (those who hold customary family titles), and government officials. In the months preceding and following my trips to Sāmoa I carried out archival and online research as part of my dissertation project, and continued this research as a faculty member at University of Hawai'i (with additional trips in 2012 and 2015, as well as to California in 2014 and local research at camps, combines, games, and related events in Hawai'i). The bulk of the material for this book was brought together over the past decade, but some insights are drawn from my time growing up on the sidelines in Tutuila, attending Samoana High School, and learning from my extended family's ongoing commitment to the game.

I spent my formative years in Tutuila, with a sense of place suffused with a distinctive culture intertwined with the global and visions of the modern. In those days, it was seen largely through commodities and media flows like weekly broadcasts of Casey Kasem's Top 40, Friday Night Videos, and nightly episodes of the *Days of Our Lives* soap opera; American fashions sold at Tedi of Sāmoa; and imported food items like Bongos and UFOs snacks from Fiji, Tim Tam cookies and pisupo from Australia and Aotearoa New Zealand, and kimchee and hot and spicy saimin noodles from Korea. Along with the excitement of trips to the airport to pick up incoming relatives bringing large bags of McDonald's and chocolate-covered macadamia nuts from Hawai'i, these things coexisted with village life and riding the 'āiga bus to school every day, buying panikeke from the market, and eating to'ona'i with my family after church on Sundays. At the same time, periodic travel took us to Hawai'i, the West Coast, the Pacific Northwest, and Big Sky country to visit family, close relations, and my father's former players who had gone off island for school and football. The early experience of living in Tutuila shaped my sense of the island as a highly localized place that was also dynamic, complex, and multiply situated in currents of international movement. This book aims to capture some of the complexities of contemporary social life in Sāmoa, and the historical experience that mixes the disjunctures of modernity and transnational flows with the "indigenous *longue dureé*" (Clifford 2001, 482).

The terms "Indigenous" and "Native" have been reclaimed by scholars as part of a worldwide movement for Indigenous rights against the dispossession of settler colonialism and empire. They index a prior claim to landed area and resources; serve as a historical, political, and ethical analytic; and reference political identities connected to sovereignty activism. In the Pacific, they have gained the most traction in settler colonial nations with ongoing and historical sovereignty struggles (Hawai'i, Australia, Fiji, Papua New Guinea, Aotearoa New Zealand) and less so in other places like Sāmoa and Tonga where settler colonialism did not take hold. However, the Indigenous or Native Pacific also connects through the concepts of tangata whenua, kānaka maoli, and tagata o le moana as part of Moana-nui-a-kea, which in the postcolonial moment draw a distinction between that which has its roots in the Pacific and that which has been introduced or imposed, and marks deep histories and genealogies of connection. In this book, I draw on an expanded sense of "Native" as both rooted and mobile, connected to homelands and overseas, as part of transnational communities (Diaz and Kauanui 2001; Tengan 2005). The terms "Indigenous" and "Native" are used interchangeably to refer to practices, ideals, and institutions rooted in long island histories, while remaining attentive to the nuances of articulation and the constructedness of "tradition" and "modernity." These elements have been woven together in complex ways to shape how we have come to understand American football in Sāmoa and Samoans in American football.

Acknowledgments

While I was in living and working in Hawai'i, I heard many Indigenous scholars say that the research finds you, and this was true in the way this project unfolded. This book belongs to the collective: to all who took part and whose stories are featured here. There were unexpected delights in learning about community connections across time and space, and different parts of our family history. Through it all my family was my foundation, my strength, and my accountability. Mom and Dad, Duke, Fele, Bal, Derek, Dart, Eirenee, and Sia have all been part of this over the past fifteen years, whether offering support, sharing knowledge, good food, or cracking jokes. Uncle Misi and Aunty Shauna's "Uperesa Inn" hosted me on many trips and was a favorite destination with 'ono grinds and warm alofa. The Uperesa and Tu'ufuli uncles, aunties, and cousins have kept me grounded and in good spirits. Special appreciation to Corabelle for support during the research, feedback, and for always believing, even when I doubted. Uncle Keith, it was fun being at UH and many of the football events with you.

To the research partners and friends who all have a part in this work, thank you for trusting me with your stories, and for your support. A special fa'afetai lava to Uncle Junior and the Ah You family; Aunty Tile, Tauanu'u, and the Lolotai family; Lealao Mel and Moana Purcell, the Samoa Bowl

Committee, and the June Jones American Samoa Football Academy/Goodwill Mission; Alema Teʻo and the All-Poly Camp; Doris Sullivan and the Pacific Islands Athletic Alliance; George Malauʻulu, Jesse Makani Markham, Kealiʻi Kukahiko, and the AIGA Foundation; and Penny Semaia and the Troy and Theodora Polamalu Foundation. Appreciation to Keith Dahl, John Hook, Robert Pennington, Jeremy Spear, and Frances Pesamino for images featured in the book. Thanks also to the staff of the Feleti Barstow Public Library for image permissions and their good humor and patience with all my requests.

My sincere gratitude to Doug Elisaia, Peter Gurr, Faleomavaega Eni Hunkin, June Jones, Mike Fanoga, Alema Fitisemanu Jr., Don Fuimaono, Ed Imo, Keary Kittles, Ethan Lake, Filo Langkilde, Jeff Lynn, Jason Magalei, Simon Mageo, Tumua Matuʻu, Rich Miano, Keiki Misipeka, Pati Pati Jr., Robert Pennington, Mel Purcell Jr., Jeff Reinebold, Riki Reinhart, Samoa Samoa, Tapumanaia Galu Satele Jr., Floyd Scanlan, Time Sitala, Paul Soliai, Brian and Brandon Smart, Suaese "Pooch" Taʻase, Solomona Tapasa, Leiataua-Lesa Fepuleaʻi Vita L. Tanielu, Jack Thompson, Al Toeaina, Dick Tomey, Daniel Tuiasosopo, Frances Tuitele, Laolagi Savali Vaeao, Brian Vitolio, John Wasko, and Vaeaosia Mike Yandall. Damien, David, Jaselle, Joey, Josh, Juju, Kapua, Tai, Tavita, Ray, Rommel, Wallace, and Vineyard, thanks for talking story with me. Much love also to Sia Figiel, who has been part of this across the Pacific and is now part of the family. If I have missed anyone, misrepresented or offended in any way, or if the academic book format falls short, tulou lava.

While research and writing can often be a solitary experience, amazing people have been part of this journey from the Pacific to the Atlantic and back. From New York, first and foremost much love to my sister comrade Adriana Garriga-López, who's been there since day one, from the late nights in Schermerhorn Hall to the virtual hugs from the other side of the world. Aroha nui to Ata, Ngapera, Tama, Alyssa, Nova, Andrea, Sarah, and the larger Indigenous network in NYC for the warm and beautiful community that enveloped our family. To Rosemary, who shared many holidays and special events with us and support over endless coffees, thank you for making part of our home away from home. There are many others who made our time in New York memorable who are too numerous to name here. Finally, a shout-out to the staff at Panino Sportivo for the caffeine that kept me going most days and Appletree for the late-night saves.

In the 808, much aloha to Jeremy and Janu for hosting me on my way to Sāmoa, and for supporting key portions of this project. I am thankful for faculty writing groups with Hokulani Aikau, Brian Chung, Jonna Eagle,

Vernadette Gonzales, Pensri Ho, Rod Labrador, and Joyce Mariano, and the feedback that shaped chapters of this book. I also want to recognize the group of brilliant and grounded scholars in Charles Lawrence's junior faculty seminar (Malia Akutagawa, David Forman, Jairus Grove, Kapua Sproat, Ipo Wong, and especially Aaron Salā for "keeping us honest"). The beautiful food and moral support in our meetings at Chuck and Mari's home helped me to face some difficult tasks at a critical point in the writing. My deep aloha and appreciation to the Ethnic Studies 'ohana for their example of inspiring commitment; I am especially thankful for Ty Tengan's work and his support of this project. Mahalo also to the staff at Coffee Bean & Tea Leaf for the hot coffee and the sweet pumpkin crunch.

A keynote invitation to Auckland gave me the push to write the last chapter of this book, and ongoing conversations with students, colleagues, and family members have shaped its final form. I appreciate the rich conversations with undergraduate and postgraduate students over the years that have influenced the writing of this story, with particular recognition to Connor Bellett, Joseph Hala'ufia, Caleb Marsters, and Caroline Matamua. It has been a joy to be with the Pasefika 'āiga here at the University of Auckland (#FollowThePac). Special thanks to Toeolesulusulu Damon Salesa, who has seen this from draft to book, and lots of changes in between. It's finally here!

This research was made possible with significant institutional funding and support from the Columbia University Doctoral Faculty Fellowship, Haynes Summer Fellowship, Scheps Travel Grant, Summer Merit Award, and Merit Dissertation Fellowship. The University of Hawai'i-Mānoa's Social Science Faculty Fund supported research assistance and travel. At the University of Auckland, Faculty Research Development Fund support and Arts Faculty research and study leave were granted for the final push that moved this book to publication.

I am thankful for my teachers, academic supervisors, and mentors at Columbia University during my doctoral study, especially Lila Abu-Lughod, Paige West, Audra Simpson, and Sherry Ortner, who were a dream team committee and the source of much inspiration. Special mention also to Vui Toeutu Faaleava, who was the first Samoan academic I ever met during my studies at UC Berkeley, and whose encouragement and example helped set me on this path.

Generous colleagues, collaborators, and mentors have shared different lengths of this journey, including Ping-Ann Addo, Juliann Anesi, Vince Diaz, Christina Kwauk, Tēvita O. Ka'ili, Marcia Leenen-Young, Sailiemanu Lilomaiava-Doktor, Alex Mawyer, Tom Mountjoy, Jan Padios, Kiri Sa'iliata,

Nitasha Sharma, Luafata Simanu-Klutz, Jemaima Tiatia-Seath, Yvonne Underhill-Sem, and many more than I can name here. I appreciate Niko Besnier's careful and generous comments on early drafts, Tamasailau Suaalii-Sauni's review of chapter 2, Neferti Tadiar's generative feedback while workshopping what became chapter 4, and Keith Camacho's unwavering support, incisive suggestions, and appreciation for good food throughout. I also want to acknowledge the influence of Brendan Hokowhitu's work, which has provided much for me to think with in this book. Many thanks to Courtney Berger, my editor at Duke University Press, whose light touch and serene support has helped me find my way through the publication process. Much alofa and appreciation to KDee Ma'ia'i for her cheerful support, keen eyes, and long hours in the final research and formatting of the manuscript. As an emerging researcher and grounded scholar in her own right, I look forward to seeing where the future takes her.

Many portions of this book and ideas included have been shared at conferences, symposia, colloquia, and other venues, and it has benefited enormously from the generous engagement and feedback provided by: University of Auckland Pacific Studies and Anthropology; University of Hawai'i Ethnic Studies, Sociology, American Studies, and the Center for Pacific Islands Studies; Columbia University Anthropology and the Institute for Research on Women and Gender; University of Michigan American Studies; University of Oregon Women's, Gender, and Sexuality Studies; Pacific University Anthropology; Bard College; the Association for Social Anthropology in Oceania; American Studies Association; Native American and Indigenous Studies Association; American Anthropological Association; Association for Asian American Studies; Hawai'i Sociological Association; and American Sociological Association conferences. The Vaka writing retreats and "Shut Up and Write" nights at UoA Pacific Studies were a huge help in that last push for the finished manuscript.

From late nights at the café to months away from home, my husband David was my constant support, and will be as happy as me that this book is out in the world. I couldn't have chosen a better partner in this life. Santana, Avienda, and Cruz, our precious bebes, this journey has been blessed by you all being a part of it.

Finally, I recognize moana Pasefika scholars past and present, and I hope this humble contribution lives up to the measina you all have created. Any faults remain my responsibility alone.

Introduction

FABLED FUTURES AND
GRIDIRON DREAMS

WE ARRIVED AT THE BISHOP MUSEUM on a bright, sunny morning to find some of the members of the Royal Order of Kamehameha (ROK) setting up the area for the formal ʻawa (ʻava/kava)[1] ceremony to welcome the inaugural class of the Polynesian Football Hall of Fame (PFHOF).[2] This first class enshrined in Honolulu included Kurt Keola Gouveia, Olin George Kreutz, Jack "The Throwin' Samoan" Thompson, Kevin James Mawae, Ken Niumatalolo, Tiaina Baul "Junior" Seau Jr., Vai Sikahema, and Herman John Wedermeyer, with weekend events including the induction dinner held at the convention center and a public event at the Polynesian Cultural Center (the permanent site of the PFHOF).[3] Prior to the ceremony, attendees greeted each other and their hosts enthusiastically as the mini-reunion brought many in the Polynesian fraternity back together.[4] They were presented with a kihei and would be arrayed on lauhala/laufala (woven mats) arranged in a half-moon shape facing those who were mixing and serving ʻawa, with chairs behind them for family members and friends in attendance. The ceremony would be led by Leighton Tseu, representative of the Royal Order, and performed by J. Keaweʻaimoku Kaholokua and Ty P. Kāwika Tengan, who were there as part of the Hale Mua o Kūaliʻi and ʻAha Kāne.[5] One of the ROK members outlined how the ceremony was going to work and expressed his appreciation for their role in honoring the inductees. He also warned them, "The longer you talk [in the optional individual speeches], the longer we will be sitting in the sun!" to laughter from the crowd.

After they assembled, Keawe began chanting as the inductees were led down a set of steps to the grassy area underneath a large, shady tree. Although it was only approaching midmorning, the air was already thickening with humidity. Once the inductees were in their places on the lauhala, Ty chanted as he mixed the ʻawa; when it was time to serve, Keawe spoke, highlighting each honoree's accomplishments before a young man with Hawaiian kakau/tatau down his left leg and clothed in a malo served the ʻawa to each one, who in turn said a few words of acknowledgement and appreciation. After the ʻawa ceremony for the inductees was completed Leighton explained, "The significance of being on these grounds are that . . . about fifty yards from us are the artifacts and the stories that come from the ancestral lands, the lands of all of our ancestors. The capes that the kings and chiefs wore, the ornaments, the traditional tools—every Polynesian island is represented here in the collection. So today's ceremony and the selection of this place is intentional. It is an opportunity not only for us to share this moment with our ancestors but also with our descendants." He invited anyone in attendance who wanted to partake of ʻawa and say a few words to come forward. Several people spoke, including chairman and founder Seiuli Jesse Sapolu and vice chairman and founder Maʻa Tanuvasa, as well as board members June Jones and Reno Mahe, inductee Vai Sikahema, and State Representative Richard Fale.

The private ceremony consecrated the mission with Hawaiian protocols of welcome and acknowledged the genealogical and cultural connections between the islands in recognition of shared histories and ancestry. That groundedness set it apart from the large, lavish induction dinner and floorshow production and the open public event with speeches and autograph signings later that weekend. In its launch the PFHOF established an identity distinct from the Pro Football Hall of Fame and at the same time was inclusive of players with ties across the Polynesian triangle and others who had played important supporting roles in Polynesian football success. It was an expansive effort to include some who (as I was told) were taking this opportunity to reconnect after many years of living in US cities without Polynesian communities.

I.1 PFHOF ʻAwa ceremony, Bishop Museum. PHOTO CREDIT: AUTHOR.

While the enshrinement and subsequent establishment of a permanent home at the Polynesian Cultural Center honored significant achievements and signaled support of football success, the vast majority of Polynesian representation in the sport to date are players of Samoan, Tongan, and Hawaiian descent, with Samoans constituting a critical mass. Focusing on one strand of this success with roots in Sāmoa, this book steps away from the celebrations of achievement to ask how we got here, what these achievements mean for players and in broader contexts, and how they are woven into larger community histories. Drawing on years of ethnographic and archival research, interviews, media analysis, and personal experience, this book weaves a narrative that winds backward and forward across the moana, connecting part of Turtle Island (the continental United States), Hawai'i, and Sāmoa.

New Voyages: Expanding Routes of Mobility

Gridiron football has become an important part of life in Samoan communities in the islands and in linked urban and suburban areas of the United States. In American Sāmoa, the sport's visibility and vibrancy are powered by its connection to the changing market of the American football industry, which for several decades now has opened new opportunities for Samoan youth at the collegiate and professional levels. Polynesian players have been racialized in ways that help them enter this line of work but restrict them from others: they are stereotyped as genetically gifted with size, girth, and quickness suitable for football as well as with a violent impulse that can be channeled into success on the field by virtue of their respect for authority, instilled by discipline and socialization in hierarchical Samoan society (see chapter 3). While this is often highlighted to explain the affinity for the game, this book argues for a more complex understanding—against the backdrop of US imperial legacies in Sāmoa and restricted economic opportunity, community histories and cultural sensibilities shape how Samoan men, most younger and some older, navigate the transnational sporting opportunities presented by American football. They are part of a global story of expanding sporting infrastructure, labor, and movement, comprising particular histories, conjunctures, and contingencies.[6]

For many, playing football is a response to limited structures of opportunity both in the archipelago and in the United States, although each context is distinct. Further developed in chapter 4 but important to mark here, I argue that the sport's rise in Samoan communities is closely tied to the recognition and forms of capital it offers players, families, and wider communities: *economic* capital in the form of college scholarships, professional salaries, and endorsements; *cultural* or symbolic capital in the form of prestige, educational credentials, and expertise; and *social* capital in the form of expanded social and professional networks (Bourdieu 1984; 1986). Capital, in Pierre Bourdieu's articulation, is "accumulated labor" in a "materialized form" that is appropriated by people or groups of people. How the different types of capital are distributed in a society reveals the "immanent structure of the social world, i.e., the set of constraints, inscribed in the very reality of that world, which governs its functioning in a durable way, determining the chances of success for practices" (Bourdieu

1986, 241–242). In this way, social privilege, access, and inequality shape one's future possibilities.

While Bourdieu's theory of capital emerges from specific historical contexts, assumptions, and preoccupations distinct from the those of transnational Sāmoa, it remains a useful lens through which to view the dreams of upward mobility and the themes of opportunity and college access shared with me by many players, their families, and their communities.[7] Still, it is a partial explanation: while the sport's rise is closely tied to the forms of capital it offers, Samoan players themselves articulate a variety of motivations for participation that are not fully determined or even encompassed by market principles and the logic of capitalist accumulation. Other elements also influence agentive decision making; for instance, cultural sensibilities shape some players' and communities' engagement with the sport beyond the market aspect (explored more fully in the chapters 2 and 4). At the same time, forward-looking imaginaries of "fabled futures" that are rooted in, and framed by, legendary sporting exploits of the past and present exert a powerful pull. Sports like football have become a new locus of fantasies of the future that are firmly linked to transnational movement and the mastery of modern institutions of education and sport in places like American Sāmoa and beyond. Exploring how the material, social, and imaginative dimensions of football are woven together in ways that draw in young players and their communities helps us to understand how football-related movement has emerged as an important gendered path of transnational mobility.

TRANSNATIONAL FUTURES

Discussions of "global sport" invoke "the global" and "globalization" with the whirring sense of high-velocity movement and connection. From intensified media linkages and ever-expanding commodity pathways to capital and labor migration capillaries that power the global economy, there is an understanding that we are living in a time with unprecedented "interactions of a new order and intensity" (Appadurai 1996, 27; see also 1990, 1991). As a concept, globalization has come to signify both a material change in social life and a shift in our awareness about the wider global context in which we live.[8] While most scholars agree that a fundamental shift in frequency, scope, and volume of economic, cultural, and social interactions across different scales (local, regional, national, transnational, and global) has taken place,[9] many questions remain about how to understand the processes and implications of this new order of movement, interaction, and blending.[10]

How do we understand the local and global as distinct, but also entangled with each other and co-constituted?

In the context of contemporary movement often driven by corporations and capital, "transnationalism" refers to the efforts by individuals and communities to forge and maintain connections irrespective of national boundaries. In this process, they "build social fields that cross geographic, cultural, and political borders" (Basch, Glick-Schiller, and Szanton-Blanc 1994, 7).[11] Activities are shaped by, but not oriented toward, state structures and policies. Beyond the focus on migrant remittances,[12] this large-scale movement of people, currency, and products has raised important questions about impacts of local–global connections, changing cultural practices, diasporic identities and experience, and the durability of transnational connections in the Pacific and elsewhere.[13]

Across the Pacific, everyday people living abroad create and invigorate vital links to Pacific Island homes and sister communities in other countries when we visit, send money and goods, share photos and stories on social media, exchange information over calls and chats, make business linkages, and so on. These transnational practices, actualized in individual and communal practices by nonstate actors, link home islands with a vibrant and expanding diaspora that crosses national, political, and social boundaries. How, then, are local politics, economies, social practices, and cultural sensibilities changing in relation to different kinds of transnational movements? How do we account for specific dynamics in particular localities while holding in tension the importance of shifting transnational geopolitical formations that shape these local articulations, and still interrogate common dynamics across different localities? In line with a push to more specificity, scholars are questioning whether globalization is more ideology than actuality—that is, in capturing aggregate shifts it obscures important particularities that attention to specific transnational histories and currents may illuminate (see Carter 2011). This book tacks between examining football as a global industry and following particular pathways taken, aiming for a deeper understanding of "roots and routes" together with critical evaluations of aspects of industry, mobility, and transformation (Diaz and Kauanui 2001).[14]

SPORT AND MIGRATION

In some areas of the world, sport has been a migration pathway for nearly a century; it has emerged in force in the Pacific since the 1970s and intensified in the last three decades with professionalization and intensive capital investment.[15] Like other transnational athletic migration streams from the twentieth century, legacies of empire and colonialism fundamentally shaped Samoan presence in American football as part of the broader history of US imperial expansion that have enabled and continue to make these paths of mobility possible. However, its vibrant growth in recent decades can be linked to the broader globalization and commercialization of elite-level sports since the late twentieth century (Andrews and Ritzer 2007; Bale and Maguire 1994; Maguire 1999; Miller et al. 1999; Miller et al. 2001). With the rise of precarious labor on a global scale, new routes of investment for future returns have emerged; sport is one of these pathways whose scope and importance has proliferated in recent decades.

Sport migration is a distinct experience built on gender-specific pathways and ideologies of class mobility and open opportunity. Young men (primarily) and their communities are increasingly drawn to this high-stakes lottery with promises of prestigious rewards and the opportunity to bring their families honor and esteem, even as the odds are not always in their favor. Unlike other forms of migrant labor, elite athletes perform a kind of specialty labor (Castells 2000 [1996]; Elliot and Maguire 2008); they are seen as national treasures and deserving recipients of the praise, adulation, and wealth showered upon them. In some sports, like rugby, they are also seen as national possessions. As anthropologist Thomas Carter has noted, this "veneer of celebrity actually obscures the processes of transnational capital, the structures of labour in a transnational industry, and how states are complicit in structuring this industry" (2011, 6). In the Pacific, for example, the emergence of a "Pasifika rugby-playing diaspora" builds on historically contingent labor migration schemes to former or existing colonial powers (Horton 2012; see also Grainger 2006, 2011; Zakus and Horton 2009), as well as a dispersed system of sport scholarships and club contracts (Besnier 2012, 2014; Schieder and Presterustuen 2014).

The critical mass of players entering the top levels of American football in the early 2000s had sportswriters declaring American Sāmoa "The Dominican Republic of the NFL,"[16] and in broad strokes, there are some similarities. Sport scholar Alan Klein's early work (1991) adopted a core-periphery framework to understand Dominican Republic history and economics, paralleling the trade in Major League Baseball players with the sugar trade, and examining how Dominican players enter American baseball as a source of cheap labor.[17] Escalating salaries underwritten by lucrative TV contracts were luring baseball hopefuls and convincing swaths of young Dominican men to turn their energy to the sport even if the actual opportunities were limited. As Thomas Carter (2007) notes, much of the sport migration literature has historically been shaped by the scholarship on the Caribbean. Yet even within the Caribbean other patterns developed that were distinct from the North–South movement framed by historical colonial relations detailed by Klein (see Carter 2008, 2011; Echevarria 2001). Carter (2007) notes, "Migration patterns vary with each sport and depend on a sport's historical circumstances in the country of origin and the destination country as well as the contemporary political economic relationships between those two countries" (377; see also Besnier 2014). Details matter, and transnational migration routes—sport included—have specific histories seeding new lifeworlds, created by people moving and connecting across borders (Basch, Glick-Schiller, and Szanton-Blanc 1994; Carter 2013).

In illuminating this route, marking key distinctions for American football is useful, particularly in the sport's infrastructure and connections abroad. Firstly, the NFL has not invested in international academies in the way that baseball or other sports such as rugby or soccer have (see Darby 2012, 2013; Esson 2013; Klein 2006, 2009). The league is pushing to develop global markets, encouraging and underwriting youth programs and expanding into new media markets, but the road to the pros is built differently. Unlike in other countries, football's entrenchment within the American school system facilitates engagement with education rather than maintaining a parallel system focused primarily on sports development. Culturally, football has become a key feature in high school and college life, inspiring dedicated fandom and providing a platform for alumni connection and continued support that is so valuable that many schools are loathe to cut their programs even in the face of economic or health complications.[18] Entities like the NFL have not had to establish "farm" systems or academies because US colleges and universities fill that space; they play a key role in developing players and situating them to connect to professional opportunities.[19] The (continental) United States remains the center of the game geographically, but continues to draw from communities abroad.

What people call the "Polynesian Pipeline" is today an elaborate network with multiple points of entry (largely though not exclusively) in the United States and US-affiliated Pacific communities; destinations include high schools, military prep academies, junior colleges, and four-year colleges and universities across the nation. This Polynesian network is constantly evolving to expand its reach, with nodes emerging deliberately and by chance, intended to connect Pacific communities to the college football system. Across the country, 73,660 athletes play football at NCAA member schools, with 48,314 eligible for scholarship support.[20] At the top level of this system, NCAA Division I[21] schools in the United States generated $9.15 billion in athletic revenue according to 2016 calculations, with their football programs averaging $31.9 million in revenue annually.[22] Football draws just over a quarter of all NCAA athletes, and remains the number one high school sport in the United States with over a million players annually.[23] In the professional realm, the NFL generated $14 billion in revenue in 2017, with roster spots for 1,696 players across the league;[24] by 2019 that revenue had climbed to $15.26 billion.[25] While many Samoan players cite family, faith, and culture as motivating factors for their entry into sport careers, their increasing numbers are made possible by an expanding sporting infrastructure (for gridiron football see Ruck 2018 and Uperesa 2010b, 2014a; for rugby league see Lakisa, Adair, and Taylor 2014).

Sport is a historical formation, and there is nothing universal about the highly commercialized US sport industry (Sage 1998, 131). Rather, American professional football is historically contingent and particular; it was developed with specific efforts aimed at growing market share and profit margins, particularly through media revenues.[26] In the battle for the nation's most watched sport it emerged victorious, dethroning baseball by the end of the 1960s (Yost 2006, 66). Daniel Grano (2014) writes, "After the NFL merged with the American Football League in 1970, earnings for national broadcasting rights grew exponentially, from $63 million in 1974 to a 2005 deal that secured about $3.75 billion a year in broadcasting rights through 2011" (25; see also Yost 2006, 75–79). With new marketing strategies designed to enhance profits and game changes aimed at making TV viewing more exciting, along with new stadium seating schemes, rising ticket prices, and merchandizing deals, the NFL has become the most successful sports league in history. Record profits and a championship game that drew over 100 million viewers in 2020 shows American gridiron football is a force to reckon with. An expanding global infrastructure in the International Federation of American Football (IFAF) and the International Pathway Program, among other formal and informal efforts, means the sport will continue to grow by attracting players and fans from places like Sāmoa and across the globe.

Yet while the story of infrastructure and pathways helps to shed light on shifting opportunities, it doesn't give a full picture of why people take them. With increasing numbers of young Pacific Islanders finding career paths through various professional sports in and around the region, it is ever more important that, rather than remain at the level of macroeconomic demographic analysis (or "the global"), we puzzle out the meanings that individuals, families, and communities attach to these movements. While many studies of sport migration focus on large-scale transfers of players from the Global South to the Global North, this book combines focused ethnography and personal experience with an analysis of the historically constituted structural constraints within which athletes move. In parsing Samoan football movement, this book approaches football as a "serious game" that illuminates changing sensibilities in American Sāmoa and US-linked communities by tracing how local agendas, orientations, and actions engage, shape, and are shaped by these larger dynamics, processes and frameworks.[27] This reveals sporting pursuits to be deeply personal journeys that resonate with family attachments, hope, and imaginaries of the future in ways that both carry and transcend cultural sensibilities in new contexts.

PACIFIC MOVEMENT AND MOBILITY

While frameworks for understanding migration have historically been dominated by macroeconomic analyses or focused on specific push/pull factors, Oceanic worldviews focused on the movement of people and goods previewed the kind of approach many scholars of transnationalism would take up.[28] For example, Epeli Hauʻofa (2008 [1994]) invoked a longer history of movement and connection among Pacific peoples whose lands are joined by massive sea thoroughfares in response to the many political-economic analyses that framed the islands as small, isolated, and without resources. Contrary to the proclamation of diplomats, bureaucrats, and various other "experts," Hauʻofa's attention to the histories, myths, legends, and cosmologies of Oceania, as well as to the movement of ordinary people, led him to proclaim that "The world of Oceania is not small; it is huge and growing every day" (30).

Decades of movement have transformed the Pacific region (Connell and Rapapport 2013, 275). The post–World War II movement of ordinary people "by the tens of thousands, doing what their ancestors did in earlier times: enlarging their world as they go, on a scale not possible before . . . expanding kinship networks through which they circulate themselves, their relatives, their material goods, and their stories all across their ocean" (Hauʻofa 2008 [1994], 34) has brought new realities into being. We continue to reckon with the legacies of empire and globalization that shape the transnational flows of people, ideas, and commodities through nodes and networks that organize movement across Oceania, and the impact of these flows on home islands and host nations.[29] As discussed in chapter 1, the movement of this post–WWII "migration generation" from Sāmoa shows how the long-standing practice of movement, concern for kinship obligations, and economic shifts intersect with local and international policy changes.[30]

Although specific pathways may be directed by national boundaries, Oceanic peoples are moving, often empowered by the social centrality of reciprocity and connection. Sa'iliemanu Lilomaiava-Doktor (2009a) argues that the focus on the migration from periphery to core or rural to urban or island to metropole casts movement as primarily economically motivated and always already disempowered when in fact it is dynamic and multivalent in practice. She reminds us that "Cultural meanings of mobility, place, and identity influence people's interpretations of migration, transnationality, and development" (19; see also Small 2011 [1997] and Salesa 2003). Likewise, Indigenous ontologies structure how these capital formations are shaped; they also mold strategies of engagement and the different meanings attached to them (Linnekin 1991; Sahlins 1988). These cultural sensibilities have historically played a large role in shaping Samoan migration, intersecting with the dynamics of globalization and transnational migration as well as American Sāmoa's territorial status to structure the kinds of pathways available.

Sāmoa at Home and Abroad

Classically imagined as an isolated culture in the sepia tones of past ethnography, Sāmoa is, rather, exemplary of the global condition in places often thought to be out-of-the-way. Movement and circulation within and beyond the Pacific has been a central part of Samoan history, contrary to curious depictions of early twentieth-century eastern Sāmoa as a chain of "remote and beautiful islands" existing in "isolation from the modern busy world," and "cut off from the history and literature of their neighbors" (Embree 1934, 51, 53). Connected to metropolitan centers and other parts of the Pacific by plane and ship today rather than 'ālia or va'a of days past, it stands (together with independent Sāmoa) at the center of a transnational diaspora dispersed across the Pacific to New Zealand, Australia, the United States, United Kingdom, and beyond. Today it is not an isolated society (if indeed it ever was).

This book presents contemporary American Sāmoa as a locality made transnationally. In one way, the Samoan nation respects no formal state boundaries—it encompasses communities in the islands as well as diasporic nodes in several countries including Australia, Aotearoa New Zealand, and the United States that are connected by an ever-expanding web of 'āiga actively maintained by movement within and across borders. Local leaders speak of American Sāmoa as a nation unto itself, as part of the larger Samoan nation that encompasses neighboring independent Sāmoa and overseas communities, and as part of the United States. Its location 8,000 miles from the continental United States serves to further emphasize the distance from the States, and the experience of foreign crossing (via international flights, with necessary documents, and through US Customs) is shaped by borders and migration regimes.[31] The movement between the islands and the incorporated United States is one strand of global mobility that is unfolding in uneven ways worldwide.

TRANSFORMED (ECONOMIC) CONTEXTS
AND SPORT OPPORTUNITIES

Comprising the larger island of Tutuila, and including the Manuʻa group (Taʻu, Ofu, and Olosega), Swains Island, and Rose Atoll, American Sāmoa is a small-scale Pacific island state with a population of more than 55,000 (US Census 2010). The state motto, "Sāmoa Muamua Le Atua," or "[In] Sāmoa, God is First" reflects a widespread Christian influence and practice across the archipelago. Whereas the church has come to serve as a new kind of village abroad, anchoring Samoan communities and serving as a site for cultural practice, in the islands it permeates most aspects of daily life from the evening family lotu to weekday church events and weekend church preparations and services. With the indigenization of Christianity in Sāmoa, cultural practices have become closely intertwined with religious ones. For example, the role of the faifeau has been integrated into Samoan cultural protocols and is highly valued. Some religious practices have grown beyond the reach of the church and include daily prayer, hymns in schools, and honorific prayer openings and closings to many secular events. Moreover, church congregations draw on and forge local and transnational networks. While not a focus in this book, it remains significant that many of the athletic service activities have been mobilized through religious networks and/or have a strong sense of calling and pastoral care that is spiritual or religious in nature (such as the Christian Athletes in Action and Gridiron Ministries, church-volunteer sport camps, and a strong network of Church of Jesus Christ of Latter-day Saints or Mormon sport leagues and organizers). These contemporary efforts connect to a much longer history of muscular Christianity (see MacAloon 2013) incorporated and transformed in the sociocentric orientation of Sāmoa to family, village, nation, and God. Sporting connections to spirituality and religious infrastructure and doctrine in the Pacific is an area that deserves further study.

Politically, American Sāmoa is often described as a model hybrid, combining the bureaucratic institutions of the US American state and a chiefly hierarchy and communal land tenure system, the long-standing indigenous sociopolitical organization known as the faʻamatai. It is unique in the constellation of US overseas empire, as it remains an unincorporated, unorganized territory. Local residents are designated as US nationals rather than citizens who may travel, work, and reside in the United States but do not pay federal income taxes and cannot vote in US elections. US territorial status in which the "foreign" and "domestic" overlap has spun a web of ties to the United States but has also maintained a precarious buffer against full application of the US Constitution, for better or worse.[32] Territorial status has provided a conduit for flows of consumer items and media programming, federal aid, and normalized movement and migration as a feature of everyday life.

In the islands from the 1950s on, American policy developed an economy largely based on cheap labor (for tuna processing and canning), bureaucracy, aid, and tourism (although the latter has never been very successful). Elsewhere I detail how the concentrated federal investment in the islands, particularly aimed at expanding infrastructure, helped to stimulate the local economy throughout the 1960s (see Uperesa 2014b). "But these projects only lasted until 1967 and focused on upgrading public infrastructure and social services. None of these programs aimed to diversify the economic base or industries in the region" (Poblete-Cross 2010, 509). The post–World War II economy was built primarily on a dependent development model of exploiting low-wage labor and territorial status to avoid import tariffs (with intermittent initiatives aimed at developing tourism, export agriculture, and local entrepreneurship over the years).

Today's economy reflects this historical legacy. From 1975 to 2000, the economy stagnated, with the tuna canneries and federal financial aid accounting for virtually all growth. Entrepreneurs power a small private sector, but turnover can be high; some businesses have been able to prosper over generations while others are short-lived. In the meantime, the federally funded bureaucracy, military enlistment, and outmigration have become the important employment options for local residents. During the same period, Samoan participation in American gridiron football has grown steadily.

While our Samoan communities are thriving through the vibrancy of local organization, work, and church activity, there are real structural challenges on the economic front, both in the islands and in the States. In 2010, the average household income in American Sāmoa was $23,892.[33] Over half (54 percent) of all families fell below the federal poverty threshold, with the percentage going up if there were children in the family, and particularly if there were children under five (64.8 percent). While income figures do not tell the whole story (for example, many residents do not pay rent or hold a mortgage because they live on communally held land), the figures are useful in the context of other rising costs like electricity, communications and transportation (mobile bills, import car purchase and maintenance, or fuel costs), building materials for homes and repair, imported food prices, rising medical fees, and so on.

Up until the fall of 2009, the two major employers of the working population had been the local government and two American canneries (StarKist Foods and Van Camp Seafood Company).[34] The canneries have supplied up to 50 percent of the US tuna market, drawing largely on nonresident labor (Poblete-Cross 2010; see also Gillett, McCoy, and Itano 2002).[35] A smaller proportion of workers were employed by the private sector or engaged in subsistence activity. Access to communal land or small-scale subsistence agriculture helps many families who might otherwise struggle in the cash economy since under half (47 percent) of all adults aged 16 and older are active in the workforce (United States Census Bureau 2013). However, because available arable land is much smaller in comparison to independent Sāmoa, agricultural ventures remain limited. Today's territorial economy is a legacy of past developmentalist approaches and the uneven integration of marginalized areas into the global economy.

Across the moana, Samoans in the United States report a median family income that is among the lowest of Pacific Islanders in the United States, with the poverty rate among the highest (Harris and Jones 2005). For those who have made their homes in Hawai'i, Alaska, or the continental United States, the 2011–2015 ACS estimates report the median family income for Samoans stood at $55,685 as compared to $62,136 for Native Hawaiians and Other Pacific Islanders (NHOPI) more widely. More Samoans than any other group of NHOPI reported income that fell below the federal poverty rate for the previous year (20.3 percent vs 18.3 percent for other NHOPI).[36] These demographic statistics are somewhat improved over the 1980 US census, which found that the population as a whole was young and highly urbanized, with 27 percent of families below the federal poverty level (Franco 1991; Hayes and Levin 1983), although they do not take account of the later shifts due to the COVID-19 pandemic. Many have clustered with family in high-cost markets, while others have moved to areas with lower costs of living like Texas and Alaska.[37] In the United States, Samoans and other Pacific Islanders more generally are fighting to hold on to any gains made by the previous generation and to ward off downward mobility in a transformed economic context.

A central pillar of the promotional ideology of sport is that success in athletics can and often does lead to career success off the field (Melnick and

Sabo 1994), whether in the form of life lessons (teamwork, perseverance, preparation, sweat equity, and so on) or using athletics to access academic opportunities that can shape one's future career and life chances. Because it is tied to individual effort and performance, sport often is said to represent a "level playing field" that does not exist in the real world; it is seen to provide a fair chance to those ready to capitalize on the opportunity. Drawing on what has become common sense about mobility, sport can be the subject of outsized expectations for deliverance from disadvantaged backgrounds.

In US-based Samoan communities and in the islands, football and the military are seen as prominent avenues to a better life (and some enlist in the military if the college football opportunity sours or does not materialize).[38] Many players I have spoken with believe that success in football can open the door to higher education, which in turn paves the way for professional opportunities. And it is not simply propaganda: our calculations for the *In Football We Trust* film based on the 2013–2014 NFL season rosters and available demographic data found Samoan and Tongans to be 28 times more likely to make it to the NFL than other ethnic groups in the United States.[39] Island-born Samoan players together with an even larger group of US-born players in the collegiate and professional ranks have come to constitute a critical mass that has raised the sport's profile in Sāmoa and among Samoan communities more broadly.

A series of high-profile firsts mark recent Samoan achievements in the game: at the college level, one of the first games of the 2008 season featured two Pacific-10 Conference teams led by quarterbacks of Samoan descent (Lyle Moevao for Oregon State and Tavita Pritchard for Stanford). The following year Jeremiah Masoli, a graduate of St. Louis High School in Honolulu, Hawai'i, and whose grandparents resided in the village of Taputimu in Tutuila, led his University of Oregon team to the Pac-10 championship. He became the first Samoan quarterback to play in the Rose Bowl and played alongside teammate Simi Toeaina, who graduated from Samoana High School, also in Tutuila. In the time since, Marcus Mariota won the Heisman Trophy as quarterback for Oregon in 2014 and his fellow St. Louis High School alum, Tua Tagovailoa, would also be considered for the honor. Tagovailoa joined the University of Alabama team as a freshman quarterback in 2017 and led the Crimson Tide to a national championship at the end of that season, accomplishing a feat no Samoan player had before him. He was made the fifth overall pick in the 2020 NFL Draft, signing a four-year rookie contract worth over $30 million. Among linemen, in 2019 Penei Sewell became the first Polynesian and first University of Oregon player to win the Outland Trophy, awarded to the nation's best interior lineman. He shared the 2020 PFHOF Polynesian College Football Player of the Year award with Tua Tagovailoa; like him, Sewell was a first-round pick in the NFL Draft. Sporting a pendant with the American Sāmoa flag on draft day in 2021, he was selected seventh overall by the Detroit Lions, later signing a fully guaranteed contract worth over $24 million. An increasing number of local players have successfully navigated their way through the college football system and to spots on NFL rosters or practice squads.[40] Building on the successes of those who came before them who are now being recognized by entities like the PFHOF, these young players have taken up the mantle of a community tradition, finding opportunities in the growing sportscape of football.

Navigating and Indigenizing Sport Labor Prospects

In line with broader trends in US society, the common sense about sport mobility has helped to orient the youth more and more toward sport as a lifeline to college access and professional opportunities. In talking with many Samoan players and community members over the years about football's attraction, it is clear that the various kinds of capital it affords have become foundational (see chapters 2 and 4). As sport constitutes a new field of labor, how then is it placed within larger genealogies of labor (local, regional, transnational), and how are players and communities negotiating sport as a new (raced, classed, gendered) labor route?[41]

In contrast to profit-oriented work toward endless productivity promoted by colonial agents of the early twentieth century, historically Samoans (and other Pacific peoples) had different drivers for when and how to work that articulated with seasonal production and family and village contributions.[42] Under colonial and territorial governments, agricultural export (copra) and military service were central to the incorporation of local people into waged work; meanwhile, local residents in turn made the most of their possibilities in a growing cash economy (see Fa'aleava 2003; O'Meara 1990; Pitt 1970). By midcentury, the military remained key to the expanding capitalist economy in American Sāmoa, and was joined by cannery and bureaucratic employment (Franco 1991). Starting in earnest during the post–World War II period, waves of emigration tied to military service helped establish Samoan communities in the United States. Cold War–era developmentalism pushed infrastructure expansion and the formal education system increasingly positioned students to continue their studies off-island; at the same time key personnel mobilized networks and local resources to expand the local sportscape and broker sport scholarship opportunities (Uperesa 2014b). By century's end cannery work and military enlistment remained two conspicuous local occupations; they were joined increasingly by an emerging pattern of emigration for education and sport at American colleges (Holmes 1992). In the rise of football movement, we see everyday people adapting and transforming the structure of politics and economy that shape the contours of their movement. For those who have the right mix of abilities, fortune, and discipline, football has become an important opportunity because it allows some to transcend the limited opportunities available locally—not to escape the capitalist economy, but rather to become better positioned within it.

Today, as players young and mature navigate the enmeshed logics and pathways connecting transnational sport industries and their home communities, they are entrepreneurs in bodily capital negotiating processes of commodification to better position themselves to ascend the interlinked football sporting circuits. Seeking out new opportunities for development and improvement, such as speed camps, summer passing camps, and other specialized training in addition to off-season "voluntary" workouts, becomes more important every year to get the edge on the competition. By undertaking a process of subjective and corporeal transformation—remaking not only their outlook, but their bodies as well—with training to ever higher-capacity standards (better times on the forty-yard dash, more weight on the bench press, higher jumps, quicker footwork, mobilizing greater power for rushing, running crisper routes, throwing more accurate passes, executing better technique getting off the line, and so on) players enhance their worth and accumulate what I call gridiron capital within the context of football (see chapter 4).

At the professional level, players are selling both their labor power (capacity to produce a socially valuable commodity in performance) and their labor (in their performance as the commodity itself). But in the neoliberal capitalist context where individuals are expected to manifest their futures through hustle and the person is increasingly leveraged into a brand, the commodity is multiplied with value inhering in the brand itself. The commodity then is not only gameday performance and merchandising, but includes brand following (which today may include social media reach) that generates value as well. Today's sporting cultures articulate very well with contemporary grind culture, which preaches constant production focused on creation of value for exchange, and appropriating other aspects (such as culture) to enhance that value.

The catch is that mobility and submission to racializing and commoditizing processes are often preconditions for realizing the unbridled potential of gridiron football for personal advancement, familial prestige, and cultural and national recognition. For players from Pacific Island communities, geographic movement is a requirement for accessing gridiron football circuits. More broadly, this very structure of movement sustains inequalities in the global sporting industry. While highly beneficial for those who are able to carve out a career, professional sport is a fickle and precarious business. The few high-profile successes obscure the narrow chances of success, the disappointing realities for many sports migrants, and the wider conditions that channel increasing numbers of young men into this enterprise. Still, many are willing to take that risk and pay the cost for the chance of playing the game at its highest levels.

For many Pacific Islander players, what makes the cost worth paying is not just the narrow potential economic payout, but the potential for one's achievements to reverberate in waves: in self-confidence, brotherhood, and social standing; access to college opportunities or winning the contract lottery; or enhancing the honor and esteem of one's family and being able to contribute to one's family, church, village, and/or nation in tangible and material ways. Among many Samoan players, the perspectives on and strategies of engagement with the game (and here speaking specifically to the professional or proto-professional levels as well as the way they trickle down to high school and earlier) have come to be shaped in part by cultural sensibilities around tautua, which has at its foundation fulfilling deeply significant cultural expectations around contribution.

As I discuss in chapter 2, the intertwining of football and fa'asāmoa through the concept and practice of tautua within Samoan cultural frameworks is an important aspect that articulates with the expanding sport infrastructure to produce the Polynesian Pipeline of the past and the Polynesian Network today. Successful players and key stakeholders have been able to take advantage of the network's sporting infrastructure provided by personal connections, travel and communications technologies, and program development, but for some the movement is powered by practices that are central to Samoan culture and sustaining family bonds sometimes across great distances. Football participation may have started as a foray into a foreign game, but with successive generations entering, it has become a Samoan game, increasingly situated within changing structures of labor and cultural scripts about service.

As migration has taken the Samoan world global, many new kinds of activities that bring prestige and honor are being recognized as tautua, invoking the alagā'upu or proverb "'E sui faiga 'ae tumau fa'avae," which is often translated as "practices may change but the foundations remain." Chapter 2 shows how within the larger expansion of tautua, sport has taken its place more prominently. Sporting prowess is one of the activities that have gained in recognition as new national and international opportunities have taken Samoans onto the world stage, and the accolades and spoils of sport contests are reintegrated in different ways into the prestige and exchange economy of fa'asāmoa. This story is therefore distinct from American cultural scripts like the individualized "rags-to-riches" tales often highlighted by sport media; here Indigenous cultural sensibilities shape the meaning of sport participation even as they intersect with the logic of upward mobility and the changing infrastructure of migration and movement.

CHASING THE AMERICAN/SAMOAN DREAM

The alliance with the premier global superpower of the twentieth century is a source of pride for American Sāmoa. With mythologized national narratives about justice, freedom, opportunity, and diversity, American exceptionalism has stood as a beacon for decades. Marking the raising of the American flag in the islands, Flag Day is the largest annual celebration, and Samoans proudly wear the badge of highest per capita enlistment in the US military as a mark of respected service.[43] Just as in the choice to serve a powerful matai realizes reciprocal benefit, the ability to proudly serve as part of the American family is an honor for many.[44]

By conquering the fabled fields of American football, Samoan players achieve both the American and the Samoan dream. With football's status as the (highly capitalized) national sport, players get paid and achieve respect. When one of the first things many NFL draftees do is buy their family a car or a house, they signal they have arrived.[45] Through hard work, grit, and perseverance materialized in their efforts on and off the field, they fulfill the imaginary of American individualism. The rugged masculine achievement makes one a breadwinner, able to secure a high standard of living for them and their family: they are living the American Dream. But football success has become a Samoan dream as well—not just as evidence of individual achievement or for conspicuous consumption but because for some it provides for valued ways of being Samoan.[46] Generally, honoring one's lineage, representing the family name, and being able to materially contribute together fulfill tautua or ideal forms of service. Specifically, sport provides a respected way of achieving markers of Samoan manhood: demonstrating valued masculinity in physical strength and prowess, obtaining prestigious stature commanding respect, and earning through hard work the resources with which to perform tautua (whether supporting one's family, matai, church, village, or wider Samoan and Pacific communities). Football success is therefore one representative of the American/Samoan dream.

Charting Our Course

The beginning of the book follows a genealogical approach to the present, asking how we got here and how significant shifts are reflected in changing sensibilities about the future. It begins to disentangle the historical conditions of possibility for the emergence of football as a route of migration and mobility. In chapter 1, "Malaga," I trace the emergence of football in American Sāmoa in the context of mid-twentieth-century US development initiatives and changing relationships to the market economy and standards of living in the islands, as well as the islands' territorial status and new cultures of migration. This chapter combines ethnography and oral history with archival research to examine the growing presence of Samoans in American football and American football in Sāmoa. It explores how individual and community desires shape and are shaped by larger (trans)national, political, and economic projects of varying scales. Woven around individual journeys, it illustrates the evolution of structures of opportunity within which local people increasingly see football as an important route of geographic and social mobility, and places it in the context of histories of Samoan transnational movement and migration intersecting with the expansion of the football industry at the professional and college levels.

"Football, Tautua, and Fa'asāmoa," the second chapter, draws on ethnographic research at selected football camps and experience in Sāmoa to trace how elements of Samoan culture are being linked to the American game of football. It examines the ways in which alternative sources of status and prestige, such as that associated with football success, have articulated with important shifts in the constituent concepts and recognized practices of tautua over time. In this indigenization of sport, we see sport being used to refract community histories, agendas, and bids for recognition (see Uperesa 2021). It also marks tensions whereby for some football success is, like many foreign imports before it, reincorporated by the powerful logic of the fa'asāmoa and the matai system, whereas for others it provides distance from social obligations and allows them to circumvent existing social hierarchies and the relations of power that structure them.

The second half of the book focuses on capital and commoditization; media narratives and the body; and cultural constructions of strength and injury to illustrate and theorize how structural pathways and material realities, together with cultural transformations and persistence, help us understand the intersection of social worlds traversed by transnational sport migrants. Chapter 3, "Producing the Gridiron Warrior," examines media constructions of Samoan (and other Polynesian) bodies in football to tease out the ways in which bodily performance and representation are infused with ideas about race, ethnographic imaginations of culture, and visions of the gendered body to together articulate a contemporary indigenous Polynesian masculinity. Turning from external representations, it then considers how some players and filmmakers are mediating these images and producing new narratives in an era of branding and social media.

"Gridiron Capital," the fourth chapter, analyzes the processes of commodification associated with the sport of football, and how Samoan players maneuver within and beyond institutional parameters. In this they negotiate a labor context of escalating expectations where the stakes have never been higher. I argue that the accumulation of gridiron capital is crucial to their success in the football environment, but through their connection to family and community, many rely on other measures of worth that allow them to resist further commodification driven by the capitalist logic that permeates the sport. The last chapter, "Fa'amālosi!" draws on recent research on traumatic brain injuries (TBIs), the high-profile debate around football's "concussion crisis," and ethnographic research to explore what legacies of players like Junior Seau mean for the way we view football and how we measure "risk" and "reward." In this analysis, I ask how Samoan cultural concepts and views on masculinity are being articulated with the hypermasculine culture of American football, and to what potential ends.

Sāmoa stands as part of the cradle of Polynesia, and as homeland to a widely dispersed diaspora. Yet as a polity, American Sāmoa has long been relegated to the margins of regional and global geopolitical power relations. A United States territory since 1900, we know little about the place of Tutuila ma Manu'a in the larger narratives of American history and globalization. Today, the islands enter the US national imaginary primarily through gridiron football; this hypervisibility works to erase Samoan history and the fullness of Samoan experience outside of sport. Moreover, it obscures a century of US imperialism and the reality of asymmetrical integration in the global economy, as well as a clear view of migration pathways that brought the players to American fields. The following chapters aim to illuminate these histories and present contexts; they also ask, in different ways, about the future and about the long-term effects of the rising dominance of institutions like football.

One

Malaga

FORGING NEW PATHWAYS IN
SPORT AND BEYOND

The "Legend"

In October 2009, a large banquet dinner was held in honor of the University of Montana Hall of Fame inductees, members of the 1969 and 1970 undefeated championship football teams. After the dinner was over, I sat at a table with my father, Tu'ufuli, and a few of his former teammates as they were catching up on news and reminiscing. He was in his early sixties then, a retired athlete and educator living in American Sāmoa. Born on the island of Tutuila, he played football through to the professional ranks in the United States and Canada, and over the years he traveled extensively as an athlete, coach, and trainer.

The atmosphere of the dinner was upbeat if nostalgic as different speakers recounted their memories of the program and the role these teams played in establishing a legacy of success at the school. The banquet hall at the hotel was full, with up to three hundred people in attendance—players, their families, coaches, and other athletic personnel. During the presentation portion, each player was featured in his uniform picture, to applause and sometimes hoots and cheers. When Tu'ufuli appeared on screen, young and athletic, thunderous applause erupted. It was only a glimpse of the

1.1 Tu'ufuli Kalapu Uperesa, team co-captain, University of Montana.

adoration that I would come to witness firsthand over the course of the weekend.

After dinner, the room bristled with excitement as former teammates reconnected after forty years, each having made his own path in life with family and careers. At their invitation, I had made last-minute arrangements to join my parents in Missoula. My father journeyed from Tutuila, and my mother drove down from Billings to support him in the celebration, reunite with old friends and family, and to revisit their university days. Long divorced, they remained civil; I was the driver, companion, and photographer, happy to document this honor. After the dinner I accompanied him, taking pictures as he met old friends; I was amused to see he was in high demand. His old coach Wally Brown took me aside and asked if I ever heard the story of Tu'ufuli's recruitment to the university. He told the story with panache and a mischievous twinkle in his eye, still quite satisfied with himself for having bested other programs with better reputations and more resources (the ordeal may or may not have led to new National Collegiate Athletic Association [NCAA] rules in recruiting at the time).

As we sat talking, suddenly an attractive, middle-aged woman walked up to us, brimming with emotion and excitement. "Is this Tu'ufuli?" she asked as she reached out, clasping his hand in hers and holding on for a moment. "I just wanted to shake your hand—We've never met but I was a cheerleader, cheering you on, and you were just legendary! Legendary!" she exclaimed. He smiled, graciously remarked how nice it was to meet her, and introduced us. With earnest excitement she told me, "Tu'ufuli was a legend on campus. You ask about professors on campus and people would say, 'Who?' But Tu'ufuli everyone knew. 'Tu'ufuli! Tu'ufuli! Tu'ufuli!' [He] was just legendary." As she walked away, I was struck by the immense satisfaction she seemed to get from greeting him and recounting the memory of his presence on campus. Although he expressed some embarrassment at the attention, over the course of the weekend I saw that he was proud of his football accomplishments and appreciated the respect many had for him.

On the following day, the University of Montana Grizzlies hosted the Eastern Washington Eagles. As the hotel shuttle dropped us off near the shopping center across the small river from the university, I glimpsed throngs of people milling about in a sea of gray and burgundy, Grizzly colors. We began to walk the path that would lead us over the bridge to the stadium, and on my left, a painted sign on the side of the Albertson's market building draped in gray shouted "Go Griz!" To my right was a small sports bar, The Press Box, surrounded by a sea of cars. The crowd slowly carried us forward to the footbridge, where we stopped to take pictures and for Tu'ufuli to catch his breath. The fall air was cool and crisp. Under the bridge the cold river water flowed downstream. I saw what this smallish college town must have looked like to a young man from the islands forty years back, before the fancy new stadium, freeway, and strip malls were built.[1]

In the crowd, the Hall of Fame players were identifiable by their copper-orange shirts, a tribute to the team colors at the time they played, before the colors were changed to burgundy and gray. As we made our way across the footbridge, several of my father's teammates slowed to greet us or to introduce us to their families. Walking into the tailgate area, it felt like a mix of a reunion of old friends and a celebrity meet-and-greet. He had donned his 'ie lāvalava, and a number of people looked and whispered as we walked through the crowd. A great many more stopped us to say hello—old teammates, old coaches, old classmates, and some of my mother's relatives. Several old friends had made the trip to Missoula just because they heard he was in town, and they greeted him with a mix of tenderness and disbelief at his presence there, truly in the flesh. Tu'ufuli in turn was energized by the interaction and the attention. He stood reminiscing and charismatically entertaining with his gift of storytelling, enthralling the crowd as I had seen him do many times before.

Lining the path between the tailgate area and the stadium were a series of UM Grizzly–themed RVs, with people cooking out in front, talking, and drinking; the whole area buzzed with excitement. At the appointed time, the inductees began to gather outside the stadium gates. Tu'ufuli walked over with his old friends and teammates, wiping the sweat from his brow, a sign of the effort required to move the weight of his six-foot-four frame, which carried the evidence of the slow pace and rich eating of daily life in Sāmoa packed on top of muscle hardened by years of dedicated sport training. Although at the time he was barely in his early sixties, his hair was a shock of white and his deliberate steps betrayed repeated knee injuries, shoulder surgery, bodily destruction from battles on the offensive line, and finally, acute arthritis and gout. Still, he walked with a perceptible pep in his step, buoyed by the buzz of the crowd and the excitement of the occasion. He was the last to enter the stadium, yet perhaps in a nod to his former status as co-captain, his teammates insisted he lead them onto the field. The crowd of more than 20,000 was on its feet with a standing ovation, honoring the team that I heard many say began the tradition of excellence at the school, laid the foundation for a solid program, and had the last undefeated football seasons. At the time, the Grizzlies were on their way to duplicating that effort, only losing to Villanova in the NCAA Division I Football Championship Subdivision (FCS) championship game.[2]

Watching from the stands, I wondered, how does a boy born in Sāmoa come to be inducted into the Hall of Fame in Big Sky country? Later, reflecting on this event raised other questions: What motivates and makes such a journey possible? What does that journey tell us about changing routes of Samoan movement and mobility, migrant pathways, and linkages to the transnational sporting industry? How do we understand what football has come to mean for many Samoan communities and their youth?

Historically, the expanding opportunities for football participation in American Sāmoa and the States intertwine with the rising prestige of the sport and changing visions of and opportunities for the future (inspired in part by the new migration generation and the development policies discussed earlier). With his permission, I share my father's story because it is both exceptional and exemplary: taken together with others' experiences, it illustrates the recent history of Samoan geographic and socioeconomic mobility in American football and how important geopolitical and transnational shifts have made contemporary movement and mobility through sport possible.[3] In the vignette above we get a glimpse of the story whose layered complexity is further unfolded below. Focused on history, economy, and transformed visions of the future, this chapter speaks to a critical genealogy of football in (American) Sāmoa and of Samoans in American football.[4]

Layered Histories and the "Polynesian Pipeline"

Born in Pago Pago, American Sāmoa, in 1948, a fraternal twin with two older siblings, Tu'ufuli (by his own description) grew up poor. With the end of the war, military personnel stationed on the island were gradually moved to other bases and there was widespread concern about the economic fallout of the postwar demilitarization. The naval station was closed in 1951, and official oversight of the island was transferred from the US Navy to the Department of the Interior, although the Navy continued to recruit from the islands. Many native military enlistees at the US Naval Station Tutuila chose to be transferred to mainland bases in the aftermath of the base closure (Lewthwaite et al. 1972). When my grandmother was five months pregnant with my father and his twin sister, my grandfather left the island as one of these Fitafita. Grandma Fa'anofo and the kids initially stayed behind on the island. I grew up hearing stories of how she cobbled together small ventures to make ends meet, including making pies and other baked goods that Tu'ufuli sold at the local market.

Many others left later: In 1952, after the base closure and once Fitafita enlistees had been transported to bases in Hawai'i and the continental United States, the ship that returned to transport their dependents carried nearly one thousand people on the voyage to Hawai'i.[5] This movement accelerated toward the end of the 1950s, in part because of transportation improvements—in 1956 regular commercial air service began at the former military airstrip in Tafuna, and the Matson liners began to call at the port in Pago Pago every three weeks on their northbound voyages to the United States (Lewthwaite et al. 1972, 137). Even though some returned to the island, an estimated one-third of the resident population had moved off island by 1960.[6] Early stateside communities were largely concentrated in the San Francisco Bay Area, Los Angeles Basin, and San Diego County in California, in addition to other West Coast and Hawai'i locations, as the Navy moved personnel to Pacific Coast bases (Ablon 1971, 140) rather than disperse Samoan enlistees to the Midwest or the East Coast of the United States.[7]

Like many other later migrants from Sāmoa, my father followed the path of Fitafita relatives to Hawai'i where he was part of a growing Samoan community. In 1959 at the age of eleven, he went to live with my grandmother's sister, whose husband was enlisted in the military, and joined their big family in Makalapa military housing. When the family was relocated to Hunter's Point, California, he moved in with my grandmother's brother in upper Halawa housing to start high school. Two years later, my grandmother and her second husband were stationed in Hawai'i and Tu'ufuli went to live with them in middle Halawa housing. Recently admitted as a state, and barely a generation removed from World War II, the military loomed large in Hawai'i. While in the latter decades of the twentieth century Samoan men moving across the Pacific were able to take advantage of other kinds of opportunities, such as jobs in manufacturing, in security, and as longshoremen, the military remained an important path of geographic and socioeconomic mobility (Franco 1991). Gradually, however, because of shifts in the sport, football became a new field of labor for young Samoan men. In recounting this time period, Tu'ufuli said he joined friends in signing up for military service while he was still a high school student, to my grandmother's fury (those of us who knew her can imagine what that must have been like). Uncle Kalapu took his name off the list—he wanted his nephew to go to college and play football. Preempting the military route, Tu'ufuli stayed the (athletic) course and became part of what would later be called the "Polynesian Pipeline."

By most scholarly accounts, the so-called Polynesian Pipeline began with a trickle in the 1930s and 1940s with the "barefoot leagues" and the occasional "local" recruit (usually of Asian or mixed Pacific descent) from Hawai'i to the continental United States (Franks 2002; see also Morimoto 2015). Over the next two and a half decades, there were other players of Pacific Islander (mostly Polynesian) descent scattered in the collegiate and professional ranks (see Franks 2000, 2009; Markham 2008; Ruck 2018). As a member of the 'Āiea High School graduating class of 1966, Tu'ufuli was part of this incipient pipeline of Samoan sportsmen from Hawai'i to the continental United States that included contemporaries like Kahuku High School graduate and Canadian Hall of Fame player Miki "Junior" Ah You.[8] Fellow player and graduate from nearby Farrington High School Bob Apisa had become a household name as a star player for top-ranked Michigan State University (MSU). He was the first Samoan All-American and helped the Spartans to back-to-back national championships in 1965–1966 with his school record for most rushing yards by a fullback. In the wake of his success, top schools began looking at Polynesian players in Hawai'i to see if they could land another "blue-chip" player. Drawing interest from coaches like MSU's Duffy Daugherty, Tu'ufuli emerged as an athletic standout in Hawai'i at a time when football was a growing presence in American life.[9]

It was a growing presence in Sāmoa as well. While the World War II era (if not an earlier one) brought early exposure to the game of football on the island of Tutuila, later American expatriate teachers, coaches, and administrators were instrumental to initial efforts at establishing the game locally.[10] An early initiative to establish a team at Church of Jesus Christ of Latter-day Saints–affiliated Mapusaga High School in Malaeimi were supported by uniform donations from the closed Brigham Young High in Provo, Utah, in the late 1960s.[11] Samoana High School was encouraged to obtain uniforms and field a team, and the new Leone High School also started a team. According to some accounts, Mapusaga's principal, Vaughan T. Hawkes, was able to connect with and solicit support from the NBC sports vice president who sent National Football League (NFL) tapes that were later included in the new educational television system's evening program broadcast.[12] These films became teaching tools for young Samoan men (some of whom became players), their families, and men in the community who would become coaches. In this way, media technology piqued interest and facilitated the sport's adoption while the expanded schooling infrastructure would come to house the sport itself. This development coincided with increasing local interest following successful Samoan players in the United States such as the locally born Apisa, whose team's national championship year was covered in the local government bulletin.

In these early years, when NFL commissioner Pete Rozelle began a concerted effort to create the spectacle surrounding the Super Bowl (and professional football more generally), television and other media coverage expanded the attendance, participation, and viewership of football in the United States (Vogan 2014). By the time Tu'ufuli moved on to Wenatchee Junior College, football had grown far from its Ivy League roots. Programs of varying size and strength offered full athletic scholarships (adopted by the NCAA in 1957 as a method of standardizing subsidies and recruiting), and in the wake of the civil rights movement, the color line was breached more regularly.[13]

The decade of the 1970s marks a watershed in the consolidation of this pipeline in which Polynesian players were funneled to the continental United States on football scholarships and across the continent from West Coast communities. In many cases, these were the sons, nephews, and cousins of the first generation of Fitafita migrants.[14] A *Sports Illustrated* article from that time, "Shake 'em Out of the Coconut Trees," heralded the beginning of a new tide (Johnston 1976). It pointed out that while Samoan players often hailed from Hawai'i and the US West Coast, they had previously been grouped with the more recognizable Polynesian ethnic group, Hawaiians. (For example, a University of Montana news release in 1968 described Tu'ufuli as a "Giant Hawaiian Ready to Go with Football Grizzlies in Spring" [Schwanke 1968].) With the new critical mass of players at the collegiate and professional levels in the seventies, Samoans were forcing recognition of a distinct ethnic and cultural identity through their success on the field, an important source of community pride.

This time period also marks a nascent pathway of football-specific movement reaching back to the islands and the beginning of a circuit that bypassed Hawai'i high schools. The 1976 article predicted a wave of scouting and recruiting direct to the Samoan islands that only really materialized since the late 1990s. In the interim, recruiting occurred largely by word of mouth and via personal contacts, a process in which Tu'ufuli was instrumental throughout the 1980s. In films like *Polynesian Power* (Spear and Pennington 2004), we see a recent snapshot of the football landscape in the islands and the experience of two sons of Sāmoa, Isaac Sopoaga and Pisa Tinoisamoa, as they are drawn through these now-established pathways.

The Polynesian Pipeline of the past has grown into the Polynesian Network today, flowing in multiple directions and forming the basis of the movement of people, equipment, and expertise between and among the Samoan Islands, Hawai'i, and the continental United States. Over the past twenty years, Tutuila (American Sāmoa's largest island) has been the site of a number of football camps and combines that are designed to expand opportunities for Samoan student-athletes. These have been hosted by the American Samoa High School Athletics Association (ASHSAA) and the Samoa Bowl Committee and sponsored by the AIGA Foundation, the All Poly Camp, the June Jones Foundation, and the Troy and Theodora Polamalu Foundation, among others.[15] The local high schools have also benefited from equipment donations from these foundations, and from current and former NFL players Domata Peko, Jonathan Fanene, Paul Soliai, Reagan Maui'a, and Troy Polamalu, among others.[16] A Hawai'i-based clearinghouse, the Pacific Islands Athletic Alliance (PIAA), and local entity, Field House 100 (FH100), also actively facilitated the recruitment of local student athletes by US colleges and universities (they have both ceased operation). In recent years a new entity, Pasefika International Sports Alliance (PISA), has also emerged. This, combined with an even larger group of US- and island-born Samoan players in the collegiate and professional ranks, has raised the sport's profile significantly.

This dynamic flow of people, goods, and ideas has transformed the local sportscape and linked it firmly to stateside nodes of sport activity (Appadurai 1990; Carter 2011). In 2010, the *60 Minutes* profile "Football Island" highlighted the visibility of the "Sunday Samoans" seen weekly in NFL games and estimated that football players of Samoan descent are fifty-six times more likely to make it to the NFL than players of any other racial or ethnic group. Calculations done for *In Football We Trust* (2014) by Christina Kwauk, Jesse Markham, and me based on the 2013 NFL rosters and US Census data estimated Samoans and Tongans to be 26 times more likely to play in the NFL than any other racial/ethnic group in the United States. As of fall 2013, there were sixty-two NFL players of Pacific Islander heritage and nearly five hundred in NCAA Division I programs (Uperesa et al. 2015).[17] The D-I student-athletes were represented in all but one of the D-I football conferences in thirty-six states across the United States. In 2010 there were an estimated thirty players of Samoan descent on NFL rosters, and of those at least five were originally from American Sāmoa; by 2020 the number rostered rose to forty-six players, with seventeen signed to practice squads.[18] With this national attention, the dream of mobility, big money, and general hype around football continues to grow on Tutuila. Building on a long-standing migratory disposition and currents of transnational movement, the *promise* of sport looms large in the public imagination, even if its fulfillment remains elusive.

Transformative Potentials

The transnational nature of football migration is key to understanding the appeal of playing football, the rewards that accrue to successful players, and how these resources have continued to transform conditions of possibility (materially and ideologically) for young people in the islands. Fui, one of the former players I interviewed who played just as the game was getting organized in Tutuila in the late 1960s and early 1970s, described a scene in which football was in its infancy but catching the imagination of the young kids. It was a game that had to be consciously taught, since some of the coaches at that time had never played football themselves. According to him, Albert "Al" Lolotai was the director of the athletic program at the time: he was the one who set up games, officiated, and began organizing the high school program. Lolotai gave each school projectors and game film to study. Fui noted that they also watched NFL Films, which, under the direction of Steve Sabol, is credited with creating the mystique of professional football.

According to Sabol, the company's 1965 documentary *They Call It Pro Football* appealed to NFL commissioner Pete Rozelle because it offered a marketing opportunity by which to catch up to baseball and college football ratings.[19] NFL Films' stylized productions—montage editing, original music, super-slow motion, bloopers—infused "rhythm and romance" to coverage of the sport. The company worked to distinguish its productions from others by making them "*felt* rather than simply *seen*" (Vogan 2014, 18). "We've always tried to stir your emotions more than your mind. Comebacks, underdogs, and a group of guys thrown together on a dream to overcome the odds are story lines that occur every season and never go out of style," Sabol says. "The NFL always had a history, but we've given it a mythology. It's the way people remember the game, in their mind's eye."[20] In this, NFL Films "changed how football, and sport in general, is represented and imagined" while providing a foundation for the future sport media landscape (Vogan 2014, 2).

It is unlikely that anyone could have predicted that not only would the enhanced media production of the sport of football inspire players (and later, some team owners) in the United States, but the glorification of the game would also strike a chord among Samoan youth in the early 1970s. Up until then, cricket and rugby had been the major sports—local fixtures well organized for different levels of competition.[21] But people were slowly building football infrastructure in a wider context of expanding educational infrastructure under the Department of Education and organized sporting activity under the new Office of Parks and Recreation. The 1968 American Samoa Government Annual Report listed island-wide rugby competitions, Little League, volleyball teams, softball competitions, and a boxing program among the sporting activities held (American Samoa Governor 1968). By 1970 a new five-year plan for a parks and recreation program was approved, as was a five-year plan for outdoor recreation. The Parks and Recreation employees organized, directed, and supervised athletic programs for the elementary and secondary schools throughout the territory; they also promoted intervillage cricket competitions (American Samoa Governor 1970, 43). In 1973 a governor's executive order placed community recreation under the Department of Education, whose Health, Physical Education and Recreation Division administered the schools' competitive sports program for upper elementary and high school students.[22] During the summer of 1974 the first reported football clinic was held with off-island coaches (organized by Al Lolotai, with Famika Anae and Alex Kaloi in attendance),[23] and the next year Faga'alu Beach Park, Tafuna tennis courts, and a running track in Utulei were designed (American Samoa Governor 1975). By 1980 "Competitive athletics and league play [were] in ascendancy," and touch flag football had been introduced at the upper elementary level. A new Department of Parks and Recreation was authorized, with the American Samoa Territorial Comprehensive Outdoor Plan noting "an immediate need for program emphasis on youth and sports" (1980, 56) and further identifying two trends needing addressing, among others: increased emphasis on Western/American sports and outdoor recreational activities in quality facilities and programs, and growing demand for organized sports with facilities capable of housing spectators (59).

In the flurry of expanding formalized sporting activity, football was drawing more and more youth. Fui remembered, "Every time it rained, all the kids would go down to the muddy malae, play fifty on fifty, tackle." When I asked him why they were taking up football when cricket and rugby were so entrenched, he said, "They were broadcasting games, NFL and college, on KVZK-TV, so there was familiarity. With the pads it was full contact, which the kids loved. Plus, you could go places with football, there was no future in rugby—with football you could go to school, make money, see places. NFL dreams." The nascent media propaganda that would come to characterize professional football, and college football later, was a contributing element in Samoan football participation. At a time when the sport was embarking on its own path of spectacle production, the visual medium of television captured the imagination of the youth as it transformed the coverage of the sport in American Sāmoa (up until then, sports news was accessed primarily through print media). This delivery was made possible by new television station, established as part of ongoing and federally funded development efforts.

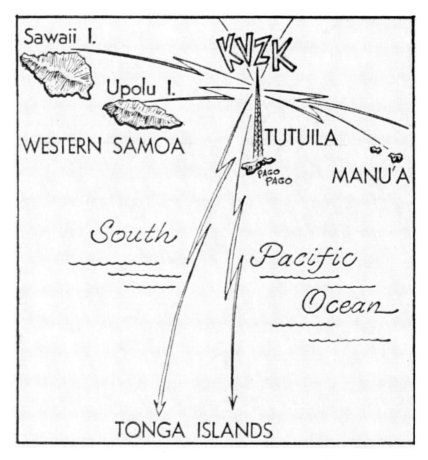

1.2 A vision of KVZK-TV's potential reach, *Honolulu Advertiser*, May 12, 1964. This illustration is part of the feature "Samoa's Bold Plan: TV Teaching" in the article series Electronic Schools in the South Seas (A4). ARTIST UNKNOWN.

Aside from the college and professional games broadcast on cable and network television in Tutuila, the local games—once simulcast only on the radio—are now recorded and replayed later in the weekend on the local broadcasting station. People who are not able to attend the games in person can view them on television. Still, while media exposure has played an important role in circulating images of the sport and in raising its profile both locally and in the United States (Dunnavant 2004), according to many I spoke with, so has personal experience of the excitement of the game, its connection to village and district rivalries, and its gendered iconography.

"IT WAS JUST COOL"

In the late 1960s and early 1970s, the local game of football was just emerging in an organized context on the island of Tutuila and beginning to draw young players, although rugby was still dominant. In our interview, Fui noted with amusement that at the time they called football a "woman's game" because you could wear pads, while rugby was a "tough man's game." According to him, for parents, football made more sense since there was no safety and no protection in rugby. By the late 1970s and early 1980s, rugby was still a tough sport, but football had far more cachet and was taking hold of young minds and bodies as a new source of masculine status. One of the former players (Galu) who was active in the sport at that time related his early experiences with the rising popularity of football and its status as the "young man's game":

> Well, rugby wasn't as popular here as [football] was then. And I think also because, for us, it was cool . . . to wear the pads and the helmet. Rugby, you just went out there and you were afraid you were going to get hurt. Someone would knock you out, you know? Then we could see there's cheerleaders, and we were like, oh, man. And at that time the booster clubs were really good . . . And it was just cool.

Part of the excitement he described was being part of the upswing of interest and excitement around the sport, when booster clubs were active and fundraising for crisp new uniforms and equipment was on the rise. As a professionalized sport and burgeoning amateur college sport, television media surrounded football, while (pre-professionalization) rugby was predominantly a local phenomenon.[24] With new efforts made at the organized game, playing football was an emerging youth pursuit, while adults were spectators and fans. It offered an expression of masculine prowess for young men where they were tested against their peers. In contrast, rugby had long been played in the villages and the inter-village contests featured young adults, but older men in their twenties and thirties still predominated. The games were fierce and embodied village rivalries, some of which ran deep; on at least one occasion I remember being caught in a crowd stampede as fights erupted after one of the Pago Park games. Football, while tough, was also regimented, with controlled plays compared to the scrums of rugby.

Galu played at the same time that Savali did, but they were on rival teams. Savali was the star quarterback for the Sharks, and sported the crisp blue and white of the new Samoana High School uniforms under Tu'ufuli's direction as coach. The fresh uniforms, outfitted by the school's booster club headed by Tu'ufuli's uncle Drury Samia, were almost as impressive as the team's undefeated season.[25] The new cheerleaders practiced many afternoons in the shade of the science building, organized by teachers Peka Solomona, Julia Levi, and others. Together, the organization and resources put into developing the sports program generated a buzz. Football continued to grow in popularity and was drawing more people into its orbit, from some parents who followed the college or professional games to young boys drawn to new competitions and performances of masculinity, and perhaps to a lesser extent, to girls who would be active on the sidelines as cheerleaders, also performing a new kind of femininity.

When I asked him what brought him into the game, Galu described a process of gradually being drawn into the sport from a young age. Having lived near Mapusaga High School, where all the high school football games were played at that time, he joined other kids on the sidelines imitating the game with a slipper as a football. As a boy he was an all-around athlete—he played volleyball, tennis, and golf, but was a standout basketball player. According to him, his athleticism in other sports gave him the confidence to compete at football even though he wasn't as big as some of the other players.

Jason, another former player I interviewed who played high school football locally but did not play in college, similarly described the lure of football excitement as early as elementary school. Listening to the games on the radio gave him the opportunity to be part of the football phenomenon even when he was too young to attend or play in the games himself. He went on to point out the influence of his cousins who played: "You know, just talking to them when they come home after their games and they're excited about the game, I guess." By the time he was old enough, he was already committed to following in their footsteps and playing at the local high school.

Getting caught up in the excitement of the game was a common theme in early experiences with football. But at a certain age many step back from the

1.3 Samoana High School cheer, Pago Park, 1984. PHOTO CREDIT: KEITH DAHL, COURTESY OF FELETI BARSTOW PUBLIC LIBRARY.

excitement of competition and the lure of football's fabled futures to soberly assess whether there is a possible payoff for the investment of time and energy required to move to the next level. Galu described his approach:

> [B]y the time I got to [my] junior year, I wanted to play really bad. I wanted to have at least one year and then I considered it my preparation year and then my last year would be my—my year to actually try to make something of it, to see if I could get a chance to go off-island to play. So I decided to play. Went to college. I played two years in college. After the second year, I sort of looked at my overall . . . goals and priorities and thought to myself, you know, although I'm a good athlete . . . realistically, I need to face reality. I don't think I'll go past this level—the NAIA Division 2 level. I don't think it's something that I'm committed enough to, to make it happen.

Realizing that his chances to again move to the next level of football in some professional capacity were slim, he abandoned the game to focus on his studies.

Galu's experience illustrates some of the affective, social, and instrumental appeals of the sport. He tried out for the football team partly to see if he could parlay his athleticism into an opportunity to play in the United States. But he also points out the draw of becoming a high school star player, a "Big

Man on Campus" in a sport with excitement, booster support, cool uniforms, and cheerleaders. Remembering Fui's remark as well, we know that for many players football was linked to the vague dream of success in football in the United States. Savali too, playing later than Fui, shared his dream of football futures: "[W]hen I was playing high school football, all I was thinking was the NFL. I was gonna go to college, finish college, go to the NFL, make lots of money, have a family." In the context of the 1980s, where portions of local youth culture looked to US imports—from Michael Jackson with his glove and jackets to the popping and locking of *Breakin'* to late-night broadcasts of the soap opera *Days of Our Lives* to Madonna, Cindy Lauper, jelly shoes, and neon bracelets—American cultural products signified both the new and the modern, consumed and displayed in ways that provided an exciting outlet for many youths chafing at the rigid expectations of daily household, village, and church obligations. In retrospect, the appropriation of new elements of American popular culture was also a source of currency and status in some youth circles—the local breakdance crews were "bad," classmates who returned after a summer in the "mainland" had stories to tell, and if anyone was lucky enough to get a leather jacket they sported it in the oppressive humidity of the tropics. As an American cultural form, football was enmeshed with imaginaries of Amelika as cosmopolitan, the source of "cool" for youth, the land of opportunity, and a fabled destination on the horizon.

New Fields of Possibility

For many players from Tutuila, that path to Amelika is a circular one and at some point brings them back to the island. Returnees with some off-island success—like Tu'ufuli and others—were local icons, symbols of off-island movement, and active agents who both facilitated the disciplining of young Samoan bodies within the framework of sport and continued to promote a change whereby players and their families would increasingly see football as a ticket to college. The young men I interviewed who described football as "the only way to get off the rock, besides the military" are in many ways inheritors of this orientation to the importance of leaving the islands—not merely as part of a larger tradition of malaga (see Lilomaiava-Doktor 2009) but also for strategic opportunities for upward mobility today. Their journeys parallel other Pacific sport migrations, but with different supporting infrastructure, contexts, and outcomes.[26]

Since the late 1970s, football has become a highly visible route to the United States. Over the same time period, the American Sāmoa economy has become increasingly credentialed and dominated by a US-funded bureaucratic welfare state with a narrative of success that often winds through American educational institutions. It is in this context that I saw an instructor at a local high school scold her students for not paying attention in class, asking if they want to end up working at the local canneries, which employ largely nonresident labor.[27] Once quite seriously trumpeted as a symbol of "development," cannery work is now used as a deterrent option when other pathways have failed. This is one example that indexes a shift in ideas about success and "the good life" that have been transformed by transnational movement of various kinds over the course of the twentieth century.

In many ways, Tu'ufuli had been a strident proponent of movement off island for education. A number of interviewees revealed to me that they had either trained with him or had him as a coach. Savali recalled him always imploring the players to "Be humble!" while Simon described him as "like Vince Lombardi" in his ability to inspire and motivate players to perform physically and to have the confidence to see themselves succeeding off island. The social and cultural capital he accrued during his years playing college and professional football allowed him to mobilize personal and coaching networks to place students at schools in the United States. At the same time, my mother Kristin, who taught high school English, tutored the players for the Test of English as a Foreign Language (TOEFL) and SAT exams and helped them sort through the paperwork required for college enrollment. They worked as a team: coming from a relatively privileged middle-class American background, she used her educational cultural capital and administrative know-how to help the student athletes navigate the labyrinth of college admissions while her domestic labor allowed Tu'ufuli to fully inhabit his role as coach and all the time commitments that came with it. In this, she represents many other women whose administrative, organizational, domestic, and emotional labor has and continues to underwrite the infrastructure of sport in American Sāmoa and beyond.

Tu'ufuli and others have also been important to improving parental opinions of the sport and increasing support for children going away for school rather than staying to take care of family obligations on a daily basis. Even within the expanding conceptions of tautua (discussed more in the next chapter), serious commitment to the game was still unusual at that point and entailed navigating existing cultural expectations for young men. One of my clearest memories involving Savali was accompanying my father to his family home in our village. There he spoke with Savali's aunt, whom I remember as a kindly elderly woman who gifted me with a red sei fulumoa.

Tu'ufuli was there to discuss her nephew's participation, and to explain why that would take his time from home. In sitting down with Savali's aunt, he was showing respect to her as an elder and guardian, and also recognizing that what he was asking was still out of the ordinary for many young men. She allowed Savali to play, and after high school he went on to play in college at a small school, earning his degree before returning to Tutuila and building a successful professional career. Looking back on his journey, in our conversation Savali (now Manu'a District Governor Laolagi) reflected on the life lessons around motivation and perseverance, and shared: "Football made me who I am today."

Alema, another former Samoana player who went on to be part of BYU's 1984 national championship team with Vai Sikahema, Robert Anae, Thor Salanoa, Kurt Gouveia, and Lakei Heimuli, described this shift in identification among the players and the support from families:

> [B]ack when I was playing ... it was kind of old-school mentality to where you know, a lot of the parents didn't see what the ... positives [of playing football] were. I think now that those athletes are starting to be on TV and it's someone that they can identify with, that came from the

1.4 Leone Lions versus Samoana Sharks, Pago Park, 1983. PHOTO CREDIT: KEITH DAHL, COURTESY OF FELETI BARSTOW PUBLIC LIBRARY.

village or was a sister's friend or someone that they know in their family or that somebody knew, now they can see the reality. There could be a possibility that that person would make it to the next level, or go to college and get a degree, using football as a vessel to get there.

The changes he describes, from an "old-school mentality" to one in which (as a result of media coverage and personal contacts) parents now recognize football as an opportunity to go to college, get a degree, or even play professionally, are important. In them we see parents and their children responding to an alternative vision of the future—one that is not only made possible by the transnational circulation of people and media images, but in turn is materialized by their own participation, substantiating the imagined possibility for themselves and serving as another narrative example for others.

The increasing support for football is not necessarily seen in systematic or direct investment in equipment, weight-training programs, coach training (although these are all part of expatriate efforts to "give back" to the community), or in other policies of sport infrastructure building or increased allocations by the governor's office, local legislature, or Department of Education.[28] (Interviews with ASHSAA staff indicated budget instability dependent on DOE allocations and not a systematic investment as one might expect given the recent years' media coverage.) What has changed is the amount of media coverage of local and US-based football; the increased presence of off-island coaches for camps and recruiting; the existence of highly anticipated games like the Samoa Bowl that drew players and coaches from the United States (and, in a later iteration, from Australia) to play the American Sāmoa all-star team; the surge of representative teams traveling to international contests like the International Federation of American Football (IFAF) Under-19 competitions; the assistance of more nongovernmental organizations providing donations and services to the island; as well as the widespread support throughout the island during the season.

In the fall of 2007 I attended the local football games every week and saw strong game attendance as well as public displays of support and personal connections (including many people wearing T-shirts with the name, number, and/or likeness of one of their friends or relatives who were in the game). One Saturday morning we were driving out to the other side of the island for a playoff game, slowly following the two-lane road that winds along the coast, when I that noticed swaths of the island were draped in school colors. From the town area to Nu'u'uli the Samoana blue kept appearing, with messages like "Go Sharks!" and "Go Big Blue!" painted on banners. Even one of

1.5 Team American Samoa coach Suaese "Pooch" Taʻase addresses the player delegation the week before they depart for the Under-19 World American Football Championship (2012) in Texas. PHOTO CREDIT: AUTHOR.

the small atoll outcroppings near the shore (Fata ma Futi) had a Samoana banner—someone had swum out and hung an ʻie lāvalava in Samoana blue up in the trees so it could be seen by people driving by. After the game, we drove further out into the western district and saw that it too was covered—but in yellow and green, the colors of Leone High School—in honor of the day's events. The island was spatially marked with school loyalties and football fanaticism, indicating an investment by the larger community in the outcome of the game, and the way football rivalries had been incorporated into existing village and district rivalries as well.[29]

Sports Mobility: A Dream, an Opportunity, an Escape?

Like those of many other young athletes, Tuʻufuli's accounts revealed different aspects of his experience in and attraction to sports. Excellence in athletics was a huge source of pride and accomplishment for a young boy, recently arrived in Hawaiʻi, who had been shuttled into special education classes because he couldn't speak English and was having trouble in school. Sports participation was also an important way to deal with and counter the racism he experienced both in Hawaiʻi and in the continental United States. In Hawaiʻi, Samoans have a long history of being marginalized economically and socially, concentrated in poorer areas of Oʻahu, and discriminated against by more dominant socioeconomic groups (local Japanese, Chinese, and Haole).[30] Like other native Pacific Islanders in Hawaiʻi, stereotypes of Samoans as lazy, incompetent breeders and violent thugs have been used to both limit their opportunities and explain their continued socioeconomic disenfranchisement (see, e.g., Merry 2000, 128; Teaiwa 1995). Even recent decades of upward mobility for many Samoan families and high-profile success stories like former Honolulu mayor Mufi Hannemann or US congressional delegate Tulsi Gabbard have not dislodged these entrenched stereotypes. While anecdotal evidence suggests that earlier migrants and their children are doing better than recent immigrants, perhaps linked to networks, educational achievement, or the changing economy, as late as 2013 American Community Survey data still reported "Samoans are Hawaii's Lowest Earners" (*Samoa Observer*, October 9, 2013).[31]

With limited opportunities for Samoan migrants in Hawaiʻi in the 1960s, Tuʻufuli used sports as a way up and out of the islands, as an alternative to opting out of the American system, becoming a beach boy, or returning to Sāmoa to eke out a living. As a "local boy made good" through sports, he made a name for himself and his extended family and also represented Samoans positively within the wider community. As for many other immigrant groups, Samoan sporting prowess was an important public demonstration of value, prestige, and belonging (Eisen and Wiggins 1994; Mallon 2012; Thangaraj, Arnaldo Jr., and Chin 2016). Tuʻufuli's mastery of sport, first as a player and later as a coach and trainer, became his expertise and an important center of self-confidence and authority in relations with others. Although he was highly recruited out of high school, his low grades put him on the junior college path. As a senior, top college coach Duffy Daugherty was interested in him, but, Tuʻufuli said, once Daugherty became aware of his grades he told him: "Son, I couldn't touch you with a ten-foot pole!" Instead, his coach at ʻĀiea connected him with a coach at Wenatchee Junior College in Washington State. There he drew fellow Samoan players from Hawaiʻi such as Leslie Kent, Jerry Lalau, and brothers John and Pati Talalotu. Later, in Missoula, Montana, he never had to pay for anything and he lived well; all he had to do was play football. According to former teammates, this he did with fierce determination, and he left the University of Montana with its first undefeated season and its first division national championship. His life as a star college player brought a number of material rewards—a far cry from his childhood in Sāmoa and Hawaiʻi.

RETURNING HOME

After several years in the Canadian Football League and with the NFL's Philadelphia Eagles, my father returned to American Sāmoa with my mother, my brother, and me in 1979 to care for our aging grandmother. He began on contract running the athletic program at the local community college (ASCC) and would eventually become active in the local high school sports scene as an administrator and as a coach. Although football had been played on Tutuila for at least a decade before his return, he joined a critical mass of returning sportsmen and women who expanded sport outlets for youth. Among them was Tony Solaita, until recently the only known major league baseball player from American Sāmoa. After Solaita retired from baseball in 1983 he moved back to the island and was instrumental in revitalizing Little League baseball; the local baseball diamond was named in his honor. Ed Imo played college football at San Diego State and did a stint with the San Diego Chargers before returning in 1979 and becoming active with the local high school sports program and later running the ASCC sports program. Lealao Melila Purcell returned with his family after retiring from the military; he and his wife Moana Purcell have been key contacts for football-related events, serving on the organizing committee for the Samoa Bowl and as part of various hosting groups for camps and clinics offered by off-island coaches. Many more have been involved with developing football on the island over the past four decades, and some of them cycle among positions in administration (whether at the Department of Education or school level), teaching and coaching, or volunteering.[32]

Like other returnees who had short professional football careers (or didn't even make it past the initial draft or tryouts), Tuʻufuli did not return a wealthy man. He instead had to rely on the experience he gained and the expertise he developed during his years in college and playing pro football. With limited economic capital, he had to parlay social and cultural capital—his personal networks, specific knowledge about different sports, their training techniques, rules, and regulations, as well as his experience and classroom-based knowledge of the body (his bachelor's degree was in health and physical fitness)—into a career on Tutuila. This he did with modest success—directing the college sports program, coaching in the high schools, directing the ASHSAA, heading up the local American Cancer Society chapter, and coaching track and field for the American Samoa National Olympic Committee. As a head coach, he regularly posted undefeated seasons and sent scores of players off island for football and schooling. In his capacity as ASHSAA director, he managed equipment, refereed games, and organized a number of summer clinics that featured coaches and NFL players (including Al and Falaniko Noga, Mark Tuinei, and Jesse Sapolu). As a track and field coach, he escorted athletes to several Olympic Games, South Pacific Mini-Games, and Goodwill Games. In those roles he communicated to another generation the importance of competing, adopting a strong work ethic, maintaining discipline for success, and leveraging sport for opportunity. At the high point of his activity on the island, he even ran for faipule of his village, narrowly losing to a more established candidate.

But my father's story is bittersweet. Today we understand NFL contracts to be highly lucrative, with deals ranging in the millions and a minimum annual rookie salary of $610,000 as of 2020.[33] The collective bargaining agreement between the players' union and owners established a minimum salary schedule according to experience in 1982, but when he played in the 1970s, salaries were as low as $25,000. Over the years, the contracts have skyrocketed with the expansion of the football industry and especially with lucrative media deals, intensifying the promise of riches in the eyes of young hopefuls. In some ways this has changed the character of the sport, with the imperative to win and capitalization reaching ever-higher levels. While you could argue that players make much more money now than they did in the 1970s (and certainly this is true), the NFL Players' Association reports that the average career of an NFL player is three and a half years and that two years after retirement, 78 percent of former players have gone bankrupt or are under financial stress related to joblessness or divorce.[34] The possibility of accumulating economic capital is a good one, but these statistics urge us not to assume the durative nature of that accumulation.

Unlike some of his student-athletes, Tu'ufuli did not go into private business or pursue a political career. He remained in education where the pay was modest, and after a series of legal troubles and physical ailments, retired early. Toward the end of his life he was on disability retirement and managed a variety of health issues, having had both knees replaced to relieve pain associated with old football and rugby injuries. The days of running a mile or more a day in the heat of the afternoon on the island, playing golf, playing rugby, and rowing with his village 'aumaga in the Flag Day races were long gone and walking for any length of time was a challenge. No longer active in the local sports scene, his extensive service to the community and his role in the early stages of sport development on the island were a dim memory for some and a complete unknown to most of the new generation of players. As a University of Montana Hall of Fame inductee, he received recognition for his football accomplishments and revisited the site of the pinnacle of his football career. In his twilight years he credited sports for providing a way to "make something" of himself, to "see the world," and to make a concrete contribution to the lives of young people on the island. May he rest in peace and live on in the memories of those who knew him.

Prestige, Recognition, and Forms of Capital

Transnational sport migration is a growing reality for people across the Pacific. But these routes have specific dynamics and histories, with both well-worn grooves and new offshoots that speak to community histories and individual experience as well as to regional and transnational geopolitical structures (Sassen 1998; Carter 2013). The "fabled futures" once rooted in paradigms of modernization and development of years past are now woven into processes of globalization and gendered prospects for mobility represented by global industries such as American football (see Uperesa 2010b).

As I address more in chapter 4, the size and opportunity structure of the football industrial complex attract many young Samoan men to the game. For my father and many other former players like him, football represented a viable avenue for accumulating economic capital (even though the potential payoff was meager by today's standards). But it was not all about money; the intense emotion and pride of accomplishment and representing one's family and community was a big draw to sport, as were other forms of social capital in the form of prestige, adulation, and connection to people invested in their performance on the field.

In Samoan communities and beyond, fulfilling the obligation and privilege of performing tautua (service, in this case expanded and transnationalized), has also been an important outcome for many like Tu'ufuli. Explored in more depth in the next chapter, this often comes in the form of publicized success of sporting exploits for younger men, and once successful and established, the opportunity to "give back" takes other forms. In this way the "escape" is from limited routes to potentially unlimited opportunity, not necessarily from family and community (although it is used in this way by some). My father's story is hopeful in that sports participation and success allowed him to make a life for himself, care for ailing parents, and give me and my siblings opportunities not available to him growing up. His experience also provides a compelling example of how individual and community desires shape, and are shaped by, larger national, political, and economic projects of varying scales. It represents precisely the kinds of aspirations many young players and their families now have, except with more money at stake. Still, the bittersweet bodily sacrifice paid for the opportunities promised by these circuits interrupts the largely celebratory narrative reproduced in popular media stories. It is a price he willingly paid (and, he said, would again).

Two

Football, Tautua, and Faʻasāmoa

WE PULLED UP TO THE FALEOʻO at Suʻigaula Beach in the morning, and the rain poured down. Penny Semaia, the director of our academic division, and I had just driven over from Sadie's By the Sea. The governor had not yet arrived but some of the local dignitaries were there, and members of the Troy and Theodora Polamalu Foundation's Faʻa Samoa Initiative were slowly arriving. It was Wednesday, June 24, 2015, the second day of the Initiative. Most of the 150-plus team members had arrived on Friday and Monday night's flights and the ceremony opening the week's events had just taken place the day before. At the edge of the faleoʻo the local hosts began to welcome the visiting guests, giving them ʻula mosoʻoi and inviting them in.

The ʻava ceremony had been kept small: Troy and Theodora and their sons, the heads of the different divisions, and a few of the doctors who came as part of the medical mission sat at posts within the fale. Arrayed opposite them were a few select local dignitaries and matai, including Governor Lolo Moliga, Secretary of Samoan Affairs Mauga Tasi Asuega, and Deputy Secretary of Samoan Affairs Tuiagamoa Tavai. Also participating were Department of Youth and Women's Affairs Director and former NFL player Jonathan Fanene and Deputy Director Paʻu Roy Ausage. Seiuli Jesse Sapolu, a matai and former NFL standout, spoke on behalf of the Polamalus and the

Initiative, and each of the directors said a few words as they accepted their 'ava (also known as kava). The 'ava ceremony was conducted to welcome the honored guests on their current visit, hosted by the governor's office, the district governors, and local government offices, with the reigning Miss American Sāmoa Annelise Sword acting as tāupou for the occasion.[1]

The next evening, we had all been invited to a beautiful dinner put on by the governor's office, held at the Lee Auditorium in Utulei. In a full house of what looked to be about three hundred people, the governor's chief of staff Fiu Johnny Saelua presided over the crowd as master of ceremonies. There was a buzz as people were chatting at their tables and watching the Methodist youth dance group's lovely siva and sāsā performance. An elaborate meal was set for the guests, and in between the different entertainment numbers the key government agencies hosting the divisions of the Polamalu camp—the Department of Education, the Department for Youth and Women's Affairs, and the governor's office—presented gifts to their guests.

What had been originally a football camp for boys in 2011, and expanded to include volleyball for girls in 2013, in 2015 also included a medical mission, an academic/life skills division, and an elementary sports component under the NFL Play 60 program. After two years of planning and organizing, the activities were held over the course of four intensive days. The articulated goals were to provide ongoing outreach, resources, and assistance to American Sāmoa along with some specific kinds of work and training.

The sport camps held on Tutuila (usually with a local organizing partner and off-island coaches) have typically centered solely on sport. While there may be cultural practices like gifting, traditional meals, hospitality and entertainment, and so on woven into the visits, up until this point few explicitly brought culture into the framing of the camps or clinics themselves.[2] In this way the Fa'a Samoa Initiative was distinct. The branding explicitly invoked Samoan culture in the naming of the 2015 initiative, but also included the logo design, which featured two crossing nifo 'oti forming the third A in FA'A SAMOA at the center of the logo. The extent to which recognizable cultural elements were explicitly integrated was unusual, and for that reason it is a notable example of how Samoan culture is being incorporated into events like this. More broadly, when combined with select features of other football-related events, we can trace some of the ways that fa'asāmoa is being linked to the American game of football, particularly through a reconceptualization of the practice of tautua (often translated loosely as *service*). In this process, elements of cultural practice and symbolism are woven into what is often (mistakenly) seen as the "culture-free" realm of sport. In the linking

2.1 Fa'a Samoa Initiative Football Drills at Veterans Memorial Stadium, Tutuila.
PHOTO CREDIT: AUTHOR.

of Samoan culture and the modern sport of American football we see the indigenization of sport, and the use of sport as a site that refracts community histories, agendas, and bids for recognition.[3] This chapter first explores how football is being selectively integrated into formal aspects of fa'asāmoa, and then turns to consider how fa'asāmoa is being incorporated into football.

"Children of Sāmoa"

The closing scenes of the ESPN documentary *Polynesian Power: Islanders in Pro Football* show a royal reception held by His Highness Afioga i le Ao o le Mālō Malietoa Tanumafili II, the late head of state of independent Sāmoa. The reception is in honor of two Samoan players in the National Football League, Pisa Tinoisamoa and Isaac Sopoaga. The footage gives viewers a glimpse of the traditional 'ava ceremony where we see men bring in long 'ava roots and gifts of contribution to the ceremony, while guests and matai sit cross-legged, arranged by rank at their designated posts, each of which provides the support to the Samoan fale in which the ceremony is held.

2.2 Isaac Sopoaga and Pisa Tinoisamoa with His Highness Malietoa Tanumafili II. COURTESY OF FILM CO-DIRECTOR JEREMY SPEAR.

The two players, honored by the reception, approach and kneel at His Highness Malietoa's side, exchanging polite greetings inaudible to the camera. In his speech, the tulāfale addresses the athletes, wishing them well in their endeavors. His words are translated on screen as "Children of Samoa who are engaged in sport on the other side of the world, your bodies may be dark, but may your vision be clear." The proverb he uses, "ia pōuliuli lou (outou) tino 'ae mālamalama lau (outou) va'ai" can also be translated as "may your bodies be invisible and your sight clear."[4] This proverb is still used to offer best wishes to athletes, and in this context clearly expresses the wish for the visitors' success in the sport of American football.

This exchange is exceptional for a few reasons. First, as narrator Dwayne "The Rock" Johnson points out, it is the first time players from the American National Football League were received by His Highness. Traditionally, the eminence of His Highness Malietoa as father of the independent nation of Sāmoa (occupying a position of paramount chief, head of state, and independence leader) would restrict his presence to the most rarefied of state and cultural events. Under usual circumstances, he would not have cause to receive Samoan football players from the United States because independent Sāmoa has stronger postcolonial ties with the British Commonwealth nations like New Zealand and Australia rather than the United States, and football is largely a sport played and rooted in areas under American sovereignty.[5] It is nearly absent in independent Sāmoa where the dominant professional and amateur sports are rugby and rugby league (although that has begun to change in recent years). Moreover, the young players had not achieved the rank of matai and so in customary circumstances would not be seated in the fale but rather outside, as taulele'a doing the bidding of the chiefs.

According to one of the film's directors, Papāli'itele Jack Tihati Thompson (who is godson to His Highness Malietoa) assisted in setting up past trips to Sāmoa for filming and helped make this audience possible. The two players highlighted in the film, Pisa and Isaac, had been in the NFL one and two years, respectively, at that point. In anticipation of the release celebrations for the film, Thompson approached His Highness about inviting the players and honoring their achievement, and blessing the film. However, as rookies in the NFL, their achievement was modest as compared to other Samoan players whose illustrious football careers preceded them, such as Seiuli Manase Jesse Sapolu, a former player whose career was significant both for its longevity and accomplishment. Briefly in the footage we see him also seated in the fale. Sapolu is an icon in his own right, having won four Super Bowls with one of Sāmoa's favorite teams, the 49ers; he had also become a mentor to Isaac in San Francisco, and was invited to join them on this trip. Part of the rookies' elevation to a status worthy of being received by His Highness came from being stars in this film, which was sponsored and released by ESPN, a global media outlet. The reception not only gave Pisa and Isaac a chance to visit Sāmoa, it was an opportunity to honor Le Ao o le Mālō and incorporate the players' achievements within the rubric of the Samoan nation, in which His Highness, as "father of Sāmoa" was a key figure.

This reception is an important example of the ways in which status, prestige, and capital afforded by football success are being incorporated within the fa'asāmoa more widely. In turn, it is being harnessed to new kinds of projects that are individual, familial, regional, and national in scope. The transformation of the matai system and its associated sources of status and prestige can be seen in the figure of His Highness Malietoa himself, whose position as head of state was the culmination of a long process of colonial centralization of government, the imposition of Western institutions of governance, and a successful independence movement in Sāmoa. At the same time, the orator's words mark the incorporation of the "Children of Sāmoa" as subordinate in the family idiom to His Highness Malietoa as father, and reveal the reclamation of their achievements in "sport on the other side of the world" to the larger Samoan nation and the fa'amatai itself. Just as can be glimpsed in this footage of independent Sāmoa, so too has the matai system been actively transformed in American Sāmoa, as paths to status, prestige, and material resources have changed with US-led "development" efforts.

Although today we often talk about it as a deep cultural practice that forms the bedrock of Samoan society and in that way imply that it is a practice from time immemorial, transformation is not new to the fa'amatai

(Meleisea 1987; Meleisea and Schoeffel 2015; Meleisea and Schoeffel Meleisea 1987). In the midst of change, however, the Samoan proverb "E sui faiga, 'ae tūmau fa'avae" is often used to reorient to a longer perspective of stability, noting that foundations remaining even as practices change. The notion of matai and the specific way we understand matai today is a relatively recent historical phenomenon that has been in transition over the past 100 years.[6] Anthropologist Serge Tcherkézoff (2000) points out that in debates about governance the role of the matai is usually presented as though it were permanent, unchanging, and central to the operation of Samoan society. Yet matai are not "out of time" nor are they the result of mere acculturation to Western values of democracy; rather, as a comprehensive class of title holders they are the result of Samoan historical transformation.[7] This interaction with His Highness Malietoa shows part of this ongoing transformation whereby alternative resources (football prestige as symbolic capital) are being woven back into the contemporary sociocultural formations known as the fa'asāmoa and the fa'amatai.

Fa'asāmoa, the Fa'amatai, and Tautua

It is widely espoused that the fa'amatai, the chiefly hierarchy of Samoan lands and titles, is a central pillar of the fa'asāmoa.[8] Briefly, fa'asāmoa or "the Samoan way" is today broadly understood to refer to Samoan culture and encompasses a wide range of beliefs, values, and practices. The fa'amatai remains a central feature of life in contemporary Samoa because it governs rights and claims to landed resources and serves as a framework for social relations. It also provides the most prestigious of full recognition to individuals who carry their family titles. Although it is a long-standing indigenous sociopolitical system, it is also a living and changing set of relationships and practices.[9]

In her book chapter "*E Faigata le Alofa*: The Samoan *Fa'amatai*—Reflections from Afar" Samoan sociologist Tamasailau Suaalii-Sauni offers a useful exploration of how the fa'amatai is translated across different geographic and social spaces.[10] Drawing on a variety of distinguished Samoan scholars including Asiata Alaelua Va'alepa Saleimoa Va'ai, 'Aiono Fanaafi Le Tagaloa, Reverend Fa'au'uga Logovae, and former head of state and paramount chief Tui Atua Tupua Tamasese Ta'isi Efi, she contextualizes important concepts and principles that serve as the basis for thought and action within the fa'amatai and reflects on the challenges to its legitimacy and longevity in the context of Aotearoa New Zealand.[11] In the discussion, alofa (translated as love or compassion) and pule (translated as power or authority) are identified as core principles of the matai system (Suaalii-Sauni 2007, 38). She points out that alofa is often manifested and measured by gifting and selfless service, as can be seen in the words used to refer to describe monetary gifts to respected people within the Samoan community or to describe contributions made on behalf of families in times of need (si'i alofa). "*Alofa* is a term that also sits within the concept of fe*alofa*ni, which refers to the idea of relational harmony" (2007, 42). Pule, on the other hand, refers to authority of individuals and groups within particular spheres.[12] It is helpful to understand these as counterbalancing principles that not only frame the fa'amatai, as Suaalii-Sauni contends, but also frame how people look after social relations in daily life (in the family, in the village, in public).

A key component of the matai system is tautua.[13] As a core feature of reciprocal relationships between family and title holder, tautua as a concept and practice is central to sustaining the fa'amatai. "The notion of 'true service' is captured within the ethical and moral imperatives of the principle of *tautua* often cited as critical to gaining *pule* or authority and respect" (Suaalii-Sauni 2007, 40). Actively contributing to fa'alavelave (ceremonial gatherings and exchanges associated with family events such as weddings, funerals, title investitures, etc.) and being present in family fono (meetings or discussions on important decisions) are ways to show your interest and commitment to family issues. "Showing face," meeting obligations, and taking part in important family functions help to sustain good relations between relatives, a central occupation in a social world in which the most important distinctions are not necessarily those of class but of status and rank. The ability to mobilize strong relationships (and thereby resources or support) can raise an individual's profile over a number of years or a clan's prominence over a generation or two. For those who are ambitious and desire a title, different kinds of personal resources or capital become important in fulfilling obligations that allow one to strengthen social relationships and demonstrate worthiness and capacity for leadership. For others, serving the family is central to the ability to make claims on land and resources that fall under the purview of the family and pule of the matai.

Esteemed Samoan historian Leasiolagi Malama Meleisea reflects, "*Fa'asamoa* is clear in principles and flexible in details" (1995, 20). This implies that although specific practices have changed, core features or values remain. For example, during contemporary ceremonial exchanges honored guests are gifted with money, bolts of cloth, and cases of canned beef, supplementing and sometimes taking the place of fine mats. The principle is properly recognizing the presence and contributions of honored guests, thus respectfully maintaining harmonious social relations and in so doing, demonstrating knowledge of the proper forms of recognition and protocol. The form of the gifts has changed significantly in conjunction with changes in subsistence and economic practice. The finely woven mats, livestock, and produce of the past have shifted toward cash, market commodities, and often mats of lesser quality as fewer people raise pigs and grow coconuts, taro, and bananas on the plantation and weave fine mats.

In tandem with the symbolism and material practice of the faʻamatai, what is seen as tautua has also substantially changed over the past century. Like many other indigenous concepts in Sāmoa, the practice, significance, and value of tautua has been transformed over a number of decades, through local innovations and opportunities made available by the association with other more powerful nations (see also Lilomaiava-Doktor 2009a). In what follows I return to the example of football to explore how tautua has been extended beyond the bounds of the family, village, or islands themselves and linked to the redefinition of belonging and citizenship in a wider transnational Samoan community.

Football as Tautua

Football, like many other opportunities made available through the association with the United States, has become another way to pursue both individual accomplishment and bring prestige to one's extended family. During the trip organized in conjunction with the filming of parts of the ESPN documentary *Polynesian Power,* Jesse Sapolu was bestowed the high chief title Seiuli by Sāmoa's head of state. People who were there on that trip with him have told me that for years he humbly resisted the call to be a matai but with this trip his family took advantage of the opportunity and organized a saofaʻi for him. Sapolu was part of a football dynasty with the 49ers, winning four Super Bowl rings and twelve division titles. His career with the team spanned two decades (1983–1997) and through his football prowess he was known not only to Samoan communities on the island and in the diaspora, but to the wider American populace as well. Over the years he has been active in the Samoan community, and his title bestowal recognized these contributions, as well as his genealogical birthright through his mother and her natal village of Sāpapaliʻi (Sapolu 2012).[14]

Another Samoan former football player (University of Miami), star, and title holder is Dwayne Johnson. He first achieved fame as "The Rock" while wrestling with the World Wrestling Entertainment organization and has since starred in a number of Hollywood films (in 2017 he topped *Forbes's* list of highest-paid Hollywood actors, and maintained that position into 2020). At the 2008 Congressional Award dinner the late American Sāmoa congressman Faleomavaega Eni Hunkin presented him with the Congressional Horizon Award in recognition of his foundation's work to promote youth physical fitness, obesity prevention, and education. Three years earlier he had traveled to independent Sāmoa and was bestowed the title Seiuli by the late head of state, His Highness Malietoa Tanumafili II. His title bestowal also recognized individual achievements as well as genealogical ties.

Both Sapolu and Johnson were high-profile stars in the United States, remained involved with the Samoan communities there and in the islands, and used their wealth and status to "give back." Yet to my knowledge, neither of them had taken up long-term residence in the islands or had performed daily tautua to a family matai in Sāmoa. Their titles recognize a different kind of tautua, and also represent the efforts of Samoan communities to both recognize and incorporate the success of their members as they venture further afield. This incorporation through matai selection by the family, if accepted by the individual, can oblige the titleholder to remain active and render faithful service when necessary.[15] Since this may represent further claims on time and resources, some Samoans in the diaspora resist becoming a matai. Many of those who are not active more widely in the islands nevertheless are active in the diasporic communities; they bring recognition and provide their own families in the islands with material resources to build family houses, purchase cars, tithe to churches, open businesses, or participate in fa'alavelave. These kinds of contributions are also considered tautua to one's immediate or extended family, and this is recognized in some title bestowals.[16]

While many young students see a move abroad to the United States (whether through football, college scholarships, the military, or other means) as "a ticket off the rock" and may settle permanently in the States, there are a number who view football and college education as tools with which to perform future service.[17] One of the coaches I spoke with, Suaese "Pooch" Ta'ase, was well respected in many quarters not only for his own journey to the United States on football scholarship, but because of his role in promoting education among the entire student body and using his transnational coaching networks to help his students get football scholarship opportunities of their own.

On the morning of our initial interview, a friend who was teaching SAT prep classes took me with her to the high school. She introduced me to Ta'ase, who was also the school's vice principal, and he agreed to do an initial interview with me. While we were talking he relayed his own difficulties as a high school student in the United States and the turnaround he experienced once his family brought him back to Tutuila to attend the very school at which he now coaches. I asked him, "Now did you think that you—you know, at that time when you went off-island, did you think that you would be coming back?" Emphatically he said, "Oh, yes. Yes. I mean it was always—I mean, I even told our [coach], I said, 'You know, may God bless I make it to the League, fine. If not that, I'm going to come back and do what I'm doing now [coaching].' It's something I envisioned, I had in mind . . . just like those guys gave me an opportunity . . . I'm here to try to give another kid an opportunity." Over the past several years as coach, his team has attended the camps and clinics held on island by US coaches, he has worked with a strong parent booster group to take the team to summer camps off-island, and he regularly sends players off-island on football scholarships to small schools. In discussions with local and off-island entities that act as brokers or clearinghouses for football scholarship opportunities, he was often noted as one of the most responsive coaches when asked for student-athlete information necessary for recruiting.

In 2015, the team made a monthlong trip to Hawai'i, where they played three of the local high schools in preseason scrimmages and regular season nonconference games. After the game I saw at the Aloha Stadium, players from the visiting team from Sāmoa each donned 'ie lāvalava as they lined up to greet and congratulate the other team. Each player gave his 'ie to a player on the opposing team, and some of the local players put them on before leaving the field. Once the home team exited, the team came to the sideline and sang the school song with the booster crowd (many of them alumni of the school who had raised funds to support the team's stay on O'ahu). As the head coach, Ta'ase gave a short lāuga expressing his thanks to all the supporters of the team. The team has made subsequent trips to Hawai'i for preseason exhibition games.

Aside from his involvement with the school program, Ta'ase also represents the school at various functions. In this representative capacity he has continued to develop his understanding of social protocol for different situations—giving and responding to greetings, giving short speeches, reciprocating gifts—and is actively enhancing his knowledge of Samoan cultural practice by calling on the wisdom and expertise of elder mentors. In our interview he relayed how one advised him, "'It's not more about speaking, it's about not being afraid.' Because another person could learn and be very fluent with their speaking but when they get out in the front . . . So I'm like, okay, just like I'm speaking to my football team, you know what I mean? [I]f you're afraid, no matter how good you know the language, it's not going to come out because you are afraid."

Ta'ase spoke about his interest in learning more about the fa'asāmoa and becoming more actively involved with the matai system—thus extending his service to the community from what is often (simplistically) seen as separate terrain: the "modern" context of local educational and sporting institutions and the customary realm of the fa'amatai. In reality, the additional knowledge required to represent the school properly shows the two are interwoven in everyday practice in Tutuila. Being able to navigate both the Samoan and pālagi contexts gave him, in his words, "the best of both worlds." Ta'ase was earning respect not only for his winning program, but for his service to the school, and through that, the district in which he lives.

TAUTUA IN THE CONTEMPORARY MOMENT

In a 2007 lecture High Chief Tui Atua Tupua Tamasese Ta'isi Efi discusses three different kinds of tautua, distinguished by frequency and location of service: *tautua nofo tuavae*, which refers to daily service in residence at the family's household given to the matai and the village; *tautua 'ai taumalele*, which refers to regular service given by someone who resides outside of the village; and *osi 'āiga*, which refers to occasional service, mainly on occasion for family fa'alavelave (Tui Atua 2007, 9). "In terms of right to title succession, Tamasese argues that those who perform nofo tuavae would traditionally, more often than not, succeed to laying claim to a matai title. However, today, he notes that all three kinds of tautua are considered" (Suaalii-Sauni 2007, 40). Although in the past families occasionally selected an individual to lead as matai even though he or she had not performed tautua nofo tuavae, it was relatively rare (Tui Atua 2007, 9).

The expansion of a family clan's access to (human or material) resources through tautua is not necessarily a new phenomenon, but it is worth exploring whether and how certain kinds of accomplishment, such as that associated with football success, are instrumental in the growing importance of tautua that is not given daily, in residence. If tautua nofo tuavae is, as Tui Atua argues, the traditionally dominant and preferred form of service that has been with more regularity supplanted over time by nonresident and nontraditional forms; and if certain kinds of accomplishment, such as that associated with football success, can be considered tautua 'ai taumalele or osi 'āiga by "children of Samoa who are engaged in sport on the other side of the world," then this signals the continued expansion of the connotation of tautua more generally to include—and, many would contend, to begin to favor—these new forms. This is not necessarily a new development—this expansion can be traced back much earlier in American Sāmoa to include early twentieth-century military service, for example. However, ongoing incorporation of new kinds of achievements as tautua recognized by the matai system can be seen as "acknowledging that traditional status thus complements modern achievements" (Lilomaiava-Doktor 2009b, 62) and is "also a sign that indigenous Samoan institutions remain paramount" in the face of accumulation abroad (Lilomaiava-Doktor 2009b, 63). These changes reflect the flexibility of Samoan cultural forms and in the era of globalization signal the changes that have produced a transnational fa'amatai. Many of these activities are being reincorporated through fundamental principles of the fa'asāmoa, but not always seamlessly or without tension.

The Obligation to Serve, Expanded and Re-signified

In Sāmoa I had several conversations with a friend who was trying to decide whether to return to school for an advanced degree.[18] To do so, she would have to not only leave her respected and well-paid job, but move her family off-island for a number of years. Like many other Samoans, she had lived abroad for a number of years for schooling and professional work before returning home to care for an ailing parent. During the years she was on island she had built strong networks and cared for relatives at substantial personal cost. Yet never did I detect resentment or bitterness when she talked about it.[19] Still, many of her closest friends were off-island, and in our conversations it was clear that she felt their absence and longed to be part of a vibrant creative community. Although she had been the one there in person, she saw her caretaking as representing all her siblings. But over those ten years she also felt she had given tautua to Sāmoa. In essence, since the passing of her parent, the primary reasons for her return were gone and she was free to move.

Her comments are revealing for a number of reasons: first, in speaking about caring for an ailing parent there was no voiced resentment as if it were an impossible burden too great to ask. When they fell ill, her siblings all had established families elsewhere while she was able to relocate to Tutuila when the need arose. Professionally, continuing to reside overseas would have been much more beneficial. Yet when she was called to serve her family she went. The obligation to show respect and alofa to her parent was deeply ingrained, so much so that fulfilling it not only demonstrated care and compassion but was simply something she needed to do. She recognized the expectation to serve her family in a way that had been part of her socialization since she was a child: to respect the wishes of her parents and care for them as needed.

This cultural expectation is reinforced in many ways, from customary beliefs that a person who mistreats an elderly parent will fall sick, to general expectation of caring for elders at home (barring extenuating circumstances like medical needs and some forms of mental illness). This is not to say that in the daily work of caring for a parent it is not experienced as a burden or does not stimulate feelings of anger, resentment, or frustration, but rather to make the point that these feelings do not usually arise from a sense of exploitation or inappropriate claim on one's time and effort. The claim in most cases is recognized as legitimate and worthy; how one responds to the obligation to serve is another matter (the reality can often fall far from the ideal). In conversations with my friend it was clear that she conceived of her caretaking as part of her tautua, laboring on behalf of her family even though her parent was not a matai.[20] Moreover, in her second reflection she groups her various activities as educator and community advocate under the rubric of tautua to the larger community body. While her work on-island surely brought prestige to her family, its primary impact was on others unrelated to her and could best be described in English terms as community or public service.

While tautua is often explained as one part of the reciprocal obligation of service and alofa between untitled family members and matai, in contemporary usage it encompasses many more activities that would fall under the idea of *service*.[21] With the emergence of the nation-state over the past hundred years, opportunities to serve the broader community rather than one's village (through government jobs, private sector employment, formal higher education, teaching employment, etc.) has multiplied, particularly over the past half century. Insofar as those activities bring recognition, prestige, and in many cases, additional monetary resources, they are considered within the rubric of tautua rather than just individual accomplishment.

In an interview with Alema, a former local high school standout and US collegiate football Division I national champion mentioned earlier, he reflected on what he saw to be shifts in tautua at the village level:

> Everyone's charged with sharpening whatever tool they've been given . . .
> whatever tool you've been given has been enhanced so that you can better
> serve for whatever calling that you have. A lot of us have responsibility

for family, village, and goals, we all have goals of going off-island, getting our university degrees, to make ourselves better so that when we return we have something to offer rather than just a high school diploma . . . So I think the tautua part of it has changed as each new person . . . has come back with some sort of enhancement to themselves, so I know that villages back home in Sa—in Apia, they're looking for the guys with skills . . . A lot of guys . . . sometimes they just don't make it back [laughs] . . . which is okay too, it's not everyone's calling to come back to the village, but as far as the needs for Sāmoa and the tautua that's needed we have far more to gain . . . the best thing is to come with all the skills that you can muster because its being asked of you now in the village now more than ever.

In his reflection, part of what is highlighted is the transnational circulation of knowledge and expertise, and how that incrementally is not only changing perceptions of what is needed, but the scope and character of service, or tautua. Since our original interview, he has moved to the continental United States and now works with a college program known for recruiting Polynesian student-athletes.

Service to one's family still remains the primary consideration in vying for matai titles, but the concept itself is no longer limited to serving one's own family matai in residence, on a daily basis. As mentioned, individual activities reflect upon one's family whether they are prestigious or disreputable. Taking up positions of leadership in a government agency or the private sector enhances one's own status, as well as that of one's extended family by bringing honor and recognition. In terms of high-profile sport, transnational media coverage of sport allows successful athletes to raise their family's profile through name recognition. (Reflecting on the importance he attached to football, a Samoan/Tongan college student explained in a team discussion I sat in on at a small private school in the Pacific Northwest in 2016: "We play for the names on our backs.") This is seen as a contribution, although once one is of age it would be expected to accompany material contribution to the family fa'alavelave or other needs. Secondly, the global transnational movement of Samoan people has created diasporic communities that recognize strong affinity beyond one's family, village, or church, which remain primary in the islands. While historically Samoans have followed 'āiga paths in migration, it is often the case that where existing genealogical linkages are not readily apparent, other kinds of relationships of care and concern are forged.[22] Many coaches I spoke with drew upon this larger notion of service to the Samoan or wider Polynesian community in the ways they articulated their own work and why they felt it was important. This was particularly true of off-island Samoan coaches who have been working to support the development of football on the island and to recruit students from the island to football scholarships in the United States.

Transpacific Ties, Service, and Sport

During the summer of 2008 three different football clinics were held on Tutuila, each run by a group of coaches from the United States. The three clinics varied widely in their duration, activity, publicity, perceived level of quality, and coaching expertise or training provided. One of the events, the All-Poly Camp, was the first local meeting of a very successful summer camp held annually in Bountiful, Utah. In previous years teams from some of the local high schools had raised funds throughout the academic year to be able to attend. This year, the camp came to the island, and students paid a registration fee to help defray costs.

At the end of the camp on the third day, the mood was light. Everyone was in good spirits; the camp had a good turnout and had gone smoothly. Players seemed happy they had a chance to go full-contact, suited up with helmets and pads. The field was wet and the air was humid; the downpour of rain was broken intermittently throughout the day by the hot tropical sun shining in a bright sky. The camp was held at the Veterans Memorial Stadium, built a few years before to host a regional sports competition. Throughout the practice, the sound of construction rang out, as workers continued to build the stage for the Festival of Pacific Arts, to be held on island in a month's time. At the sound of the final whistle all the players hustled into the covered stands, grouped by their school and jersey colors. The coaches were lined up to speak to the player crowd, leaving them with words of wisdom to consider. Without exception each stressed two key points: taking advantage of the opportunity football provides for earning your college degree, and that football will only be a small part of your life.

What was perhaps more salient for many of the players was the fact that in contrast to the other clinics held that summer, the majority of coaches associated with this camp were of Polynesian descent, and most of them were Samoan. Several of the coaches who spoke to the players that last day had direct ties to Tutuila—three of them graduated from local high schools, while two more were raised in local villages. Speakers included Alema Teʻo, Mike Fanoga, Johnny Nansen, Doug Elisaia, and Solomona Tapasa. Their ties to the island and to the Samoan community more broadly were reflected in how they spoke to the students and how they articulated their role as coaches. As one remarked, "Our goal is to help you succeed." Each one emphasized the personal stakes of the journey off the island. One of the coaches who had left the island at a young age admonished the students not to "forget where you come from." The next insisted: "Take the opportunity that's available!" Others echoed that sentiment, and told the students to remember "how your family has sacrificed for you, that you need to represent your family and your people to the best of your ability." All of the Samoan coaches stressed the importance of using the opportunities available to put yourself in a position to support or "give back" to your family. They recognized how success or failure is not just an individual event but one that reflects back on your immediate and extended family (and on Samoan people more generally in off-island contexts).

Sustaining the determination to succeed in order to help your family was a key point made by another coach as he stressed the impossibility of failure once you begin your journey. In our later interview Taps spoke more at length, citing our cultural heritage as a drive to success: if you fail then everyone will know and everyone will "faikakala" about it and it will reflect poorly on your family. "Fear of failure was a huge motivation," he told me. As we talked story, he revealed that my father had trained him for fall camp before he left for junior college and told him flat out, "If you fail, I don't want to see you back here. I don't want to see you fail, so go to the military or do something else but don't come back." He kept those words in mind when things were difficult.

The coaches' affiliation with the camp, as one expressed to me, is part of a larger commitment to Polynesian students, and serving the island and diasporic communities with the talents and resources available to them. The head organizer, Alema Te'o, was well respected even though he was not affiliated with the biggest or most recognized football program, precisely because of his long-standing commitment to serving the larger community by providing opportunities for Polynesian (and other) players to improve their skill and gain exposure.

What football (and other forms of access to capital like the military) has enabled is a measure of freedom to choose whether and under what circumstances one might fulfill expectations of tautua or involve oneself in the fa'asāmoa. In many cases the demands are experienced as too great a burden: some in American Sāmoa speculated that some current and former NFL players who had been active on island in the past no longer sponsor activities such as summer football camps and clinics because the expectations for

2.3 All Poly Camp, Veterans Memorial Stadium, Tutuila.
PHOTO CREDIT: AUTHOR.

their contribution are so high they are unsustainable in the long run.[23] For those who are able to mobilize their networks and resources to continue serving the islands in this way, their service is an opportunity for the youth as well as a chance to recognized ties of affinity to local communities. Local communities, in turn, value and recognize the tangible (skill coaching) and more broadly symbolic (prestige) contributions to the islands.

Football and Faʻasāmoa

In projects like the Faʻa Samoa Initiative where organizers largely come from off-island, many of the aspects of faʻasāmoa that are incorporated are the work of local partners, and so the way it is approached as a partnership is important. In this process, cultural practices partake of the sheen of a modern, highly prestigious sport and where the efforts toward the game also benefit from a different kind of cultural capital and prestige. Local partners receive a boost in status through the honor of hosting prestigious guests, while organizers benefit from a grounded legitimacy, social capital, and network of contacts that make the whole event possible.

While the program itself, organized over two years with many people involved, had a spine of activities, agendas, and objectives, in the execution of the program with local partners and student and community participation, Samoan ways of being in the world infused it with life. In the football sessions one of the things that stood out to the Initiative coaches was the spirit of the players, reflected in the morning hymns sung by the teams. As the boys lifted their voices in unison singing the morning prayer, the coaches were impressed by the unity and lack of ego or showmanship they had become used to in the States. This they attributed in our conversations to solid cultural foundations. In Sāmoa, singing a hymn to open a school event is so routine that it is unremarkable, but the coaches' open appreciation reminded me that most of them lived in the continental United States and may not see that on a regular basis, if ever.

In a later reflection with my cousin Keith Uperesa, who was one of the coaches on the trip, he remarked, "Football is a passion, it's not a priority. Getting off the island is a priority, and football is a way to do it." He saw that for the student-athletes, family was a priority, and football was a pathway that provided an opportunity to serve the family. But church and culture were also centrally important, which was a different orientation from many of the student-athletes they work with in the continental United States. Many coaches and volunteers were actively involved in the Church of Jesus Christ of Latter-day Saints (LDS) or other Christian-denomination churches, and were impressed with the integration of church into daily activity, with students being able to stand up and pray on invitation, and a strength in cultural foundations that youth raised outside the islands often struggle with. The beauty of the choral hymns sung with spirituality and humility were something special to witness, as they infused the sporting day with peaceful effervescence. Those moments when their voices took center stage quieted the crowd and held many of us in rapt attention.

Meanwhile, in the academic division staged at Samoana High School, different cultural values, ideals, and practices related to peace and wellness, such as *fealofani* (kindness/support), *filemū* (peacefulness), and *faʻafetai* (thankfulness), had been painted by an artist on the walls of the science building as part of an exercise run by Maria Toʻotoʻo, the Director of Guidance and Counseling Services (DGCS), that linked mindfulness, meditation, and Samoan culture. The mornings began with students and the elder volunteers (Toe Afua Mai Matua) singing prayer hymns and a blessing given by

Upu Tuiasosopo, also of DGCS. Having the elders volunteer that week reinforced the culturally inflected behavior of respect expected of the attending students while providing the opportunity for intergenerational transmission of knowledge through pese. The academic division's portion of the closing ceremony included a Samoan song taught by elders to the students, as well as a sāsā that was choreographed by the juniors in Ti Kinikini's class, capped off by a taualuga by the elder group with the academic facilitators, counseling staff, and Troy and Theodora Polamalu. Largely through Maria and Upu's organizing, aspects of faʻasāmoa infused the academic sessions, which were otherwise focused on the academic development and life skills curriculum selected by Maria as educational administrator and Penny as session director.

In addition to aspects of Samoan sociality shaping the ongoing program, specific events or engagements were designed to showcase other aspects of culture and hospitality. In this, cultural exchanges enriched the Initiative and the experience of the visiting team while boosting the standing of their hosts. Early in the week the team had been taken to Tisa's at Alega Beach for a traditional Sunday umu toʻonaʻi as part of welcoming everyone and

2.4 Organizers, facilitators, and supporting elders of the Faʻa Samoa Initiative, Academic Division. PHOTO CREDIT: UNKNOWN.

2.5 Raw fish and 'ulu (breadfruit)   **2.6** Gifted items (including fine mats, wahoo, and tapa cloth). Overall caption: Governor's Dinner, Fale Laumei.
PHOTO CREDIT: AUTHOR.

starting off the week. As the umu was unveiled and food was set out, Tisa explained to the attendees a little bit about the making of the umu and what each of the dishes were, for the benefit of those who were less familiar with the traditional meal. Guests watched the unveiling of the umu, and once dishes were set on a long table, Tisa identified the fai'ai eleni, palusami, talo, 'ulu, and other dishes. It was also a nice bit of showmanship for everyone who had their GoPros and iPhones out recording; Tisa is a very graceful and gracious host.

In the coming days the 'ava ceremony and the governor's dinner, sponsored and organized by local government entities, incorporated cultural protocols of gifting and recognition, speeches, and food and hospitality. At the dinner, presentations of tapa, fine mats, buckets of salted beef, cases of wahoo, and umu were gifted to Troy and Theodora, and each of the heads of the Initiative divisions by the Department of Education, the Department for Youth and Women's Affairs, and the governor's office. The event, replete with music, dancing, speeches, and an impressive feast, honored the work of the guests and the tautua of Polamalu and other returning Samoans while enhancing the status and prestige of the hosts, who commanded a notable amount of resources distributed over the course of the evening in Samoan style. (I was happy to get a case of wahoo from Penny, which a friend in New York many years ago referred to as "Samoan gold.")

Earlier in the week during the 'ava ceremony Governor Lolo, in his remarks, said:

> Troy, Theodora, this has been a great experience for our young men and women, to have you as a role model in their lives. We'd like to thank you for taking time to come home and work with our children in making their future a bright future for our country. High Chief Seiuli and to all sons and daughters of Sāmoa who join this great vision we'd like to welcome you home. Thank you for being part of this wonderful vision. To all our friends from abroad, thank you for helping Troy make this vision possible. You really make a big difference in the lives of our young people. I hope that you have enjoyed your stay here in American Sāmoa and hope you'll have a good time on our island. Soifua![24]

Of all the Initiative events, the 'ava ceremony was the clearest example of the indigenization of sport. In this moment, in the acknowledgement of the relationships that brought local representatives and Initiative organizers together, recognized in the sacred space of the fale through the unique language of Samoan cultural protocol, the intersection of football and fa'asāmoa materialized in a shared moment of prestige and respect.

Over the course of the week and in the time leading up to his arrival, I sensed (from the buzz among young people to conversations with adults ranging from old classmates to shopkeepers) that local people appreciated Troy Polamalu's efforts in coming to Tutuila. There appeared to be appreciation for his accomplishments, the way he has made Polamalu a household name, and his contribution to positive recognition for Samoans in a game that is carried globally by contemporary media. But in many interactions over the week it also appeared that he was appreciated because as a humble, funny person with mana and integrity he has important personal traits that many Samoans value and respect. In accepting the gifts at the governor's dinner from the American Sāmoa government on behalf of the group, he became visibly overwhelmed with emotion and his wife Theodora stepped in to eloquently articulate their gratitude to the local hosts. When Troy spoke later, in his remarks he said, "You don't have to speak Samoan to be Samoan," and in that moment many in the audience might have agreed with him. In his choice to pour money, energy, and time into helping the youth of

2.7 After the 'Ava Ceremony, Suigaula Beach Park: Jonathan Fanene, Troy Polamalu, Jesse Sapolu, and Shaun Nua. PHOTO CREDIT: AUTHOR.

American Sāmoa, where he has ancestral family ties but where he himself was not raised, he had given selflessly and without expectation of immediate material return—an admirable act of tautua to the wider community.

Transforming Tautua

The matai system in Sāmoa has been transformed over the past century in tandem with development efforts in the islands and the transnational movement of Samoan people to metropoles around the world. As a power structure, it has both narrowed in scope (as individuals are no longer bound to the authority of the matai for their daily livelihood) and increased in stature (as some matai have more material resources at their disposal and cultural knowledge, recognition, and capital has become more valued). In conjunction, the concept and practice of tautua has also been notably transformed over the course of the last century. Since the 1960s football has been one particularly visible strand of development in which this transformation can be seen. The issue of whether the fa'asāmoa and fa'amatai, and their associated principles, will continue to be significant and meaningful in everyday life as frameworks for action and the structuring social relations rather than simply fetishized symbols of national belonging and ethnic difference is an open question for the future.

For now, as players and their communities navigate these new opportunities made possible by an expanding global sporting industry, and partake of the fruits of their labor, many choose to share the largesse in ways that are consistent with cultural sensibilities around service and contribution. As shown in the footage of His Highness's reception and the reception by Governor Lolo, the status, prestige, and capital afforded by football success is being incorporated within the chiefly system rather than necessarily undermining it (although this is true as well in some cases). In addition to the expansion of forms of service, the entities one serves are not only one's matai and village, but may also include the larger transnational Samoan community. In this way tautua not only serves as an investment in material claims (such as that to land and other family resources) but as an important practice signifying identification with a particular cultural heritage and claims to national belonging. In the recognition and incorporation of football prestige into customary protocol, and in turn, the inclusion of distinct cultural elements into football events, Samoans are localizing or indigenizing the American game of gridiron football on their own terms and claiming it as their own.

Three

Producing the Gridiron Warrior

What is coming on is a swarm of Polynesian warriors—not your run-of-the-reef, gin mill flamethrowers, but strong, fierce men, six to seven feet tall, who seem to have stepped into the 20th century from some secret museum of oceanic antiquities. As, in fact, they have. The museum is a tiny (76 square miles) island cluster in the deep South Seas called American Samoa. Not only is it the least known and most remote of the U.S. territories, but, together with Western Samoa, it is also the only island group where the Polynesian culture—and the Polynesian race—has survived virtually intact . . . Along with natural selection and racial purity (unlike the Hawaiians, few Samoans married missionaries, traders, sailors or marines, and no intruders ever got possession of Samoan land), hard work accounts for the Samoans' extraordinary size and strength.—RICHARD W. JOHNSTON, "Shake 'em Out Of The Coconut Trees," *Sports Illustrated* (August 16, 1976).

It's as if the football gods, searching for the perfect conditions to breed players, found them on this remote isle, with its singular mix of Polynesian culture and modern American influence.—BILL SYKEN, "Football In Paradise," *Sports Illustrated* (November 3, 2003).

IN POPULAR MEDIA stories about Samoans in American football, a common script emerges of a natural athlete gifted with size, quick feet, and cultural conditioning to respect authority. With repeated iterations, the image of a muscled young man, with long wavy or curly hair and occasionally tattooed with Polynesian motifs, has become iconic in the representation and recognition of Samoans and other Pacific Islanders in the sport of football. The two quotes above, printed decades apart in a major American sports publication, highlight the imagination that informs media productions of these players for consumption by mainstream America. These epigraphs are useful not simply to highlight an outdated view, but to begin to trace the important continuities and disjunctures that shape the way Samoans and Samoan athletes are represented to the American mainstream, even in recent years. As Stuart Hall argues, practices of representation embody "concepts, ideas and emotions in a symbolic form which can be transmitted and meaningfully interpreted" to different communities (1998, 6). Moreover, "because of their extensive accessibility and scope, mass media can serve as both reservoirs and reference points for the circulation of words, phrases, and discourse styles in popular culture" (Spitulnik 1997, 162). These recognizable narratives shape the ethnographic imaginations with which non–Pacific Islander coaches, fans, and residents of the United States perceive and engage with Samoans and other Polynesians as a racialized group invested with an excess of culture. However, it is not only the mainstream media portraying Samoans as modern-day warriors; these iconic depictions resonate with our communities too, although they may be shaped by different perspectives and points of reference. Beyond the warrior trope, Samoan players have come to be represented as (cultured) laborers in a global sporting industry and relatives of a vast Samoan cultural diaspora. Mainstream media depictions have real-life impact, and those representations both intersect with and stand apart from the ways athletes and communities are producing their own narratives and mediating these existing images today.

Images of Pacific Islander football athletes are viewed through a range of lenses as they circulate through and among various sites, and as they do they are interpreted by people with dynamic and distinct frames of reference. This is part of a larger dialogic emergence of narratives depicting players representing their communities and heritage, in a context of media fascination with and the public consumption of exoticized difference. Drawing on the ESPN documentary *Polynesian Power: Islanders in Pro Football* (2004) and the CBS *60 Minutes* "Football Island" segment (2010), together with the media portrayal of select NFL players, this chapter pursues two major lines of argument. First, it examines key American mainstream media portrayals of Samoan football players, employing an intersectional analysis of the racialized, cultural, gendered, and class dimensions of these productions. These narratives draw on long-standing discourses about Polynesia and indigenous Pacific peoples in the production of the iconic Polynesian "Gridiron Warrior." The traffic in stereotypes about physical capacities of male Pacific bodies then shapes opportunities and experiences in everyday life in contradictory ways.

In the second part of the chapter, I consider some of the impacts of these narratives on Samoan and Polynesian communities more broadly. This is not a straightforward story about oppressive (colonial or racist) representation and resistance. Rather, there is complexity in how these discourses have defined the dominant horizons of possibility for Samoans in the US diaspora and in the islands, and how Samoans are challenging the parameters of those horizons in practice. In the contemporary moment, as more and more players are in the limelight and are actively shaping the stories told about them, Polynesian athletes and communities are both mediating preexisting imaginaries and producing new ones. Through their active presence, athletes and their communities are engaging with, drawing on, and transforming long-standing discourses about Samoan and Polynesian bodies and masculinities, and the stakes and significance of sporting excellence.

Creating the "Polynesian Gridiron Warrior"

The first epigraph of this chapter marks a critical mass of Samoan players entering the college football ranks in the mid-1970s and distinguishing themselves as an ethnic group from their predecessors, who were widely known as "Hawaiian" (a catchall for those both of Native Hawaiian ancestry, and those who were born or raised in Hawai'i regardless of ancestry). Writing for a popular mainstream American audience, the author depicts these college student-athletes as ancient, physically superior forebears of awesome size and fierce temperament.[1] This "swarm of Polynesian warriors," described as "strong, fierce men, six to seven feet tall, who seem to have stepped into the 20th century from some secret museum of oceanic antiquities" at once reveals the author's own ethnographic imagination of Samoans as premodern (prehistoric?) and that of his audience, or perhaps what he expects will resonate with his readership.

The scenario draws on recognizable tropes in anthropological and media representations: a fantasy of a "secret museum of oceanic antiquities" discovered, ancient peoples come to life as though they were stepping out of a diorama in the Pacific Hall in the American Museum of Natural History in New York City.[2] The "swarm" is reminiscent of the Hollywood "Paciflicks" of old that show the "natives" descending on the beach to get a glimpse of the

Western visitors arriving by ship, narratives which draw on a longer genealogy of sensationalized accounts of the native-explorer encounter (Vercoe 2004; Kahn 2011, 30–60). At the same time, describing the student-athletes as "Polynesian warriors" who are "strong, fierce men" of "extraordinary size and strength" invokes culture while setting them apart from their fellow teammates and placing them in anachronistic time (Fabian 1983). The sensational aspect here is their exotic difference manifest in the "sign of spectacular corporeality" (Desmond 1999, xv) of the Polynesian warrior. It enacts a politics of looking that is shaped by imperial perspectives of native peoples (Pratt 1992; Rony 1996; Lutz and Collins 1993).

The invocation of the "Polynesian warrior" by Johnston in 1976—nearly a century after meddlesome foreigners stoked the flames of localized warring in Sāmoa to their own capitalist and colonial ends, and then conspired to impose stability and peace on their own terms—is a heuristic device for American audiences no doubt familiar with primitivist depictions of Pacific men.[3] It links a historical legacy of warriorhood with a practice seen as particularly modern: American football. In the second quote opening the chapter, the author draws this linkage directly: he alleges the "singular mix of Polynesian culture and modern American influence" to be a divine discovery wherein America's "modern" influence improves upon (non-modern?) "Polynesian culture" and in turn, states that it is this mixture that provides the "perfect conditions" to improve on the game of football.

This "singular mix" has been a point of fascination for a number of media segments in recent years, one of which was produced as part of CBS's regular Sunday program *60 Minutes*. In the month before the 2010 Super Bowl was played in Miami, CBS aired a special segment of the show. In it, correspondent Scott Pelley reported on the Samoan football phenomenon emerging from American Sāmoa, or as he referred to it, "Football Island." He noted the familiar story elements: the "paradise" setting, the long distance from the US mainland, the island's long association with the United States, and the size of the players.[4] But in addition to size, then-governor Togiola Tulafono pointed out that the players emerge from a farming culture that prizes hard work, respect, and discipline. Pelley notes that this makes them attractive to college coaches and remarks, "It turns out the South Pacific was raising football talent before there was football." Here we see a teleology of gridiron participation in which the "nature" and "culture" of Samoan bodies renders the young men always-already players in the eyes of the American mainstream (see also Henderson 2011).

Pelley describes the performance of the "haka" for the camera by the Leone High School players as the "haka war dance" and explains it as "something

3.1 "Football Island" on *60 Minutes*, 2010

that's been passed down for ages to teach agility to warriors of size and strength." He omits the fact that it is a performance tradition adopted and adapted from Aotearoa New Zealand. He also does not mention that its presence in American football is a relatively recent development, having been most recognizably linked to global sport by the New Zealand national rugby team (the All Blacks) and widely popularized after the professional turn in the 1990s. It was later adopted by Kahuku High School and the University of Hawaiʻi football team, beginning its movement into the US gridiron landscape. Here the clip of the haka serves as a metonymic representation of Polynesia; it also points to the ways in which the haka, and its response in the Samoan siva tau, Hawaiian haʻa, Tongan sipi tau, and Fijian cibi has become a modular form through which to express a specifically indigenous Polynesian masculinity.[5]

REPRESENTATION AND MEDIATED IMAGES:
CULTURAL EXCESS AND THE SAVAGE SLOT

Describing the Gridiron Warrior as a polyvalent image marks the ways in which a single image carries within it multiple meanings that elicit different kinds of emotions and attributions of value depending on the audience. It draws on what Boyer identifies as a "productive tension" between "technological or representational aspects of media" and "what we might gloss as processes of social mediation . . . the movement of images, discourse, persons and things" (2012, 383). On the one hand, the repetition of imagery has created shared transnational cultural codes for recognizing "Polynesia" and the "Pacific" that are then used as the backdrop for the raced, classed, cultured, and gendered figure of the Gridiron Warrior; and on the other hand, those images are socially mediated in the islands and the States toward contradictory ends that cannot be separated from linked processes of production, consumption, commoditization, and transnational circulation (Spitulnik 1993, 306; Appadurai 1990). In this mediation process of translation, interpretation, and meaning-making, Hall writes:

> One soon discovers that meaning is not straightforward or transparent . . . changing and shifting with context, usage and historical circumstances. It is therefore never finally fixed. It is always putting off or 'deferring' its rendezvous with Absolute Truth. It is always being negotiated and inflected, to resonate with new situations. It is often contested, and sometimes bitterly fought over. There are always different circuits of meaning circulating in any culture at the same time, overlapping discursive formations, from which we draw to create meaning or to express what we think. (1998, 6)

In this ever-shifting process, then, the "reader" is not a passive blank slate receiving messages simply transmitted in their entirety, but rather perceives, comprehends, and understands them within their own frameworks (Hall 1998, 7).

Moving away from conceptualizing media messaging as overly directive, researchers have engaged the "crucial problem of where to locate the production of meaning and ideology in the mass communication process, and how to characterize processes of agency and interpretation" (Spitulnik 1993, 295). Hall argues that these interpretive frameworks vary depending on preexisting knowledge, prior experience, context, and so on; there are shared cultural codes that sustain dialogue and make "effective 'translation' between 'speakers' possible" (Hall 1998, 7). Articulating an important direction for anthropologists and other scholars in the early 1990s, Deborah Spitulnik argued that illuminating "the broader cultural conditions that enable the emergence of these new media processes and products, and the wider political economies that impel their circulation in diverse societies across the globe" was a key priority (1993, 307). Since then, scholars have addressed a wide variety of socially significant media and representational practices, arguing the importance of media analysis that is articulated with local, national, and transnational frames (Ginsburg, Abu-Lughod, and Larkin 2002).[6]

The excerpts above highlight a recurring theme in media portrayals of Samoan and other Polynesian athletes, and while individual interpretations of these portrayals may vary, one of the notable aspects is they draw on shared mainstream US cultural codes shaped by the "savage slot" (Trouillot 1991) that reproduce Samoans and other Pacific Islanders as Other (Said 1994 [1978]). The representation of these athletes draws on a parallel history of "Pacificism" or perhaps "Polynesianism," where the space of Polynesia has been crafted as a backdrop with particular cultural elements, recognizable to Euro-American audiences through their repetition over centuries.[7] Heather Waldroup helpfully describes the discourse of Polynesianism, as "a set of Western literary and visual texts that renders tangible and visible the geographic space of Polynesia and the Polynesian body, especially those shaped by primitivist and Orientalist desires" (2004, 3).[8] Power circulates in and through the representations, the knowledge they convey and produce, and the meanings attached to them. These media are "dynamic sites of struggle" (Spitulnik 1993, 296), and the effort "to fix meaning is exactly why *power* intervenes in *discourses*" (Hall 1998, 7).

In their obsessive focus on exoticized cultural difference these media portrayals link a long-past practice of warring to the modern sporting context of football and, like the *60 Minutes* segment, maintain a teleology in which young Samoan men are always-already players. They are part of the global capitalist sporting infrastructure that participates in the market for consuming things Pacific. In this portrayal of a Polynesian warrior tradition, writers are not just capturing what exists but participate in a dynamic dialogue that has shaped mainstream and community understandings of this linkage. The narrative appears to have shifted over time, and not just among mainstream sports writers, but by players themselves who have come to connect their activity on the field with their deep community histories and ancestry. As the images and accompanying narratives travel through different sites, being read with multiple, overlapping, intersecting, and divergent lenses and frames, various social dynamics and attachments shape the way these images are mediated, as well as the contours of power relations and interest that propel their consumption.

Forging "Polynesian" Power

The promotional flyer for *Polynesian Power: Islanders in Pro Football* (Spear and Pennington 2005) is an excellent promotional tool—striking in its simplicity and powerful in the way it brings together different elements to forge a visually compelling and meaningful narrative. It both captures the viewer's interest and communicates immediately and imperceptibly the subject of the film as the publicity is distributed. For the flyer to garner interest, the directors must choose a highly effective ensemble to both "hook" viewers and communicate key elements of the film. In that, they must rely on potential viewers having a set of interpretive frames with which to decode and make sense of the image (Hooper-Greenhill 2000, 15, 116–123; Hall 1998).

In the photo Isaac Sopoaga stands clad in an 'ie lāvalava and a kukui nut 'ula. These two items serve as one visual indicator of what his background might be: the 'ie lāvalava is a customary clothing item in Samoan villages while the kukui nut 'ula has been popularized in Hawai'i and circulated transnationally, from the streets of New York City to the shops in Sāmoa to graduations in Aotearoa New Zealand. Together with the beach background and Sopoaga himself, there is no mistaking this is a Pacific story. His arms and torso—brown, bare, and muscled—stand at the center and draw the viewer's eye. Along with the title, these different iconic elements (clothing and adornment, the naturalist landscape of the beach, and the brown body) articulate to frame the narrative as tied to Polynesia as a geographically bounded place and a space of visual imaginary.

Yet the forging of this imaginary is not a new one in this format; this has been the preeminent way to invoke Polynesia specifically and the Pacific more generally for a very long time (see Smith 1985; Edmond 1997; Grainger 2009). We are reminded that "communications that emanate from mass media . . . are preceded and succeeded by numerous other dialogues and pieces of language that both implicate them and render them interpretable" (Spitulnik 1997, 161). The "island" elements of the promotional flyer are widely enough distributed in tourism advertisements, cinematography, and art to be mobilized by many as signs of Polynesia. Meanwhile, the vision invoked in this chapter's epigraph is one in which the social and historical distinctions of the many cultures that evolved in the region are conflated or erased. It mobilizes a singular "Polynesian culture," of which Samoan student-athletes are supposedly now the "guardians," to highlight cultural difference for the benefit of captivating a mainstream audience.

While the landscape, adornment, and subject of the photo are recognizable as signifying Polynesia, what is different is the helmet Sopoaga wears and the football he cradles in his arm; both marked are with the (then recently rebranded) University of Hawai'i Warrior motif (see Tengan and Markham 2009). For the bricolage including the helmet and the football amid the beach setting with 'ula and lāvalava to make sense, one may need

3.2 Promotional film poster for *Polynesian Power*.

to know a bit more about the visibility of Polynesians in American football; but even if one has never seen a football game, one might have already been exposed to the image invoked by the way his hair, long and textured, escapes the helmet. As *60 Minutes* correspondent Scott Pelley claimed, the "Sunday Samoans" are recognizable by their "vowel-laden names" and "trademark hair" (2010)—and, I would add, their (distinctive) Polynesian tattoos, which increasingly draw on multiple cultural art forms (Samoan tatau, Hawaiian kakau, Maori tā moko, and contemporary stylings) to express ethnic and cultural identities in the uniformed context of the field. All underscore an indigenous Polynesian masculinity that has become visibly and publicly aligned with visions of warriorhood, in large part, though not exclusively, through this kind of media narrative. By the late 2000s, this was a widely circulated image through media coverage of high school, college, and professional games.

The web promo and opening sequence of *Polynesian Power* begin on the beach with Sopoaga looking out to the ocean, hands on hips, clad in an 'ie lāvalava and kukui nut necklace.[9] As the opening shot pans the beach, he has his back to the camera so we see only his long hair flowing and muscled upper body. Narrator Dwayne "The Rock" Johnson says in the voiceover (backgrounded by the sound of the Ka Mate haka), "This is the story of two young Samoans sustaining a warrior tradition in American football" as the beach view fades to the pregame haka for the University of Hawai'i and a shot of Sopoaga on the goal line facing Vili the Warrior.[10] The voiceover continues: "One straight from the 'hood [close-up of Pisa], one straight from the islands [close-up of Isaac in what appears to be a Hawaiian shirt and woven launiu hat]." Over the sound of the Manu Sāmoa siva tau we see a fiery cartoon transformation of Isaac that adds a facial tattoo and a head covering. He jumps, muscled superhero style (FWHOOSH!) from the islands of American Sāmoa (labeled with a flag and shown as a small, lush island with two coconut trees) to the Hawaiian Islands where Pisa, with his UH-logo hat turned sideways, white tank top, a boar's tusk necklace, gray baggy pants, and construction boots awaits (presumably having just made the same jump from the "'hood," labeled in the background as Los Angeles, California). Against a backdrop of foliage, they are transformed by lightning into their football personas—clad in the green, black, and white uniforms of the University of Hawai'i. With a stomp [BOOYAH!] the foliage melts away in a cloud of smoke to reveal the football stadium.

In informal discussions with Jeremy Spear, one of the film's directors, he explained that the cartoon intro was added to quickly portray and dramatize an important part of the background story—Sopoaga as an island boy and Tinoisamoa as escaping the urban life (and literally as we see in later scenes, imprisonment). Yet it also accomplishes the narrative functions of portraying the transformation of these players as individuals and members of their communities into football players. The visual transformation erases social and cultural markers, replacing them with the standard uniform of a player on the field as part of their documented journey.

While the opening depicts a common meeting ground of football, in the film the sport signifies different things for each. Tinoisamoa tells us that sports came easily and was linked to family functions, saying it "was our time to escape a lot of the other stuff that was going on around us." In his senior year, he explains, he was arrested for his part in a fight and the judge, considering his prior record, sentenced him. In the words of June Jones (then UH head football coach), "We got him out of jail, basically." Later in the film Tinoisamoa connects his journey with those of some of his relatives and is thankful for the opportunity to continue the family football tradition. Yet at the outset his individual experience with the criminal justice system frames his as an urban-escape-through-sport story. Hailing from urban Oceanside, California, we are told that football was almost literal salvation for him, who otherwise might have joined the rising number of young Pacific Islander men in US prisons.

Meanwhile, Sopoaga's path is framed not as an escape or salvation, but as an opportunity: he tells us that he switched from rugby to football in his senior year at Samoana High School to give it a try, and went on to play at the College of the Canyons in California and at the University of Hawai'i. Sopoaga explains (in Samoan, translated into English on screen): "The factors that motivate me to play football are my Dad, my family . . . my village from Samoa and my people from Samoa." On a recruiting trip, the film narrative continues, his body size and athleticism caught Coach Jones's eye even though he had not been playing the game long. Jones describes: "The first time I ever saw him I walked in the gym and he was dribbling the basketball and he took it between his legs and slam dunked the ball from about the foul line. I said, 'You gotta be kidding me.' This guy doesn't have an ounce of fat on him, he's 6'3, three hundred twelve-fifteen pounds that is like, unheard of." In some of the footage Isaac is shown in his home village and with his family. Like many others coming from the islands before him, his journey is framed as a quest to represent his family, village, and nation on the gridiron.

The best parts of the film highlight the family connections and close kinship networks that constitute the fabric of Samoan communities at home

3.3 Pisa Tinoisamoa and Isaac Sopoaga. PHOTO CREDIT: ROBERT PENNINGTON.

and in the United States. At the same time, these kinship contexts are expected to serve as sites of socialization that may or may not bear out given the particular challenges faced by youth in US urban areas. When asked why Samoans have had such success in football, after citing genetics, I have heard many coaches resort to a cultural explanation (especially applicable to players from the islands) and talk about "coachability." Here coachability is explicitly linked to Samoan culture, values of respect, disciplinary practices, and respect for hierarchy and authority. One (non–Pacific Islander) Division I assistant coach I interviewed echoed this interest in "Polynesian culture" as "powerful" because the "old-school respect" and "really good culture" can be harnessed successfully to football. The cultural training to respect hierarchy and authority, as well as the sway parents hold over their children, render the players paradoxically docile subjects in the view of some coaches.[11] While many coaches expect this socialization from Polynesian players, the expectation relies on and assumes a certain family dynamic and community context that is the reality for some players and not others, particularly away from the islands.

Today, many Samoan players at the professional level are characterized as low-key, friendly jokesters off the field. Many of them are churchgoing, "respectable" and respectful, and it is this image that makes their intense performance on the field even more palatable to the public, and ingratiates them to the coaches. This corresponds to a more general expectation of athletes to be humble, obedient to authority, and grateful for their success (Romo 2017; Wiggins 1994). But more than that, as Polynesians are the second most visible non-White group in the sport, this view also raises the question as to whether there is an implicit contrast with Black athletes whose image in popular culture is often portrayed as dangerous, unmanageable, and even criminal (see Leonard 2012). Is the excess focus on culture constructing Samoans and other Polynesians as "model minorities" in the game and helping to hide a differential racialization at work?

Race, Gender, and "Physicality"

If the cultural element is overdetermined in media narratives of Samoan and other Pacific Islander football players, it stands enmeshed with undercurrents of racialization and preferred scripts of gender and masculinity. In the highly visible figure of the football player we see how Samoans become inserted into larger hierarchies and narratives of race in America but in particularly gendered ways. The first quote that opened this chapter reveals the kinds of language used to racialize Samoan bodies and the way they are linked to visions of culture and performances of masculinity.

The "strong, fierce men, six to seven feet tall" are cast as survivors and perpetuators of *the* "Polynesian race" through "natural selection and racial purity." The contrast with Hawaiians assumes an essentialist view of Polynesians as a distinct race and relies on particular frameworks of racial purity that have long been debunked while placing the blame for land dispossession in the occupied territory of Hawai'i on intermarriage rather than on US colonial capitalism.[12] Yet the author's narrative implies that rather than enhance physical capabilities, Samoan mixture with (largely Euro-American) "missionaries, traders, sailors or marines" would weaken them. In the context of sport, this "racial purity," coupled with hard work, is cast as a pinnacle achievement: the avoidance of *racial* mixture is what retains the physical characteristics of "extraordinary size and strength" for Samoan men, and the "hard work" required of any successful student-athlete is almost an afterthought.[13] This contrasts with the second quote, which claims the *social* mixture of Polynesian culture and American influence to be the key to the "perfect conditions to breed players." Taken together, the aims of racial purity and social transformation are seen to underlie the success of the football project in American Sāmoa.

In the *60 Minutes* segment, Scott Pelley makes a point of lining up a handful of the Samoana High School players, and as he looks up to each of them he asks them their height (all are more than six feet tall). Pelley continues to focus on body size in his interview with Governor Togiola, affecting a somewhat sheepish tone when he says, "Well, not to be indelicate about it—your people are big." The governor in turn, smiles slightly and responds, "And big is beautiful." In this small exchange it is clear that Pelley is aware of the social codes that make commenting on body size, and particularly larger physiques, "indelicate," yet he is determined to highlight this point of difference for *60 Minutes* viewers. The focus on the substantial body size of the players reinforces "the absolute centrality of physical size to the stories told about Samoans in the United States" (Henderson 2011, 277). It also reveals that the standards by which the body size of the players (and all Samoans as indicated by "your people") are judged are not local, or even regional standards, but rather come from the perspective of the continental United States. Governor Togiola's response then is quick and tongue-in-cheek, reframing the meaning of "big" as "beautiful" rather than problematic.

In the second quote that opens this chapter, players from American Sāmoa are depicted as emerging from "the perfect conditions to breed players" as if found by the providence of the "football gods." Here the author invokes biogenetics to explain the phenomenon of Samoan success on the gridiron, and he isn't alone. In 2014 a writer for online magazine Elite Daily used "Football Island" to address "How Samoa is Breeding the World's Best Football Stars," and several months later the same author wrote "Why Polynesians Are Genetically Engineered to be the Best Football Players in the World."[14] Citing a "warrior-like intensity" and ability to play the game with "supreme toughness" these "behemoths of athletes," the author continues, "are just born big-boned and have frames perfect for any NFL position, especially linemen down in the trenches." While one could question whether these statements are true, exaggerated, or simply reproductions of claims already circulating in the ether of media, we can pay attention to how the focus on breeding and genetics produces a naturalized overidentification with the body, and a common sense (shared by those within and outside the community) in which Samoans are seen as "natural" athletes.[15] This discourse participates in a stereotyping of body size that does not hold across the islands and diaspora.[16] This is particularly relevant since Polynesian players, and especially those recruited from Sāmoa, have historically been overrepresented as offensive and defensive linemen, and these are viewed as first and foremost physical, smashing positions.[17] As linemen, they are often animalized in mainstream sports coverage—described as "studs," "prime beef," or more recently, "beasts" (see Reiss 2007 for example). Coupled with ideas about antiquated savagery, Samoan players have often been depicted as the "embodiment of primal, savage warriorhood" (Tengan 2002, 249) in a way that enhances their football stock.

THE RACIAL SLOT?

Here the discursive construction of African American sporting excellence is enlightening, since the framework for the ideological and structural positioning of Samoans and other Polynesians in the US context is already shaped by the history and presence of Blacks in America and American sport. Black athletes have dominated accounts of non-White sporting experience in the United States, both numerically and ideologically. While many writers have analyzed the central role of racism and racialization in shaping the lives of and attitudes toward African Americans in sport and American society more generally, no one has examined the important role of racialization for Pacific Islander players as specifically both non-White and non-Black.[18] This shows the ongoing importance of racial logics even for groups for whom it is often ignored or disavowed, and highlights the processes and effects of differential racialization. Finally, analyzing the intersection of racial logics, ethnographic imagination, and gender performance allows us to see the important nuances of this representational formation and how they shape subjectivity and real-life chances in ways that both challenge and reproduce racialized social inequalities.

Sport sociologist Harry Edwards warned long ago about the high-profile media propaganda espousing sports as an open field for Black social and economic mobility while there was a lack of a critical mass of comparably high-profile Black role models in other professions. Against "a longstanding, widely held, and—at its root—racist presumption of innate race-linked Black athletic superiority," Edwards claimed, Black families were channeling their children into sporting pursuits, to their own and their communities' detriment (1988, 138). Other scholars have been equally critical of the use of Black players on the "new plantation" of collegiate sport, arguing that the burden of commercialized sport and its diversion from educational pursuits disproportionately affects Black student-athletes (Hawkins 2001; Beamon and Messer 2013). Moreover, examination of labor practices in the NFL, specifically around the draft, show current practices shot through with symbolic racism (Dufur and Feinberg 2008). Conscious and unconscious racial bias is also shown in the way ideas about physical attributes for Black players and intellectual/intelligence attributes for White players shape different patterns of media coverage (Bigler and Jeffries 2008; Billings 2004) and "stacking" of positions (Lewis 1995; Roderick 2002; Sack and Staurowsky 1998).[19] These ideas and practices maintain a ceiling on Black mobility in sporting infrastructures, as Whites continue to dominate coaching and upper-level administration at the college and professional levels (Kukahiko 2015; Lapchick and Robinson 2015; Lapchick et al. 2014). Finally, the portrayal of Black masculinities in and through sport has been a subject of criticism, as scholars point out that these portrayals provide a narrow view of Black masculinities and often reinforce stereotypes already rampant in American society in ways that limit Black horizons of possibility (Leonard 2012; Oates and Durham 2006).

Popular discourse relies on terms like "breeding," "genetics," and "studs" to describe Samoan and other Polynesian athletes in football. It employs the language of racial biogenetics and draws on terms reminiscent of discussions of African American physicality and the legacy of slavery in the United States. Much like how the focus on athletic excellence for African Americans has reinforced a split from intellectual capacity that has been used to justify rather than contest racialized inequality (Dyreson 2001; Hoberman 1997), these discourses about Pacific Islanders construct them as physical laborers and in turn, naturalize their standing at the bottom of the US class hierarchy.[20]

There are important connections between aspects of African American and Samoan/Pacific Islander experiences in American sport, such as the increasing focus on sport as an opportunity for socioeconomic mobility, position assignment, and providing "grist" for the collegiate football mills. In narrating the gridiron dreams that have been cultivated among young Samoan hopefuls over the past several decades, the mainstream media has turned to a familiar script of underprivileged, "at-risk" youth whose only potential escape from poverty is sport—a script popularized through coverage of African American sporting experiences.[21] Insofar as their realities coincide in urban centers where resilient African American and Pacific Islander communities survive, endure, and flourish in the face of major economic and social shifts, neoliberal state policies, and structural stress, the scripts may ring true.

In an on-camera interview for the *60 Minutes* segment "Football Island," Pelley asks NFL player Troy Polamalu, "What does football mean to a kid growing up in Samoa?" Polamalu answers, "It's our meal ticket. Just like any marginalized ethnic group, you know, if you don't make it to the NFL, what do you have to go back to?" he asked. "That's the beautiful thing about football," Polamalu continued. "It's allowed us to get an education. Football is something that comes naturally to us." Football offers an opportunity for a college education, which otherwise still remains out of reach for many Samoans and other Pacific Islanders, who together have come to constitute a "marginalized ethnic group" in the US context.[22] This acknowledges the positioning of Polynesians in the United States in ways that may resonate with other ethnically and racially minoritized groups. Racialization is a diasporic experience.

Yet while there are overlapping diasporic histories that converge largely in US urbanized metropolitan centers, Samoans and other Pacific Islanders are positioned differently from African Americans in relation to the US social structure due to historical circumstance and relatively smaller population numbers. With a background of (largely voluntary) migration conditioned by imperialism rather than forced migration and enslavement, Samoans have a fundamentally different relationship to racial hierarchies in the United States than African Americans. Their history and contemporary engagement with the sport, the way their presence in the sport is narrated by mainstream media, and the different kinds of meanings attached to the sport for many Samoan communities share some aspects with the African American experience, but remains distinct in its own right.

In parallel but divergent stories featured in *Polynesian Power*, the escape-from-poverty narrative is configured differently in coverage of the pipeline from the islands versus the city. In these stories, place matters in how it shapes structures of opportunity for youth and in the way recognizable narratives are drawn. For example, stories that focus on athletes' successful escape from the urban context, like with Tinoisamoa, are more likely to portray the inevitable dead end of the "hood" and escape through sport in a way that parallels the African American experience but with particular emphasis on family or community supports. Meanwhile, stories that focus on leaving the island, like with Sopoaga, are more likely to highlight the underdevelopment of island areas and a connection to culture, adhering more closely to the longstanding construction of Sāmoa and the Pacific in the US imagination more broadly (see Uperesa 2014b). In each case, important historical and social contexts are finessed or elided (including imperialism, neoliberal disinvestment, and racism) and the sport is represented as salvation, even if it has a ceiling and is governed by a White-dominated power structure in the NCAA and NFL (Dufur and Feinberg 2008; Lapchick et al. 2014).

PHYSICALITY AND INDIGENOUS MASCULINITIES

In the framing of these stories recognition and legibility are important— what stories and pathways are recognizable to a wider audience? What are their key markers, assumptions, and typical outcomes? The media coverage of Samoan players is shaped by preexisting discourses that intertwine latent racial attitudes and ethnographic imagination. The understanding of them as non-White players in a particularly physical sport reflects to a certain degree how African American athletes are portrayed, with some of the subtle messages carried by assumptions about racialized biogenetics. And yet in contrast, as Henderson (2011, 286) notes, "while Samoans sometimes inherit racial US mythography originally crafted for peoples of African ancestry, it is their presumed connection to an indigenous culture that is understood as anterior or outside the West that casts them as 'primitive' in a manner different from American blacks, whose culture—as Paul Gilroy (1993) and others have noted—is precisely a *product* of modernity." The focus on heritage and culture in the contemporary articulation of native Polynesianness draws on a long history of gendered representations; for men, these have been configured differently against a colonial backdrop as the noble or threatening savage, ward in need of tutelage, or threatening leaders needing containment.[23]

This genetic discussion is powerfully determined by both gender and race. That is, it makes a difference that it is the male Samoan body in a predominantly male sport. From early European explorer accounts of the eighteenth century, Samoans were known as fierce fighters and expert navigators. Making war was a predominantly male preserve, linked to the traditionally male institution of the 'aumaga and notions of fierce strength, bravery, and physical prowess. It is this legacy that is being connected to the contemporary arena of football. Yet the 'aumaga, comprising the untitled men of the village, was not a mercenary standing army at the beck and call of the chiefs. Rather, the 'aumaga is one (albeit an important) aspect of life for Samoan men in the village setting whose counterpart is the 'aualuma, or women's organization, also drawn from women of the village. Citing Suaalii (2001, 164), Schmidt notes that "Samoan men ideally provide food, shelter and protection for their families and villages, and their maturity is marked by 'forming a politically successful union, having and raising successful children, and gaining status through tautua, or service, to one's [family] and village'" (2016, 290). The historical legacy of warriorhood in Sāmoa is linked to ideas of service to one's family, village, and district.

Contemporary media narrations, on the other hand, carry the notion that violence is a part of Polynesian male nature writ large regardless of context, and indeed that it is a strong component of traditional (read: authentic) Polynesian masculinity (Tengan 2002). In this way, we can see how Samoans in the United States are often invested with an "excess of culture," but in particularly gendered ways. Here Susan Birrell's notion of "physicality" as the connection between gender and race in sport is useful, because it is a key element in the construction of dominant images of racially defined groups (1989, 222) as well as competing masculinities (Connell 1995).

One of the common explanations for Samoan success in the sport links culture and aggressive physicality. One coach I spoke to noted that Samoan kids liked to be "physical" and "aggressive" and football was a good outlet. In *60 Minutes*' "Football Island," Samoana coach Pepine Lauvao discusses his players: "They're soft spoken, they're gentle, but when they put on the equipment, they just become monsters. I mean they just want to go out and hit and hit and hit." While he may have been playing to the camera some, in Samoan villages physicality is a central part of body culture that is valued and respected, with appropriate performance in context.[24] Locally, especially but not exclusively for men, courage and steadfastness on behalf of yourself, your family, or your village is valued; cowardice is disparaged but indiscriminate aggression is also discouraged. Strength of will, political savvy, and being able to hold your ground physically if necessary are characteristics worthy of respect in both men and women, although particularly valued for men, given expectations for them as providers and custodians of extended family resources in many parts of Sāmoa. Shifts over time and space also factor in, as some acts of aggression or violence that may have in the past been seen as permissible or honorable have since been criminalized or are no longer socially acceptable (see Irwin and Umemoto 2012, 8, and Kamau'u 1998 cited in Tengan 2008, 11). For Samoan representation, the transnational element is also essential; the movement back and forth from the islands strengthens cultural and social ties such that contemporary ethnographic representations of culture are an important feature of perceptions and expressions of Samoan "physicality." In these representations physicality and violence are cast as "cultural."

When this aggression is harnessed to the football field it becomes a controlled, domesticated violence, a "fantasy of Otherness" (hooks 2006, 370) that can then be pleasurably consumed by the American public. Writing about the "drama of Otherness" that finds expression in the "cultural marketplace" of the commercial realm, bell hooks notes, "Encounters with Otherness are clearly marked as more exciting, more intense, and more threatening. The lure is the combination of pleasure and danger" (370). Off the field and on the street this aspect of sociality is threatening to the mainstream population and becomes pathologized, contributing to rising rates of incarceration for young Samoan and other Pacific Islander men in the prison industrial complex (Irwin and Umemoto 2012).[25] The implicit violence of the "warrior," then, is only desirable when enacted in the context of institutions such as the military or sport.

Impacts of the "Gridiron Warrior": Stereotypes and Athletic Labeling

The view of football as a "natural" fit for Samoans, and Samoans as "natural" athletes, has opened particular doors for many young men in recent decades, as we see clearly illustrated in Tinoisamoa's case. Yet it is also arguably the most widely circulated stereotype that marks everyday life for Samoan and other Polynesian youth in transnational communities. Just as for African Americans historically, this stereotype mobilizes a complex imaginary to contradictory ends.

On the one hand, the athletic stereotypes have helped to open sporting pathways for Pacific Islander youth, with sport constituting an important site of inclusion and belonging. Yet on the other hand, even though the stereotype is more positive than others (like security worker or gang member), its focus on physical performance has helped to reinforce the view of Samoans as laborers and the narrow expectations for achievement in non-physical areas like education.[26] This is true in the United States as well as in the Pacific, and in Pacific metropoles in New Zealand and Australia (Hokowhitu 2003; 2004; McDonald and Rodriguez 2014). This pushes more and more Samoan and Pacific Islander youth into sport. Speaking to the issue of stereotypes in *Samoan Youth: Ensuring Our Success*, Josiah Fanene describes people thinking "We were just kind of dumb jocks, we were really good at sports, and when it came to the classroom work we didn't really take care of business." In the same clip, Glendal Tautua pointed out a similar issue, with people thinking "all we're good at is sports."[27] On his blog post "The Annoying Yet Inevitable Stereotype of Being a Polynesian College Student," Tautua describes, "Before people even ask me what my name is I get a confident point aimed at the middle of my ribcage followed by the question 'football? or rugby?'"

In the years I taught at the University of Hawai'i (2011–2016), college students would often come up to comment on these issues after my colloquia lectures. Several of the young men noted how they were always expected to play football, and it was the first thing people would ask about when they met. Others described the disappointment when they did not live up to the football expectations, even though they continued on in their college careers as students. At the University of Washington, Benning Tamatane Potoa'e writes, "It is important for me to help others understand that I am more than just a football player and more than just a stereotypical Samoan. Be yourself and go against the grain when you are put into a false stereotype—it does not feel good to be boxed into an image that society creates."[28] In many Samoan communities this escalating value of football performance—driven both internally and externally—produces a tension that manifests in different ways for youth and families.

In Southern California, for example, this was one aspect of the Pacific Islander young adult experience that emerged in the Pacific Islander Health Careers Pipeline Program (PIHCPP) community-based participatory research effort conducted in 2007–2008. This effort was a needs assessment of educational concepts among Pacific Islander young adults aimed at providing information to help in developing and addressing a health career pipeline. In it, researchers found that participants felt keenly the weight of Pacific Islander stereotypes, and that those stereotypes reinforced existing barriers to educational achievement (particularly the lack of expectation of success for Pacific communities or Pacific youth in education) (Tran et al. 2010, 28–30; see also Miyamoto 2005; Lee and Kumashiro 2005). In their view, educators kept their expectations low and provided little support for students to dream big. Pacific Islander students, on the other hand, had begun to internalize the prevalent stereotypes, limited their educational efforts, or dropped them altogether (Tran et al. 2009, 25, 33). The exception was sports. Researchers noted:

> Unless a student is a promising athlete, the belief is that the chance of that student getting into college and succeeding are very small. The result is a cascade effect—if a student is not a talented athlete, there is little chance for him/her to get into college, and thus, the student develops a fatalistic attitude toward education and gives up. Often times, students who are athletes, spend so much of their time thinking about excelling in sports that they forget to think beyond the athletic scholarship and about their future as a career professional. (Tran et al. 2009, 25)

Focusing on sports as the path to college, many Pacific Islander students were not well informed about alternative pathways to higher education, and for those without scholarship offers, postponing education or dropping out became more likely (Tran et al. 2010, 31–32). "As a result, stereotypes were further perpetuated within the PI community and contributed to the pressure on youth. The added task of combating these inflicted stereotypes stressed the already overwhelmed students as they seek to establish their identity as PIS" (Tran et al. 2010, 31). Sports—especially football—sustained the dream of success through high school, but participants reported not being well prepared for the academic side of the athletic scholarship game.

In Hawai'i, Samoan high school girls have reported similar struggles: low expectations for educational success from teachers, negative stereotyping from peers, and domestic demands from parents and family members. In a study of how Samoan girls negotiate challenges around bias, racism, sexism, and various social pressures, one youth observed that many people "stereotype Samoans to be good in sports and yet when it comes to like academics and stuff, they think we're like dense" (Mayeda, Pasko, and Chesney-Lind 2006, 10). They went on to criticize the sport stereotyping and the wealth of resources directed at keeping the boys eligible for college athletic scholarships while they were left with few role models outside of their family and community circles. Without the strong push toward sports that has been ingrained in the boys, the girls reported struggling with fewer opportunities and less support for college from teachers, counselors, and family. In discussions weighing gendered effects of the emphasis on football in Pacific Islander communities, I was surprised to hear one of my students critique what she perceived to be an expectation for girls to either marry or birth the next NFL player: "If you're a Polynesian woman and you want to be taken care of you will find a Polynesian man that plays football and you will generate a line of sons to play football." This "fandom standard," as she called it, positions boys and men at the center, and women as fans and supporters. These kinds of critiques point to the heteropatriarchal elevation of contemporary Indigenous masculinities that contribute to the marginalization of women and nonbinary people (Tengan 2014).

It is clear that athletic labeling has highly gendered outcomes. The stereotype of the Polynesian Gridiron Warrior that produces some positive outcomes for boys—increased access to specific sporting pathways, sites of belonging, and masculine social currency—does not extend to girls in the same way. There has been concerted effort in recent years to cultivate athletic pathways for girls, given the time and effort involved in fostering pathways for boys. For example, in recent years in American Sāmoa, camps and clinics have added volleyball and softball to provide training opportunities for girls. While this is helping to foster more gender equity in athletic opportunities, it remains underdeveloped in relation to the infrastructure supporting boys' football in the islands. Gender inequality in the sports realm has meant that the infrastructure drawing boys and girls into sport and the kinds of rewards they can earn remain unequal. While this has changed more in the States than in the islands, largely due to Title IX challenges and requirement, the larger structure of capitalized sport in the United States remains heavily skewed in favor of men's sports, and so the potential for college access and status attached to women's sports is not yet on equal footing. One effect is to push girls to be more serious with their studies, and boys with athletic talent to be less so.

Meanwhile, divergent expectations for performances of (hyper-) masculinity and (hyper-) femininity have shaped the social meanings of sports participation differently for boys and girls in the United States.[29] To the extent that Samoan communities resist extreme performances of gender, the kind of physical strength and prowess required to dominate in mainstream sports do not dissuade girls from participation for fear of being less "feminine," and many do find sites of belonging and confidence in those arenas. However, cultural sensibilities around gender roles and household labor have historically encouraged Samoan parents to favor boys' sports participation while restricting that of girls, perhaps in part because access to sporting-specific pathways changed for boys earlier and more dramatically than for girls.[30] This may well change in the future, and there are some signs that change is already under way. Still, gendered stereotypes about Samoan sporting have real-world consequences, as they work to reinforce channeling boys into and supporting them in particular sports like football while restricting the growth of robust sporting infrastructure and participation for girls.

Mediating the "Gridiron Warrior"

Samoan and other Pacific Islander communities have been responding to these stereotypes and fixed narratives in ways that show a complicated mediation of the figure of the Gridiron Warrior. Representations are not always rejected outright; they are received, interpreted, and engaged in different ways by diverse audiences. Their social circulation is made possible by a "transportability, or detachability" that allows them "to seem to have lives of their own yet also be fibers of connection across various social situations and contexts" (Spitulnik 1997, 181). In the process of responding to media, players actively mobilize notions of culture in responding in complex ways to encounters with the media and the larger American public. They also narrate their journeys in ways that give credit to their families and cultural heritage. With the particular ethnographic interest outside media brings, it raises the question of whether public framings and private interest compel the players to narrate their cultural backgrounds in ways that are recognizable, given the media representations that are already circulating.

The tension produced by emergent pathways and racialized, gendered stereotyping recognized by US West Coast Pacific Islander youth above is illustrated in a 2011 piece on "Samoan Stereotypes" by Sāmoa-born artist Francis Pesamino. Pesamino moved to Auckland as a child and spends time in Sāmoa visiting family; he started watching American football years ago (his favorite player was Troy Polamalu) and he followed the sport through ESPN, American television broadcasts, and online sources like YouTube (personal communication, February 24, 2015). In figure 3.4, Pesamino's black-and-white drawing takes the uniformed figure of Troy Polamalu as its base, and illustrates it with the many positive and negative stereotypes about Samoans. In our interview, Pesamino described wanting to explore how people outside Samoan culture view Samoan identity, as well as how those inside the culture, especially the younger generation, views being Samoan. Compared to his other pieces created around the same time that addressed viewpoints mostly within Samoan communities, he noted that "Samoan Stereotypes" features Polamalu as someone who is well known and whose image speaks to Samoans and non-Samoans alike, incorporating both views since he took many of the stereotypes from the way people inside and outside the community described Samoans (including on newscasts).

Although some labels in the artwork are more resonant to the Auckland context (like *Factory and Meat Workers*), most can describe stereotypes in many other places. In our discussion Pesamino noted that others may stereotype Samoans as: *Loud, Short Temper, Obesity, Fresh, Abusive, Fobs, Ruthless, Fat,* and *Trouble,* while inside Samoan communities, ideas we associate with being Samoan are: *God, Values, Respect, Family, Morals, Sporty,* and *Athletic.* The sporting stereotypes dominate today, with labels like *Fearless, Physical, Big Hitters, Strong, Wrecking Ball, Natural Talent, Solid, Muscles, Bone Crunching Tackles, Flair,* and *Speed* used both within and outside our communities. The sporting stereotypes offer scripts that are preferable to ones like *Abusive* and *Ruthless,* or *Bad Diet* and *Fresh* (which in the Aotearoa New Zealand context notes one's recent immigrant status or lack of sophistication, as in "fresh off

3.4 Samoan Stereotypes. IMAGE CREDIT: FRANCES PESAMINO, ARTIST.

the boat"), but as we see with the youth in Southern California, they are as limiting as they are promising. As they come of age young Pacific people can see the contradiction represented by sporting pathways, but entrenched ideas, as well as structural and economic realities, reinforce the belief in upward mobility through sport.

The media narratives (on the surface, largely positive) of imposing, powerful young men drawing on a cultural heritage to both claim victory on the field for their contemporary communities and honor their ancestors is a story attractive to the writers, the fans, and the players and the communities themselves. Like in Aotearoa New Zealand and Australia, where rugby union and league provide an important site for articulating Pacific identity and connecting to diasporic communities (Bergin 2002; Lakisa 2011,

2014; McDonald and Rodriguez 2014, 237; Panapa and Phillips 2014), in the United States football provides an important space, for Pacific Islander boys and men especially. Set against a backdrop of minoritization and colonialism, football success has been an important source of pride.[31] As June Jones noted on screen in *Polynesian Power*:

> Ever since I came to Hawai'i, 1973–74 to play, there was many Polynesian players and every time we walked out onto the field there was a different energy, a different type of feeling . . . it was almost like it was more to it than just this game we were getting ready to play . . . here in Hawai'i the kids had been told for so long, and it doesn't matter where the Polynesian players come from, they've been told that they're not as good as these mainland US players. And so, every time we go to tee it up, it's almost like it's not just about playing this game, it's about proving we are something special.

Activities on the field then often come to symbolize a kind of serious game (Ortner 1996) where the performance and outcome of the game encompass much more than a tick in the win-loss column, and this complicates both the engagement with the sport and larger issue of athletic stereotyping. This athletic labelling is taken up in different ways by transnational Samoan communities in the islands and beyond, as part of a wider circulation and mediation of these images and narratives. Taking account of how particular players engage with the media narratives, artistic work, and film media, we can see more clearly the shifting discourses that emerge from this circulation.

BRANDING NEW NARRATIVES

Drawing on the examples of Troy Polamalu, Marcus Mariota, and Danny Shelton, we can trace some of the different ways that players are both recognized by mainstream media and shape their own public images. Perhaps one of the most well-known players of Samoan descent, Troy Polamalu (retired, Pittsburgh Steelers) was not the first football player to wear his hair long on game days, but when his ability put him in the national spotlight, his hair—flowing and wild—captured the imagination of the American media. In a 2005 story (DiPaola) he attributed his long hair to laziness in college; when he found that his repeated concussions ceased with his longer hair, he decided to keep it long. In the story he does not make an explicit connection to his Samoan heritage, but notes that his mother-in-law remarked that many warriors from ancient times wore their hair long. In 2006, a reporter narrates the significance of his hair and connection to culture in a different way: "His grandparents hail from the island village of Ta'u, which is part of American Samoa. The long hair is a symbol of his heritage and the Samoan warrior tradition".[32] In late 2008, the tag line of his personal website was "The Samoan Warrior of the NFL."[33]

In the years following, he successfully cultivated a strong personal brand, including a lucrative advertising contract with Head & Shoulders. In those commercials he pokes fun at the obsession with his hair, and brings a light-hearted and self-effacing humor to the screen. The commercials, as well as other brand ventures, position him to be marketed to a wider American audience. In 2016 the home page of his website, troy43.com, had a photo of him in uniform against a Pittsburgh city backdrop, with text that narrates different aspects of identity "TROY POLAMALU Husband. Father. USC Trojan. American. Samoan. Safety. Student. Movie Buff. Green Thumb. Pittsburgh Steeler." The Troy and Theodora Polamalu Foundation supports a wide variety of charitable organizations and causes that serve both Samoan and wider American communities. Their work with American Sāmoa high school sports and the Fa'a Samoa Initiative (discussed in chapter 2) has been a direct conduit for connecting to and benefitting the islands and its people, but it is one of many projects they are involved in. It is unclear what specific decisions shaped the growth of Brand Troy, but it is clear that there was a shift in his marketing, with an effort to narrate him increasingly as a multi-dimensional public figure where his Samoan heritage remains an important, but not singular, aspect worthy of focus.

Shifting to a new generation of players, Danny Shelton immediately stood out at the 2015 NFL Draft in New York City. Instead of a typical suit, he opted for an island-print vest and matching burgundy 'ie faitaga along with an 'ulā fala. In true island style, his outfit was coordinated with those of his entourage. His sartorial choices had a commentator asking if he was wearing a skirt, only to be corrected by a fellow commentator in the know: "That's a lāvalava." The lāvalava has become something of a signature for Shelton: he chose to wear an 'ie faitaga also at the Senior Bowl media night, and wore a lāvalava while doing position drills at the University of Washington's Pro Day, as well as in other public appearances and after practice. One story noted, "Danny Shelton Brings Polynesian Culture to Browns Locker Room" (Jones 2015), as he had his teammates also wearing them around the team facility.

In media interviews he has been clear on his intention as someone who largely grew up on the US West Coast to represent his Samoan heritage while recognizing both his American influences and his Samoan and Polynesian cultural influences carried by his family. Marked with an 'ulā nifo tatau around his neck and a tatau sleeve on his left arm, Shelton actively shaped his public image also through video blogs as part of Grit Media's "Unfiltered" series on YouTube.[34] In his first vlog he described grappling with identity issues around being mixed Peruvian and Samoan, and not being accepted by youth peers because he was a "half-breed" and did not speak Samoan.[35] In the segment he credits his athletic and academic success starting in high school with helping motivate him to work harder: "It made me realize that I could be a representative of my community, the Polynesian community." It was later, as a college student, where he says he found a Samoan and Polynesian peer network, and connected more to his heritage through studying anthropology and playing football. Finding a Polynesian community at the University of Washington helped him to consciously resist the pull of assimilation to American mainstream culture, choosing to learn more about and consciously represent his Samoan roots. He outlines his own vision for tautua to a larger entity: contributing to what he calls the Poly Movement, he hopes to represent his Samoan heritage and validate Polynesian cultural communities (in predominantly White contexts like Washington State) through his own success in a highly visible field. As an Academic All-American as well as an All-American for football, Shelton took his studies seriously and was a role model for academics as well as for sports.[36] In this revealing clip, he is negotiating not only the meaning of his cultural heritage for himself, but also in how he is represented to Samoan and Polynesian communities, as well as the wider public.

The third player, Marcus Mariota, has been represented differently from both Polamalu and Shelton, even though like Shelton he is also of mixed ancestry (Samoan and pālagi/White). Keeping his hair short, and of a slimmer build than Shelton without visible tatau, in media coverage leading up to the 2014 Heisman Trophy vote he was referred to often as Hawaiian, referencing the place of his upbringing rather than his ancestry. Yet like Polamalu and Shelton his media presence is not just constructed by others—his own speeches, interviews, and advertisements show an intentional self-representation that eschews pre-existing discourses about Samoan players. These new mediations are successful, in part, because he blazed a new trail for Samoan players with his enormous success as a quarterback at the top of the college game, and in that way disrupted expectations for what Polynesian players are expected to do in football. While he wasn't the first Samoan Division I quarterback (preceded by Jack "The Throwin' Samoan" Thompson, Samoa Samoa, Marques Tuiasosopo, and others), as the first Samoan

Heisman Trophy winner, his success in the college game at the position is rivaled only by Tua Tagovailoa's achievements.

In his Heisman acceptance speech Mariota showed it was not just an individual accomplishment: he explicitly narrated place and recognized relationships that had shaped him into the person he had become, thanking a variety of people who had contributed to his success.[37] After recognizing coaches, the university, the city of Eugene, St. Louis High School, and Ducks fans, he said: "To Hawai'i nei (beloved Hawai'i), thank you for teaching me humility and respect." He went on to address the Polynesian community specifically: "Young Poly athletes everywhere, you should take this as motivation, and dream big and strive for greatness." After thanking his parents and brother, he closed the speech by saying, "Fa'afetai tele lava. God bless, and go Ducks." In the lāuga he recognized the different communities that had shaped his success, and specifically marked his heritage by referencing his genealogical links and using Samoan in his speech while addressing both Hawai'i and the wider Polynesian community.

These multiple affiliations bear out in the crafting of the Heisman Trophy display at the University of Oregon that features Polynesian tatau design, a relief of Diamond Head and map of the Hawaiian Islands, the 2014 University of Oregon football roster, tributes to family, and *AIGA*, the Samoan word for family.[38] His choice of advertising sponsors also reflects multiple aspects of his identity, even while they highlight particular place-based cultural influences. For example, a 2015 spot for Beats by Dre themed "Ohana" features his own 'ohana, or family, as well as clips of early-morning beach workouts and him in the gym to the sound of Leon Bridges's "River."[39] Toward the end, different people from Hawai'i are featured on screen as we hear a voiceover of a blessing that notes, "It's not just your mom, your dad, your brother. It's the people of Hawai'i that stand behind you. You are now carrying us. [Translated from Hawaiian:] God please bestow upon us your warm aloha . . . Mahalo, mahalo, mahalo. Go get 'em."[40] The visuals and sound of the ad evokes a nostalgia of place while also conveying the vibrancy of Hawai'i communities, and a specific schema of affect, relations, and responsibilities encompassed by the concept and practice of 'ohana (and tautua in a more general sense). The theme is repeated in a later 2016 NFL TV spot, "Football is Family," which talks about football in Hawai'i, the meaning of 'ohana, and the communal orientation where what you do reflects on your family and community.[41]

While place-based associations interrupt some of the dominant discourses about Samoan players in Mariota's case, we can also ask whether his mediation of his public image is shaped by being racialized differently from some of the other recognizable players in diverse mainstream interpretations of him. His taller and slimmer build, shorter hair, skin tone, and phenotype may signal race and culture differently than the figure of Shelton, who is also of mixed ancestry, or others like Haloti Ngata or Domata Peko. The latter figures are more likely to be positioned within dominant US discourses and images of indigenous Polynesian masculinity and bodies. Differential racialization and coding may open more space for Mariota to narrate multiple cultural affiliations. At the same time, his association with Hawai'i invokes different cultural scripts that already carry with them a certain set of assumptions people have about the place, even prior to their specific articulation in media (the focus on 'ohana, for example).

New Mediations

The mainstream media coverage of Samoan and other Pacific Islanders in American football has consistently been framed as a "Polynesian" story. The early coverage like the Johnston article (1976) expanded the frame from Hawai'i and included Sāmoa; in later coverage the emergence of the figure of the Gridiron Warrior was not specifically Samoan, even though players of Samoan ancestry were largely the ones being profiled. Shaped by a longer history of ethnographic imagining of the Pacific in general and Samoans in particular, the pan-Polynesian Gridiron Warrior has emerged as a raced and gendered cultural icon. In this coverage, the narrative mobilizes particular aspects of culture that suit the football endeavor. The production of this image, then, and its circulation in different interpretive communities elicits a variety of attachments and meanings.

The figure of the Samoan football player is in many ways a new transmutation of visions of Polynesian warriorhood. It has been more than a hundred years since the practice of war-making was outlawed by colonial powers in the Samoan islands. Still, the Samoan football player is presented as a modern-day warrior, and in the context of the sport the difference that he embodies is at once dangerous and domesticated, with displays of physical dominance and exciting, full-throttle power plays rendered pleasurable and valuable to home and mainstream audiences. Their increased visibility has compelled an ethnographic account of the players themselves that is often figured, as in the journalistic selections above, in the premodern savage slot (Trouillot 1991) or recuperated in the suffering slot (Robbins 2013). In this sense, the interest in the players reflects not only their possible performance on the field, but also a fascination with the exotic that in the moral and material economy of football heightens their value because of the explicit linkage with fierce strength. Players then navigate these double-sided opportunities in the sport context, but also in community contexts.

Received narratives have been taken up in different ways by players, and figure in the marking of young bodies in ways that portray pride in their Samoan heritage especially in the form of long hair and tattooed arms (the "sleeve" being a contemporary undertaking of tatau that is distinct from the mālofie). It is one way to claim the field as a cultural space, disrupting the repetitive anonymity of the uniformed gridiron. This contemporary inscription of culture and heritage on the body by Polynesian players garners visibility for their home communities in and through, but ultimately beyond, the individual's performance on the field.

Although representations of Samoans in football often mobilize a warrior tradition, the sport is clearly not traditional at all. In some ways, it is at odds with customary normative expectations of young men to work on the plantations, serve the family, participate in the village 'aumaga, and in years past, to apprentice with tufuga. In others, it complements and fulfills the expectation to honor one's family and ancestry, and becomes a vehicle for enabling future tautua. That both Samoans and non-Samoans now discursively mark football as linked to a tradition of warriorhood points to the transnational sport experience, the success of Samoan players, and the media coverage of that success. But it also raises the prospect of "gendered memory work," wherein coordinated "personal memories, historical narratives, and bodily experiences and representations" shape subjectivity, and this is worth considering carefully (Tengan 2014, 214).

The branding of the Gridiron Warrior as "Polynesian" has also been taken up as a way to unite Pacific Islander communities in the sports endeavor. The geographical marking of a Polynesian triangle that spans Hawai'i, Aotearoa New Zealand, and Rapanui, and encompassing the islands in between, does reflect the largest groups of Pacific Islanders playing the game in the United States. From the Polynesian Coaches Association to the Polynesian All-American Bowl to the Polynesian Football Hall of Fame, players, coaches, and organizers also highlight the particular aspects of culture that suit the football enterprise, while taking control of the circulating messaging and images.

As a widespread stereotype, though, the Gridiron Warrior has helped to enlarge a highly gendered sporting mobility pipeline for boys, perhaps impinging on other paths of mobility. While artists and other community members are engaging the image and producing different kinds of stories about the role of football in Pacific communities, players themselves are also interrupting stock procedures of how media highlights sport labor. In recent years Samoan professional football players have resisted playing to type and have taken control of their own branding and image in ways that both engage and transform that image. Like Polamalu's humor (in the Samoan tradition of faleaitu) or Mariota's lāuga showing humility and giving respect to those who supported his journey, players negotiate commercialized platforms and infuse them with cultural sensibilities.[42] In so doing, they are refusing to be captured by images not of their own making, but not disarming them altogether.

Four

Gridiron Capital

ON A HOT, SUNNY DAY IN MAY, I attended the Pacific Islands Athletic Alliance (PIAA) annual combine held at a private school on the island of O'ahu. The school's long-standing football program is well known, particularly recently, for graduates who have earned top accolades in the college game and secured NFL contracts. When I arrived in the morning the combine had already begun, and the field and gym were set up with a series of stations designed to test skills and quantify performance. On the field, players did the broad jump, pro-agility shuttle, and 40-yard dash. They also ran through different drills to show their ability and performance in specific positions. In the cool shade of the gym, players rotated between stations that measured the height of their vertical jump and how many pounds they could bench-press. Players and their families were there: some were simply watching the events while others were volunteers, providing drinks to the players, taking pictures, or helping out in other ways. Families were set up in the stands and at the edge of the field; some had brought their chairs, coolers, and umbrellas and had settled in for the day. The combine was open to players from all backgrounds, but the majority of participants appeared to be Polynesian students from the state of Hawai'i. I attended at the invitation of PIAA's executive director, Doris Sullivan, following a lunch meeting where she described the workings of the organization.[1]

Talking story over lunch, Doris explained that the goal of PIAA was to increase Hawai'i and American Sāmoa students' access to college athletic scholarships. The geographic focus meant that many PIAA members and participants were of Pacific Islander descent, although the organization's services were open to all. In practice, PIAA acted as a clearinghouse and broker, matching players with college recruiters. It served a large number of students (male and female) in a variety of sports, but football had been the main focus since its inception. Each combine participant was able to create a profile with their contact information and statistics from the combine, in addition to athletic or academic honors and any football camps they had attended, for interested coaches to access on the PIAA website. Doris was active with a wide network of coaches and would get requests for particular player positions, which she either answered or forwarded on to high school coaches and other contacts.

The combine and events like it had become an important part of the process in part because of the increasing move toward standardized measurement, but also because for some it was the first step in scouting and recruitment, providing a measurement profile of a particular player for evaluation by coaches.[2] Following that, there might be requests for game film or transcripts, SAT scores, and other instruments of measurement. For students from Hawai'i, it allowed continental US coaches access to some information on potential recruits and acted as a conduit into athletic networks. For students from Sāmoa, there was often no film available for coaches to view, so either endorsements from trusted sources or initial measurements like those provided by combine profiles served as sources of information for coaches seeking to recruit new players. In the contest for visibility both sets of student-athletes are at a significant disadvantage, although those from Sāmoa are more so: games are generally inaccessible to college scouts, and clinics and camps where they might be noticed are largely inaccessible to players. In this sense, organizations like PIAA that hold these kinds of events help to mitigate an uneven field that is getting more unequal every year.

A combine is an event where a measure of participating athletes is taken, initially in terms of particular body aspects like height, weight, wingspan (measured length from one fingertip to the other, arms outstretched horizontally), and handspan (length of the tip of the pinky to the tip of the thumb). It also measures skill performance in the execution of particular drills and through in-person observation, providing an initial gauge of the unquanti-fiable: effort, presence, and heart. As competition for college scholarships and spots on high school rosters has increased, so have a plethora of cost and no-cost activities outside of the regular season. Together with camps, clinics, private gyms, and weekend workouts, the combine is one of a con-stellation of events that have proliferated in recent years to give student-athletes an "edge on the competition." Their expansion dovetails with the growth of youth sports nationally (Coakley 2004, 124–130) and what Eitzen has described as the conflation between the possibility and probability of upward mobility through sports (1999).[3] In Hawai'i and Sāmoa specifically, the compressed economies compel youth toward opportunities for upward mobility like those provided by sport while the highly capitalized system draws them in.[4]

The camps were a singular opportunity for some of the college coaches to cross the Pacific Ocean and scout Hawai'i and American Sāmoa players (and enjoy a trip to the islands and maybe earn some money).[5] In addition to the clearinghouse and combine events, PIAA had also organized clinics, and in 2014 lent its support to the first Ultra Performance Camp.[6] The 2014 camp had nearly sixty coaches from college programs at different levels of compe-tition from across the nation in attendance. Activities typically started with a morning check-in and warm-up, a variety of offensive, defensive, and spe-cial teams drill stations with instruction provided by participating coaches, lunch, a full-contact scrimmage, and short motivational speeches peppered in during breaks.

While living in Hawai'i (2011–2016) I volunteered at PIAA's combine twice, as well at as the 2014 camp. I had also been an invited guest speaker for two of their National Letter of Intent Signing Day events at the Elks Club in Waikiki. The year I helped with the combine height station, we moved play-ers through quickly to get all the measurements done so they could move to the next assessment. The students came through the different stations with their Under Armour PIAA Combine dry-fit shirts and bags, congregating in small groups. The atmosphere of the combine was energetic—the kids joked around on the sidelines and some parents and family watched, but at the stations they got to work, pushing for the highest vertical, longest broad jump, and stacking all the weight they could handle on the bench. The all-volunteer staff was guiding the students through the stations, recording but not evaluating. The event with high school student-athletes had a fun com-munity feel to it, with many long-time PIAA volunteers, including parents of current and former local players.

At the highest levels of the sport, including the professional leagues and the top tier of the NCAA, the capitalist market logic directed at winning and accruing profits is a major driving force of football programs. This ethos of maximum performance has slowly permeated lower levels of the sport, fueling the winning imperative even when there is little money at stake.[7] For many players there is a shift in high school as they prepare for the potential jump to college: in order to compete successfully, football players undergo processes of commodification that enhance their value to their teams, accruing what I call gridiron capital. Drawing on the "the existence of multiple, coexisting, and variously related 'regimes of value'" (Myers 2001, 4), the production of football players as they enter the college game and continue upward as a category of laborers raises questions about local contexts, sport circuits, and the peculiar nature of sport as cultural commodity. Players at different levels are negotiating structures of athletic labor and forms of capital, exercising agency as they navigate within and beyond narrowly construed economic frames of value.

To examine the various ways in which players are commodified and how they move within and among various regimes of value (Appadurai 1986, Graeber 2001, Myers 2001), we engage ethnographically with "the athletes, the multiple agents that surround them and shape their decisions and actions, and the multiple contexts in which they must operate simultaneously" (Besnier 2012, 504). One of the unique aspects of Samoan participation in football I explore briefly here, and more fully in chapter 3, is the market commodification of players' cultural heritage in order to stress their exotic difference from other players and the general public. This plays well in the media—attracting viewership and interest, selling magazines, and drawing clicks—and also helps brand particular players and teams.[8] But this enterprise is not for the weak or faint of heart; the last section offers a preliminary analysis (more fully developed in chapter 5) of the social and physical costs of participation that are often obscured by the spectacular propaganda surrounding the sport.

Corporeal Transformation and Gridiron Capital

Visually, the PIAA combine may have held a passing resemblance to the NFL Scouting Combine shown in the documentary *Polynesian Power*, but the difference was significant. The former was on a much smaller scale, organized by volunteers and held to assist student-athletes better their chances for college scholarships; in the latter, organized by corporate rather than community entities, the stakes were much higher, as there were onlookers and evaluators that were directly responsible for future NFL contracts. That footage features then-prospect Isaac Sopoaga and others as their bodies and performances are measured in a high-stakes evaluation leading up to the NFL Draft. One by one players are examined, notated, and profiled by combine staff and by the interested consumers, NFL coaches. How well a player prospect performs in the combine is also obsessively reported by media outlets, generating a lucrative seasonal mini-market within the sport. The process leading up to and encompassing the draft, what Oates calls "the contemporary flesh market" (2007, 86), "is startling for its invasiveness, comprehensiveness and studied dehumanization" (Oates and Durham 2004, 310). Perhaps because the players were stripped down and appeared to be paraded before NFL coaches and staff, in my first viewing the footage resembled accounts of slave inspections on the auction block, as prospective owners examined all parts of the body up to the teeth to ascertain the health and potential for physical productivity of the individual in question. This impression has been echoed by African American players who have experienced the draft process, describing the combine as a "slave trade" (Dufur and Feinberg 2009, 65).

The players' value in the eyes of management is directly tied to their prospects for productive labor. In the 1989 *Sports Illustrated* cover story "Maximum Exposure," New York Giants general manager George Young declared bluntly, "It's a livestock show, and it's dehumanizing, but it's necessary. If we're going to pay a kid a lot of money to play football, we have a right to find out as much as we can. If we're going to buy 'em, we ought to see what we're buying."[9] While front office personnel might speak more tactfully today, the impetus remains the same: intense scrutiny of the team's investment. Focusing in on the purchase, we see that "while they occupy the front lines of a global industry of extraordinary public visibility, professional athletes operate in the only sector of the global labor market in which workers can be legally bought and sold" (Besnier 2012, 494).

This raises a prickly moral issue concerning "the commoditization of human attributes such as labor, intellect, or creativity," according to Igor Kopytoff (1986, 84). These concerns show the "conceptual unease of conjoining person and commodity,"[10] in part because of the legacy of slavery built on the extreme and totalizing commoditization of people (85). Yet "we do not—we cannot at this point—object to the commoditization and sale of labor . . . [even if] we do object to the trafficking in labor that a complete commoditization of labor would imply" (85). In the United States, as elsewhere, the capitalist economy is largely structured so that workers sell their labor for a wage paid by individuals or companies. What allows a moral acceptance of this sale of labor is the caveat is choice: "the commoditization must be controlled by the laborer himself," or at least appear to be (85).

Clearly NFL prospects are far from slaves with no recourse or options of their own. In the case of sporting contracts there are a number of ways players manipulate the negotiation process (such as holding out for a more lucrative contract before reporting to training camp, publicly demanding to be traded, or not performing at their best). Players are agentive: actively evaluating and accepting college offers, entering themselves into the draft, and working out with particular teams; they are not one-dimensional objects at the whim of institutional power currents even if they are navigating a system over which they have little control. Moreover, their selection to highly visible events like the NFL Scouting Combine is an occasion of excitement and celebration. Spots are coveted and hold the potential to be well rewarded, with performance linked to one's evolving "draft stock." As one former Samoan NFL player told me, "It's amazing to be part of an elite group of athletes invited" to an NFL combine and to have the opportunity to be selected as a player. For many, it is a joyous culmination of many years of hard work.

Even though it is often obscured by the view of sport as high-profile entertainment, the players provide a particular kind of well-compensated labor in an industry. While players attempt to manipulate the negotiation process, they must actively maximize their marketability as players and maneuver within constraints set by coaches, teams, owners, and fans. As Niko Besnier (2012) writes, sport is "one of the human activities in which the body is most objectified by intense scrutiny: trained, disciplined, modified, displayed, evaluated and commodified, the sporting body is the focus of not only the person who inhabits it but also spectators, trainers, and 'owners'" (494). Under this scrutiny, players enhance their performance through training, where they hone their skills in daily workouts in anticipation of the combines or team workouts. They build muscle, gain speed, perfect their footwork, and build endurance; players transform both their bodies and subjective understanding of themselves as player-products in order to compete to the best of their ability.

Football players are entrepreneurs in bodily capital. To this end, they undertake a slow process of training the body and the mind for performing a particular set of movements in competition. Players train to maximize their performance on the field, leading up to and throughout fall training camp:

the "peculiar institution concocted for the intensive protection and prolification of corporeal capital" (Wacquant 1995, 78). During this training players (ideally) are turning themselves into high-value products that are then selected by coaches, and eventually—if one is both lucky and talented—idolized and consumed by fans.

In the course of transformation in which bodily sensitivity is acquired through a slow and protracted process of sedimentation in which one gains practical mastery over the sense and action-execution of various body parts (Wacquant 1995, 72), football players are accumulating gridiron capital. Here gridiron capital is a specific set of bodily practices, abilities, and orientations that can be converted profitably in gridiron football. This value is both accumulated and convertible, but not always economic. Distinct from economic, cultural, and social capital players may accrue with football success, gridiron capital accrues in the specific process of training one's body. It inheres in the specific sets of skills and abilities valued for their on-field performance, the social currency attached to playing the game, and enhanced brand value. The process of accumulating gridiron capital is also the route by which one transforms the body in anticipation (or perhaps continuation) of successful commodification and thereby conversion into the forms of capital.

In the neoliberal US postindustrial context where discourses and policies enact and reinforce diminishing expectations for social support and instead push increasing acceptance of precarity and expectations for entrepreneurialism and personal responsibility, sport labor as a pathway for mobility has become ever more important.[11] "The business of recruitment works best when it has an ever-replenishing pool of highly motivated, even desperate, youths without access to quality education and facing diminishing job prospects" (Runstedler 2018, 160). Mobilizing a form of masculine individualism and self-sufficiency, and promoting "the transcendent power of labor" (Trimbur 2013, 349), the pursuit of gridiron capital is one way young men navigate increasingly uncertain futures.[12]

"I know I'm a product but . . .": Resisting Commodification and the Logic of Capitalism

As I concluded an interview with a college coach from the United States, he asked me about Mark, a football player from American Sāmoa who was a relative of mine: "How come he never came out [for the team]? . . . He never called . . . tell him to give me a call." I was a little confused, as I understood that Mark had transferred from his previous school to his current one in large part to play on the coach's team. I assumed that the details got confused (transfer eligibility and such), or perhaps the workout had not gone well. The coach made it sound as if he did not follow up with the coaches about walking onto the team.[13]

However, at dinner later that evening Mark told me a very different story. According to him, the previous winter when he came to visit one of our relatives (then a starting player on the team) he worked out with the coaches and talked to them about the possibility of transferring. In the spring he initiated the transfer, with a verbal agreement that he would walk on, without scholarship, in the fall. If things worked out, he could be offered a scholarship as early as the following semester. After making the decision to move and initiating a transfer, news reports indicated that the head coach was leaving the program. Still, Mark moved over the summer, wary but hopeful that the plan would materialize. According to him, after the head coach left, the other coaches, including the one I interviewed, showed little interest. At first, they told him that he had to sit out a semester because of the transfer and could not work out with the team, but he noticed another transfer working out and meeting with coaches. It became apparent to Mark that they were giving him the runaround. As he recounted the events, he said, "I know I'm a product, but I'm not going to get down and kiss their feet." He felt he had held his part of the bargain: he transferred from his school, leaving a full scholarship to move thousands of miles amid uncertainty but with faith that the coaches would give him a fair shot. When he felt that they were not interested in maintaining their agreement (and in fairness, the circumstances had changed since the departure of the head coach), he drew the line, unwilling to humble himself before coaches who clearly were not invested in him.

One might wonder why Mark would choose to leave a full scholarship for an uncertain situation at another school, a few years into college. In the end, there were a number of reasons that pushed him to go through with the transfer. One, as he told me, was the desire to be part of a winning program. After experiencing the thrill of winning in high school, he said the disappointing losses year after year "kinda took the football out of me." I doubt he was looking forward to another losing season in his fourth year, yet did not have much of a choice as an athletic scholarship recipient. His visit to the new school came on the heels of a very successful season, including a postseason appearance in a bowl game and several players selected in the NFL Draft. After years of lackluster seasons, the head coach had built a strong program with much success. Another draw was that one of our cousins would be entering his senior year at the school and they would have the opportunity to play together again as they had in high school. There were a number of friends and relatives who lived locally. Moreover, there were a number of Polynesian players on the college team, and elements of pan-Pacific cultural identity were consciously cultivated by the coaches in service of the program. This gave the camaraderie of the team and performance on the field a very different feel from what Mark experienced at his previous college. All things considered, there was not much tying him to his previous school.

But there was something else as well: in many ways his body size and type overdetermined his participation in the sport from an early age. At six-foot six-inches in height, 300-plus pounds in weight, and coming from a family of football players, there was an expectation by people outside of the family that he would (and should) play football. His mother at first forbade it, insisting that he concentrate on academics, but when he kept his grades up, she allowed him to play. It might have been the case that others were more invested in his football participation than he was: friends and family were proud of him and hoped he would be an NFL prospect someday like some of our relatives had been. But at different points he had talked about wanting to build a house for his grandmother, for whom his mother had been caring for a number of years, and of building a new family home. When I talked to him that summer, he seemed excited about the transfer and thought that being part of a successful Division I program would boost his NFL prospects.

PLAYERS AS COMMODITIES

Players navigate the conditions of their labor in a multimillion-dollar industry,[14] but to do so successfully they must actively participate in honing their bodies and performance as commodities. While subjective "intangibles" like leadership and drive are important, without talent and skill players don't have a chance at a second look. Foundationally, they are evaluated for their game-day performance (labor) and potential performance and contribution to the team and organization (labor power) always toward winning, driving profit, and eventually, accumulation of capital for owners and/or organizations.

Whether paid (pros) or unpaid (college and high school),[15] players are part of producing an experience and mobilizing the excitement and emotion of hundreds of thousands of people toward long-term engagement and affiliation with the sport. In the wave, touchdown celebrations, and shared mourning of devastating losses these experiences shape affect and form the basis of connection and memories. In the emotion of the game, it is easy to forget how the magic is produced. Focusing on the production of entertainment/labor in the consumption and creative use of cultural commodities helps to shed light on sport and sport labor as a particular kind of commodity. In the highly developed production of commodity items, production is mystified or hidden from the consumer. The fetishism of the commodity[16] lies in the way its own history and embeddedness in wider social relations and relations of production is hidden so that consumers remain unaware of how it was produced and under what conditions. Commodities are thus endlessly "honed, however imperfectly, always to the future of individual consumption rather than the past of collective production" (Willis 2000, 52).

Distinguishing "cultural" from "classic"[17] commodities, Paul Willis argues that the former offers "actual or potential cultural meaningfulness, the ability to supply expressive resources available for local creative cultural practices" (2000, 55). Unlike the general form, cultural commodities must "enable meaningful communication" by both emitting information and being open to re-signification. Further, cultural commodities cannot completely disavow the labor associated with their production, because there exists "a continuous reminder throughout of embedded expressive labor *in* the commodity" such as can be seen in a song, a film, or in the present case, a play in the game. With the body as the medium of performance, we are continuously reminded that the play/performance is both the culmination of work and the work itself.

Samoan and other Polynesian sporting bodies are certainly not objects in the classic sense, but they are often objectified and do circulate in particular contexts and institutions. In their movement they become enmeshed in and may also transform different regimes of value. In the context of the football industry, players' bodies undergo a process of self-transformation and commodification in which individual players try to maximize their opportunities to play, and teams recruit, draft, trade, and cut them based on an elaborate arithmetic of evaluation. Insofar as the sport of football exerts a dominant presence in American popular culture that is carried through media network linkages globally, football players themselves become cultural commodities in certain situations.

Building on the argument that cultural commodities rely on being de-fetishized in order for consumers to make deep and meaningful attachments to them, others argue for a continuous process of fetishization/de-fetishization. Rather than a continuous or dialectal process, I suggest commodities are multiply fetishized as a simultaneous dynamic wherein the cultural commodity of performance, brand, or icon is re-signified in real time by disparate communities of consumers. Using the example of English football (soccer), Paul Willis points out that "TV football cannot exist apart from the football community" (2000, 56): the sport is a fetishized commodity that must be portable—alienated from its production and circulated as widely as possible—but it must simultaneously elicit desire, affect, attachment, and meaning from fans in order to be viable. He highlights this contradictory process wherein cultural commodities are fetishized as a condition of their commodity quality (in order to travel to new markets and reach ever larger consumer bases) while at the same time necessarily must defetishize themselves in order to be intelligible and consumed.

Similarly John Hughson and Marcus Free claim, "Sport is also a very special cultural commodity" because the meaningfulness of sporting contests is highly dependent upon the active participation of consumers through ticket sales and physical expression in attendance numbers and vocality at games (2006, 75–76). They argue that in the process, sport becomes a "defetishized commodity with deep communal significance and attachment" (Hughson and Free 2006, 72). The entertainment/labor of the San Francisco 49ers, for example, has to cultivate fan loyalty beyond the San Francisco Bay Area to be commercially viable. There has to be some aspect that resonates with those outside the area to forge meaningful attachments that spur people to tailgate, watch games, buy merchandise, and travel to see the games in person, and even get body tattoos of the corporate logo. "The *usefulness* of cultural commodities, the precondition of their profit-making potential, must be with respect to their specifically human role within communicative and cultural meaning systems which are inherently social" (Willis 2000, 67). In this way, they are continuously integrated into frames of meaning and re-signified by individual and communities of consumers.

This perspective is useful to understanding the position of players in the realm of sport and sporting economies, especially the insight that the labor in a cultural commodity such as sport has distinctive attributes. Players are both part of the cultural commodity of football, and in themselves become cultural commodities whose bodies, labor, and images are circulated, re-signified, and consumed. In this sense, the value of their bodies and their images are intimately intertwined not only with the past labor undertaken to hone their skills as players, but with the promise of future labor, value, and profit in their performance on the field. At the same time, however, we must keep in mind commodities in general are never *fully* fetishized in any context: they are never completely removed from their history of production. When they are taken up simultaneously by different interpretive communities, they become re-signified, and the relations of desire, affect, and consumption that shape the meaning of these cultural commodities in these different contexts help to mystify the conditions of their production, hidden as they are by the spectacle of performance.

COMMODIFICATION OF (WARRIOR) CULTURE

Players-as-commodities absorb other kinds of worth that are not directly related to the value of their labor on the field (Willis 2000). As demonstrated in chapter 3, the figure of the Polynesian Gridiron Warrior draws upon specific frames of reference, including visual cues, historical narratives, and visions of culture, nature, and racialized bodies. These sedimented and continually reproduced framings tend to boost Pacific Islander players' value in contact sports, especially for particular positions.[18] In this way Samoan and other Polynesian players are distinct from others who enter the football industry. In an example drawn from the *Polynesian Power* documentary, one of the coaches described the increasing visibility of football players from the island and the rising interest among all sizes of football programs. He declared that Samoans "are made for the game of football . . . People know the reputation of Sāmoa, they know that these kids eventually turn out to be great football players, good students, and uh—just—everybody wants one." His claim that Samoans are "made for the game of football" is a sentiment shared by many. This highlights how the narrative of the "natural" body (albeit raced, cultured, classed, and gendered) dominates as an explanatory factor and shapes the overdetermined participation of Samoans in football. His remark that "everybody wants one" highlights the demand for these players, particularly by coaches and fans who are not part of Pacific Islander communities. This example also draws attention to the larger context of racialized dynamics that infuse the structure of the industry.[19] The industry capitalizes on culture, selling alternate forms of access and currency such as can be seen with the long-standing profitability of Black urban culture (see Collins 2006; Mower, Andrews, and Rick 2014; Rhoden 2006; Runstedler 2018).

In the context of ongoing commodification of Samoan football players, the ways in which their bodies become invested with different kinds of meaning and serve as potent symbols is striking. In some ways it parallels the performance of culture and nature in contemporary Pacific tourism, as their intertwining in bodily performance is a defining aspect of the tourist experience. The packaging of culture through bodily performance illuminates the "visual and kinesthetic basis of codifying 'difference' on which tourism relies" (Desmond 1999, xiii). Jane Desmond writes, "In common discourse, bodies function as the material signs for categories of social difference, including divisions of gender, race, cultural identity, and species" (1999, xiv). Bodily performance authenticates the commodity of difference. Drawing on Desmond, Ty P. Kawika Tengan maintains, "In Hawai'i the apparatus of global tourism has most visibly appropriated the Hawaiian body as a commodity" (Tengan 2008a, 90). Similarly, I argue that in the contemporary United States (as well as Aotearoa New Zealand and Australia), the apparatus of global sport has most visibly appropriated the Samoan body as a commodity. At the iconic level the player becomes a fetish, abstracted from the unique personal attributes and conditions of his own production and reproduction to symbolize power, strength, and success. In this appropriation the constant invocation of the warrior marks difference in cultural, racial, gender, and temporal terms, thereby producing a new opportunity for consuming Samoanness, Polynesianness, and Indigeneity in an economy of fantasy.

The College Football Industry

Mark was drawn to the sport in the way that many others have been: through the appeal of being part of a family and community tradition, player prestige, the lure of potential NFL riches, and the intense emotion and pride of accomplishment. Playing organized football in American Sāmoa is no longer just mere pastime though, linked as it is to the football-industrial complex of the United States. The "football-industrial complex" term refers both to the scientific pursuit of performance efficiency and rationalization that Maguire (2005) describes, as well as the structural and institutional aspects of player production bolstered by ideological and cultural commitments to maximum performance and the consumption of sport products by the mainstream.[20]

In the wider context of late twentieth-century deregulation in global sports and media markets, this enabled countries to compete for prestige on the sporting fields, and sports organizations to accumulate capital in a global marketplace fueled by the proliferation of sporting spectacle in media markets, the rising consumption of sporting commodities like apparel, and viable sporting infrastructures in developed nations (Manzenreiter 2007; Burstyn 1999). The football-industrial complex also references the industrial production aspect that some authors have highlighted wherein at "big-time" programs, student athletes in so-called revenue sports are used up in the process of accumulating profit for the program and the school.[21] Critical feminist scholar Varda Burstyn writes, "College sports scholarships—the basis for the entire football and basketball systems in the United States—do not, as a rule, provide good college educations for young athletes. Instead, the athletes are temporarily employed, exploited, and then discarded. The system makes money for some colleges and their sports departments, but it does not profit most of the young athletes who exit the system with no sellable skills, and often without basic competence in anything other than sport" (1999, 141). This has been true for decades, but changes are afoot with recent court rulings and a new (2021) NCAA policy allowing student-athletes to monetize their name, image, and likeness (NIL), and thereby share in the profit generated by the wider athletic-industrial complex. Still, it is too soon to predict the impacts of this policy change and to determine how much players will be able to recoup of the considerable value they generate.

Gridiron football in the United States comprises of a number of intersecting institutional enterprises that together form interlocking networks that draw boys as young as five years old into the game. Programs like Pop Warner and Big Boyz leagues cater to the elementary school–age children and feed into high school programs, which then position players for leveled college programs (such as the NCAA and NAIA divisions, as well as junior college programs).[22] These college programs act as launch points for professional opportunities in the NFL, CFL, or overseas leagues (up until 2019 there was also Arena football, and the XFL is slated to return in 2023). The ultimate goal for many players—because of the associated money and prestige—is the NFL, although many will end up in the other leagues. The more successful the feeder route is in terms of providing access to the upper levels of the sport, the more desirable it becomes for players who want to "go pro."

Mark's statement, "I know I'm a product but I'm not going to get down and kiss their feet," indicates a savvy understanding of the forces at play, and his own position of power, or powerlessness, in relation to the coaches. First, his understanding of himself as a kind of product is significant because it shows a sophisticated perception of players at the college level. Far from the dream of amateur sportsmanship and the character-building function of collegiate sports as initially imagined, college football is a multimillion-dollar venture. The top five highest paid college football coaches all earned over $6 million per year in 2021, with the highest topping out at $9.75 million.[23] Meanwhile, under the College Football Playoff system, postseason participation brings conferences $300,000 to $57 million via revenue-sharing agreements.[24] Television exposure is both a source of revenue and an important recruitment tool for the football team as well as the school more generally. Moreover, merchandising is a significant source of profit for many schools that are well known for their programs. The economic model of capitalized sport has shifted from primary dependence on ticket sales and contributions to diversifying revenue streams based on mass marketing, merchandising and licensing, and television media contracts (Rowe 2010). For college "revenue" sports—particularly football and basketball—media contracts have provided a windfall for some programs and conferences. With the College Football Playoff, the stakes of the game have never been higher.

College football is big business any way you measure it, even if the current business model is recognized by many to be unsustainable. In the 2007–2008 school year, an NCAA report noted that, "nearly 80 percent of major athletic programs reported operating deficits, with programs in the red losing an average of $9.9 million." At that time, "even football-generated revenue [did] not cover the operating cost of the football team at 44 percent of the institutions playing major-college football."[25] By the 2013–2014 school year, only 24 of the 230 public schools in the NCAA Division I were self-sufficient according to NCAA standards (revenues covering operating expenses without subsidy from university funds, student fees, or direct government support).[26] When subsidies and revenue transfers between the athletic programs and university were considered, the number of schools meeting the self-sufficiency benchmark rose to fifty. Most of them are part of the Power Five conferences: the Atlantic Coast Conference, Big Ten Conference, Big 12 Conference, Pac-12 Conference, and the Southeastern Conference (Brady, Berkowitz, and Schnars 2015). Schools outside of those conferences are struggling to "keep up in the high-stakes world of major college football" by increasing spending on coaches' salaries, facilities, travel, and recruiting in the hopes of having a successful team that will win a bowl bid and its lucrative payout (Kirwan and Turner 2009).

The athletic directors, coaches, and other team personnel at schools with major college programs are under relentless pressure to win. Players themselves, while they might also reap other intangible benefits, learn quickly that their scholarship, and their value, is directly tied to their performance on the field.[27] In that sense, many are athlete-students rather than student-athletes, particularly at the higher end of the college football system where the drive to competitive success and high stakes go hand in hand.[28] As football players in a highly lucrative business model, they are not always valued primarily for their academic ability or performance but for what they contribute to the team, and in that way are "products." Having been involved with a smaller college football program for three years, Mark was not a newcomer. He understood that coaches were not always concerned with his best interest as a person or as a student, but rather the performance of the team.[29] When the coaches' interests cooled, Mark also pulled back and walked away from the game.

Limits to the Commodity Framework

Mark's story is enlightening on a number of levels, one of which is in highlighting the different contexts in which Samoan players move—circumstances that are materially and symbolically organized by different interpretive communities and their ideals and imperatives. As a student-athlete, Mark's coaches estimated his worth based on his labor on the field and his ability to bring surplus value to the team. His ability to embody a particular kind of value was tied to a process of self-fashioning that is captured in bodily measurement of various kinds. This process included participating in one of the PIAA combines held in Hawai'i when he was a high school senior, a crucial step in the process of him presenting as a viable prospect and matching him with the small program that initially recruited him.

In negotiating different regimes of value and navigating disparate contexts, commodification is not straightforwardly teleological or categorical, but contingent and processual. While a person may embody commodity attributes in the moment of the hiring contract when their bodily presence and labor power is given a value, people are never fully or simply commodities. "Commoditization, then, is best looked upon as a process of becoming rather than as an all-or-none state of being" (Kopytoff 1988,73). One navigates the commodifying relationship and may enter and exit the commodity state in a fluid fashion even as they are actively committed to the process of building their value through bodily training and discipline. While young Samoan men may become commodities as players at certain points in their football journeys, their worth or their choices as individuals far exceed their experience in the commodity context. While Tu'ufuli's story in chapter 1 illustrates the forms of capital accessible by successful players, Mark's story suggests how others (including coaches) accrue capital based on the bodily labor of players. Yet far from being fully interpellated by capitalist logic of commodification and accumulation, Mark resists further commodification by pursuing other avenues of mobility and meaning.

Mark references his own understanding of himself as a product, but he also points to an important limit. The regime of value represented by the coaches and the team, the game itself, is only one of several in which he was moving. As a potential walk-on, his identity and status as a student was distinct from his position as a football player. His friends and family too represented a different community that valued his growth, his success, and his happiness both on and off the field. While close friends and family were differently invested in his football success, it was not the only thing valued, or even the most important. Most of us had no idea what he could bench-press, how fast he could run, whether his footwork was quick and sharp, or if he could jump high. We didn't see him from a fan's perspective: there was no awe, no idolization, no hero-worship. In his physical stature he was like many of our relatives. His hair did not resonate as an image of "savage warriorhood" (a trope examined in more detail in the chapter 3); his mother complained about it while some of us wished ours was as long. Returning home on break from college, he seemed to fit back into his place in the family (as son, cousin, and older and younger brother to siblings), alternately doing chores at home and hanging out with friends and relatives. Immediate family members cared more about whether he graduated and could build a career after college than how much playing time he might see. As a student, his ability to perform in the classroom was most important to his grades, and anything on the field was irrelevant. Finally, from conversations with his mother, I know that some of his relatives were hoping that someday he might be interested in moving back and assuming responsibility for family lands in Sāmoa—a set of obligations far removed from how American coaches assess his value as a player.

Still, we might ask why Mark was able to turn his back on the opportunity provided by football when others were not. While personality and relationship to the game certainly factor, Mark never "needed" football. His parents were both college-educated and he did well in high school, taking advanced courses like physics and calculus. He likely would have gone to college one way or another, although a scholarship for playing football presented a clear pathway. While it may not have covered the entire cost of attendance, it removed a significant obstacle to enrollment. Still, with the availability of financial aid and loans, he could have gone to school whether or not he played football. When it came to the point of humbling himself before the coaches, unlike many others he didn't have to; he had other options and walked away.

A Costly Endeavor

While there are a number of different forms of capital that can be accrued in football participation and success, the hyper-visible success stories obscure the physical, emotional, and social costs that are borne by players, their families, and their communities. Tu'ufuli's body was an example of this accumulation of gridiron capital through bodily destruction—with specific ailments encoded with memory of repeated action. I once asked him why the last joint of each of his fingers was permanently angled, unable to fully straighten. He explained that it was from years of crouching on the line in wait for the ball to snap and the play to begin, set in the stance of a lineman with the fingertips on one hand touching the ground for balance and support. The pressure on his joints took a toll over a number of years. The damage betrayed the vulnerability of his large, muscular hands, which at first glance appeared invincible. His forehead bore traces of the constant reverberation caused by helmets crunching bodies, pads, and the unforgiving ground: just above the eyebrows sat a protrusion created by years of contact with his helmet.

It was the physical costs that at a moment in time were too much to bear, forcing his decision to eventually retire from playing. According to him, during the season his knees would swell up with fluid as a result of repeated injury and lack of adequate time to rest and heal. The team doctors would then drain the fluid, perhaps give him a shot of cortisone, and clear him for playing. One day, the story goes, he brought in a large bottle and told the doctors to deposit the fluid in there; the day it filled would be his last with the team. When that day came, he walked away from football. But he carried his injuries with him; remaining physically active, he still struggled with stiffness and pain and eventually required knee replacement.

In addition to physical costs, many student-athletes in Division I programs navigate a variety of social experiences at university. Some include challenging instances of racialization and stereotyping that impact their college experience (explored more fully in chapter 3). As a doctoral student and faculty member, I had many student-athletes talk to me about how they were stereotyped as non-academic or less intelligent by both student and faculty members while navigating a much more challenging schedule than most students; on top of that, the way Pacific Islander players were racialized added another dimension to that experience. Particularly at predominantly White institutions (PWI), they stand out. In one master's study with Polynesian players at a PWI, a football player expressed that a negative aspect to their student-athlete experience was that "others may perceive us as just jocks. Polynesians are on the football team and they don't even get good grades" (Morita 2013, 83). In the same study, a Samoan player described being paired up for group projects: "And then you could tell that the student was sitting there looking at me like I was just a dumb jock . . .

sometimes it'd be harder to work with because they assumed that I didn't want to do my part, that I was trying to just coast by and let them do all the work" (Morita 2013, 85). A third student-athlete (Tongan) pointed out that being large and visibly Islander or Polynesian also made it difficult to avoid their athletic identities in other contexts: "Just, we're bred larger so people automatically assume you're a football player even though you might be in a situation where you're trying to avoid, avoid that conversation, you just try and go to the store and buy something and not be harassed by fan or just somebody wants to talk about football and then come talk to you about how their son can get recruited and how can they meet the head coach" (Morita 2013, 84). In GritMedia's "Unfiltered" vlog series, Danny Shelton shared the importance of finding a Polynesian student community at the University of Washington and subject study areas that resonated with his background. His experience suggests a key role for supportive peer groups in helping to shield against the burden of stereotype threat as one price of admission to the student-athlete pathway.[30]

Finally, players may also deal with emotional and social costs related to strained relationships or mental health struggles, and often in silence. In the next chapter I delve more deeply into the injury and mental health impacts especially around concussions and masculine expectations, but here it is worth marking many of the stories that were shared with me by and about student-athletes who had poured their all into this pathway just to have their dreams derailed and lives disrupted with injury. In more extreme cases, worries were buried in the bottle or channeled into other risky behavior that led them to the criminal justice system. Others found refuge in family and community, coping until they were able to turn things around. Everyone eventually went pro in something other than football.

Negotiating Gridiron Capital

Corporeal transformation and commodification are central to accessing American football as a path of transnational movement and mobility. Players are not only commodified by the market of the football-industrial complex, but actively cultivate their own commodification in order to maximize their chances of success, accumulating gridiron capital. In this, they are producing their own mobility.[31] However, the varied contexts within and across which players are moving are not reduced simply to regimes of consumption and commodity exchange, the terms of which are determined by owners, agents, or cultural elites. Clearly, these are important elements but are not the whole story. The examples above reveal how Samoan players draw on other aspects of their identities (as players, as students, as family members, and so on), as they actively bridge distinct cultural-geographic milieus in their movement between American Sāmoa and the United States. This difference is not a totalizing or essentializing one but does signal different frameworks that dominate or organize the realms in which the players are moving. The variety of meanings and motivations that Samoan players bring to the field are only partially explained by capitalist logics of accumulation, and therefore complicate our ideas about the sporting industry, transnational movements, and paths of socioeconomic mobility.

Five

"Faʻamālosi!"

STRENGTH, INJURY, AND SACRIFICE

ON MAY 2, 2012, I received a call from my mother in Montana, tearful on the phone. She asked me, "Have you heard? About Junior Seau?" I had been offline that morning, so I had no idea what she was talking about. Her voice cracked as she blurted out the story of his passing in between sobs. I sat stunned on the other side of the line as it went silent for a few seconds. It didn't make sense; it had to be wrong. Was it an internet hoax? Would the truth come out later? I finally had the presence of mind to ask the expected questions: "What happened?" "How did they find out?" "How did you hear?" My mind was reeling. I just couldn't believe it.

As my mother continued talking, her grief came through as she choked back the tears. I did not understand the depth of her reaction until she told me how she remembered Junior as a young kid at the family barbecues, when my parents spent time with our relatives in Oceanside, California, and my father played rugby there during the professional football off-season. Out tumbled another piece of our family history that I had never heard. She reminisced about those early days and described how she had followed his career from college at USC, to the San Diego Chargers when we lived in California in the late eighties and early nineties, and then to the Miami Dolphins and New England Patriots before he retired. Much later it occurred to me that the news was such a shock that many in the Samoan community, and the wider Polynesian football fraternity, would remember what they were doing and where they were when they heard the tragic news. To my mother he had been a boy whose journey she followed with interest and pride; to me he was an icon, connected to our community but distant in his shining success.

When I left Sāmoa for San Diego in 1991, Junior had recently been drafted by the Chargers and was one of the best players on the gridiron. His professional success there loomed large, compounded by his status as a local boy who conquered the fabled fields of the NFL. Junior was unlike so many hopefuls whose gridiron dreams washed out under pressure of injury, physical performance that didn't make the cut, bad timing, bad fit, or the cold calculation of value and investment. He provided a model of success that reinforced community support for brothers, cousins, sons, and nephews playing the game. When I came to San Diego, for example, my older brother Duke was on football scholarship with San Diego State University as a redshirt freshman. We attended SDSU games that were held at the same Jack Murphy Stadium where the Chargers played. Later, as a visiting college student excited to eat at Seau's sports-themed restaurant ("pronounced SAY-ow!" patrons were advised), I was proud of his success. Junior's meteoric rise in his football career from Oceanside High School to the University of Southern California to the Chargers and later the Dolphins and the Patriots—twenty years strong with countless accolades—stood as a shining example to a generation of Samoan youth. However, the news from the phone call and its aftermath complicate that vision and raise important questions.

By many accounts of people who were close to him, Tiaina Baul Seau Jr. was a special person. He had a charismatic way about him, reached out to others, and was kind and compassionate. His loss as a person was felt deeply by many, as the countless tributes to him after his passing attest. Yet just as his success rippled far beyond those who knew him personally, so did his loss. In reckoning with this public legacy, Junior Seau's biography is important not only because he was a football icon for Samoan and other Pacific Islanders (and many others across the nation), but also because his successful career encapsulates the stakes of the game while also highlighting the significant potential cost. In it we see clearly the themes of hope, mobility, and achievement complicated by physical violence and brain trauma. His tragic death also raises the question of how Samoan masculinities are being fused with American sport, and to what potential ends.

Part of the attraction to football and other contact sports like it (such as rugby league and rugby union) is that it elevates a preferred embodiment of masculinity for young men that articulates with aspects of valued expressions of Samoan masculinities. In this, new generations of Samoan and other Pacific Islander players negotiate both outsiders' racialized expectations of their bodies as indestructible and Pacific communities' expectations of resilience, strength, and sacrifice. This chapter examines how this unfolds within the context of football, sport injury, and emerging medical research, and how the emergent knowledge about concussions and their long-term impacts might affect the next generation of youth, their approach to the game, and assumptions about informed consent and participation. Drawing on recent research on brain trauma, the high-profile debate around football's "concussion crisis," and discussions with Polynesian athletes, it explores how the legacy of players like Junior Seau shapes the way we view football and how we measure its inherent risks and rewards. In closing it suggests how elevating different aspects of Samoan masculinities might provide a countervailing force to safeguard against the perils of injury and promote well-being for our youth.

Opportunity and Cost: Football's "Concussion Crisis"

The hyper-visible success stories like Junior Seau's may sometimes obscure the physical, emotional, and social costs the sport exacts. These are largely borne in silence by players, their families, and their communities. On any given week during the football season one may witness spectacular injury to players; this risk is not only accepted as part of the game, it elevates the sport's standing in the eyes of the public. Boys and men are routinely expected to play through pain to prove the depth of their commitment to the team, their character as people, and their worth as players. In the course of the action, players literally sacrifice their bodies for the gain of the extra inch, the extra yard, or to make the play. "The commercialization and commodification of men's sport in the television era have played a large role in turning professional athletes into modern-day gladiators, exchanging alienation, injury, and pain for material and social rewards" (Burstyn 1999, 138). Yet perhaps more dangerous than the damage to sinew and bone players frequently sustain is the less visible prospect of neurological injury. While critics have long suggested a link between the sport of football and long-term neurological complications, only recently has scientific research been able to substantiate that link.

In October 2013 the book *League of Denial: The NFL, Concussions, and the Battle for Truth* was published; a companion documentary, *League of*

Denial: the NFL's Concussion Crisis, aired concurrently on PBS *Frontline.* Helmed by journalists Mark Fainaru-Wada and Steve Fainaru, the book and film chronicle the emergence of research on football and CTE, or chronic traumatic encephalopathy, and the NFL's knowledge of and role in discrediting early research and withholding information from the players and public. As American media was ablaze with the story, some outlets asked, "Does CTE, The Brain Disease Found in NFL Players, Really Exist?"[1] A slew of articles and broadcasts raised questions about concussions and the long-term effects of traumatic brain injury (TBI) not always accompanied by a concussion event. In the wake of continued fallout, some have asked, "Can the NFL Survive its Concussion Crisis?" (Drummond 2014).

Critics suspected a link between the sport of football and long-term neurological complications for some time, but it was only in 2009 that the National Football League released a report from a University of Michigan study that found that Alzheimer's or similar memory-related diseases were diagnosed in the league's former players at a rate of *nineteen times* the normal rate for men ages thirty to forty-nine. In releasing the study findings, the NFL reversed a long-held position that claimed there was no reliable data that linked cognitive decline and professional football (Schwartz 2009). In a more recent study of 202 deceased former football players, CTE was diagnosed in 87 percent of the participants, and was distributed across the highest levels of play including 99 percent of former NFL players. The findings suggested a link between CTE and football participation (Mez et al. 2017).

While the professional leagues have sought to contain that conversation, the NCAA enacted policy changes intended to stem the fallout of these revelations. Many high school athletic governing bodies have adopted new policies in an effort to address concerns of parents, who must consent to their children's participation in the sport. CTE has garnered much media attention in the United States because of high-profile suicides of former NFL players, who upon autopsy were found to have developed the disease. Junior Seau was one of these players: before the age of fifty he died by suicide after a steep slide that included behavioral, mood, and personality changes. His tragic demise raises questions for Pacific communities that have been channeling their sons into this sport for at least three generations now.

CTE AND THE RESEARCH ON TRAUMATIC BRAIN INJURY
According to researchers at Boston University's CTE Center, one of the premier brain research facilities in the United States, chronic traumatic encephalopathy is a "progressive degenerative disease of the brain found in athletes

(and others) with a history of repetitive brain trauma . . . The brain degeneration is associated with memory loss, confusion, impaired judgment, impulse control problems, aggression, depression, and, eventually, progressive dementia."[2] In 2005 the first confirmed case of CTE was identified in highly decorated former NFL player Mike Webster (Omalu et al. 2005); the following year the same physician confirmed another case (Omalu et al. 2006). For over a decade now, researchers have been exploring traumatic brain injuries and what circumstances cause conditions like CTE to develop (see, for example, Omalu et al. 2010; McKee et al. 2009; 2013; 2014; Lakhan and Kirchgessner 2012; Gavett, Stern, and McKee 2011). While the visibility of CTE research has surged since those groundbreaking findings, repeated trauma to the head had been linked to brain damage and degeneration for much longer. As early as the 1920s, for instance, some boxers were said to have "punch drunk syndrome" (Martland 1928), which was later identified as *dementia pugilistica*, a distinct neurological disorder (Corsellis, Bruton, and Freeman-Browne 1973).

The term CTE emerged in the 1960s among researchers to identify and describe the neurodegenerative effects of repetitive brain trauma (Stern et al. 2011, S461). As research progressed, it became clear that these effects were not confined to boxers but afflicted many in contact sports and the military. People who suffered from CTE in the past were likely misdiagnosed, and while new research is working toward being able to identify CTE in living patients, at this time CTE can only be diagnosed after death (Omalu et al. 2018; Dallmeier et al. 2019). Brain researchers have also found that the pathways of this disease are distinct from other neurological diseases like Alzheimer's or ALS (Lou Gehrig's disease). CTE is associated with traumatic brain injury, but there is not yet a clear picture of how prevalent it is, whether there is any genetic predisposition toward it, or how much or how little traumatic brain injury is needed for it to develop.[3] Some research suggests that the type and frequency of trauma may play a role, as could the type of sport, position played, and level of competition, but research on CTE is still developing (Stern et al. 2011; Campolettano et al. 2019).

While CTE has been driving the high-profile conversations on brain trauma, other research is aimed at trying to better understand concussions more broadly, including long- and short-term impacts, and variations according to age, gender, and genetic disposition (Broshek et al. 2005; Dick 2009; Daneshvar et al. 2011; Castille et al. 2012; Montenigro et al. 2017). This research raises some important questions. The first research study to examine new versus recurrent concussions in a large national sample of US athletes was the National High School Sports-Related Injury Surveillance Study (2005–2010). This study found that among boys' sports, football had the highest rate of both new and recurrent concussions, far outstripping the others. "Nationally an estimated 732,805 concussions occurred among US high school athletes participating in the nine sports studied (636,053 new 96,752 recurrent); concussions represented 10.5% of all injuries. Football accounted for nearly half of all reported concussions (48.5%), followed by girls' soccer (17.7%), boys' soccer (12.2%) and girls' basketball (6.3%)" (Castille et al. 2012, 605). The study also found evidence that "athletes returned to play while still symptomatic" (Castille et al. 2012, 608), which can have serious consequences.

As of January 2014, when Mississippi's governor signed the Mississippi Youth Concussion Act into law, all fifty states had passed laws addressing the management of traumatic brain injuries in youth sports. The passage of youth concussion laws began with the Lystedt Law in the state of Washington, named after Zackery Lystedt, a boy who suffered severe brain injury and was permanently disabled following a concussion in a middle school football game in 2006. His story raised awareness of the significant risk posed by secondary concussions in youth sports, and served as an important catalyst for a wide range of lobbying efforts. Zackery Lystedt's case galvanized the community, which in turn lobbied the state to pass the first law of its kind that mandated treatment of concussions in youth sports, named in his honor. All states now have mandated annual education for program athletes and parents. They require the removal of athletes from play if they exhibit concussion symptoms, and clearance by a health professional before a concussed athlete can return to play. However, a review of the state concussion laws passed between 2009 and 2013 revealed that the laws were aimed at managing traumatic brain injuries after they occurred and reducing secondary injuries stemming from returning to play too soon. None of the laws focused on preventing primary injury (Harvey 2013). Although there have been some policy changes on this front (for example, California's 2014 change limiting practice time in youth sports), there is wide variation in state laws on training and concussion protocol (Kim et al. 2017).

Research on the long-term consequences of TBIS or repetitive head impacts (RHIS) like concussions is still in development. Although a Centers for Disease Control study estimated that 300,000 TBIS involved the loss of consciousness annually, if unreported injuries and those with no loss of consciousness are included it raises the estimate to between 1.6 million to 3.8 million sports-related TBIS every year (Thunnan, Branche, and Sniezek

1998; Langlois et al. 2006, 376). Some argue that in football, those who play middle linebacker, like Junior Seau did, are even more in the line of fire than most. Riki Ellison—a player of Māori descent who was an NFL linebacker for nine seasons with the San Francisco 49ers and the Los Angeles Raiders—has noted, "The middle linebacker, apart from every other position in football, endures the most violent and most repeated contact using the head and helmet and, as a result, sustains the most concussions" (2012).

While the spotlight is on concussions as an identifiable flash point for injury, research suggests that one does not need to have a concussive episode to suffer trauma to the brain. Some studies have found that "Athletes at certain positions (e.g., linemen) may sustain up to 1400 impacts per season, and high school players who play both offense and defense potentially sustain closer to 2000 impacts" (Stern et al. 2011, S460; see also McKee et al. 2009). Others have found players showing cognitive impairments (neurocognitive and neurophysiological deficits) at postseason testing even without exhibiting observable concussion symptoms (Talavage et al. 2014, 334).[4] They suspect that these players have experienced sub-concussive events with neurological trauma, but not at the level that would qualify as a concussion or require health professional intervention. As a result, they continue to play and sustain impacts, potentially contributing to long-term cognitive and physiological damage. This raises the issue of long-term damage for players in linemen positions even if they have never had a concussion event. Where are Samoan and Pacific Islander youth playing on the gridiron? Still overwhelmingly on the offensive or defensive line, in positions that sustain a significantly larger number of head impacts than most other positions on the team (Campolettano et al. 2019).

CONVERSATIONS ON RISK AND INJURY

In January 2014 I was invited to attend the Polynesian All-American Bowl (PAAB) in Los Angeles, an event that was organized by the AIGA Foundation with assistance from Gridiron Ministries and many long-time Southern California football organizers. I had been supporting one of the AIGA Foundation members on new research with Pacific Islander high school players making the transition to college (see Kukahiko 2017). When we sat down with the high school student-athletes participating in the PAAB, we talked about their entry into football, the recruiting process, and their hopes for college. Given Junior's passing and continued media coverage of concussions at the time, the sessions often touched on how they were thinking about these issues and whether the media conversation was making any waves in their schools or communities. Several described basic policies on concussions that included sitting out a certain number of games or practices following a reported concussion and having to be checked and cleared by trainers. Concern with long-term risk or the potential for permanent disability did not arise in any of the conversations. Instead, there were two key explanations that emerged as we continued with our discussion.

The first was an *awareness* of risk as being inherent to the game. One of the players noted that football was about risk: "It's part of the sport, when you think about it. I mean there's a risk to everything you take. I mean of course, we know what we're getting ourselves into. And I don't think, in my opinion it affects the way [I play], I was gonna play as hard as I can. If whatever happens, happens." This sentiment was echoed by the others (and matches what I have seen over the years in the various camps, combines, coaching sessions, and player discussions). In and of itself, this is not surprising: part of the socialization to the sport is aimed at reorienting one to embrace or at least disregard risk. What is worth noting is that for youth players, by their senior year in high school (and likely much earlier) the presence and acceptance of risk is drummed into them and then presented as a badge of honor that motivates a good deal of the social currency provided by football prowess. In a reflection on Junior Seau's passing, Riki Ellison writes that middle linebackers like him "are a different breed. They are very aggressive and are often monumental risk takers. They lead by action and love contact, perhaps more than any player on the field."[5] The players who embrace contact and take risks are some of the most respected on the field because their fearlessness often yields spectacular gains.

The second key theme that emerged from our conversations was the *minimization* of risk (and the potential for long-term impacts). This aligns with other reports that suggest parents' concerns are allayed by the sense that new technology and tackling techniques are making a difference, even if those involved with the game question whether risk has actually been reduced (Fainaru and Fainaru-Wada 2014). Each one of the players either said that they thought they were less at risk than earlier generations and players like Junior Seau because of advances in technology and rule changes, or they indicated that it was unlikely to happen to them. They viewed those cases as an exception rather than as a cautionary tale.

What was most striking was that many of them also indicated that they do not report potential concussions. One player said, "I did get a concussion in a game, my sophomore year. Kinda how I knew, is when I'd go out there it was almost like tunnel vision, and I didn't remember any plays. Like they called some blitz and I wouldn't know which gap I had to take but it never crossed my mind to go tell somebody." After a brief pause he added, "that could really harm you though." Looking back, he recognized the potential for serious harm but in the moment he not only played through, it didn't even cross his mind to report it. Another chimed in with a similar experience where he didn't report: "The offense that we run, we do a lot of pulling. There was one play where I pulled and I hit someone. My vision blurred too. I was like, oh what the heck. And I walked back to the huddle and I was holding someone's hand and they were like 'are you hurt?' and I was like 'yeah just keep huddling.'" Rather than alert the coaches or trainers and have to leave the game, he just shook it off and stayed in.

This is consistent with many discussions I have had over the past ten years or so with Samoan, Hawaiian, and Tongan student-athletes who play college football, and the underreporting of concussions more generally. A 2004 study based on surveys of high school football players found that more than 40 percent of the respondents did not report a concussion because they were concerned they would be pulled from competition (McCrea et al. 2004). A more recent study found the rate of underreporting to be much higher—about 55 percent, because players did not think it was serious, did not want to lose playing time, or did not want to let their team down (Wallace et al. 2017; see also Kerr et al. 2017). While athletes in general self-report significantly fewer concussive symptoms to trainers (Meier et al. 2014), football players in particular are more likely to underreport concussions (Kerr et al. 2014). Unlike a broken ankle or a back injury that cannot possibly be hidden, concussions or other brain trauma—depending on severity—can. Although there is new training and awareness about the seriousness of brain injuries, there is still a lingering view of getting one's "bell rung" or "wind knocked out" as an expected but temporary setback in a game. Moreover, many involved in the sport may not have the training to recognize and respond to TBIs properly (especially if there are changing policies).

In American Sāmoa, a move in that direction a few years ago had been training sessions for local coaches on concussions, conducted by nurses as part of the June Jones Goodwill Mission to Sāmoa. Yet aside from these sessions, there has been a dearth of voices championing the issue; at that time it was not a topic I raised with those involved with the mission or the sport more generally, and neither did others bring it up. Without ongoing support or training, and in the absence of a catastrophic injury like the one that affected Zackery Lystedt, it appeared there was little sense of urgency to make brain trauma a serious and consistent part of the football conversation.

One might argue that all we need to do is provide better training to players, coaches, and other support staff and it would lead to more players being able to identify head injury; more coaches concerned about head injuries and applying team, league, and institutional policies about treatment and follow-up; and more support staff trained to identify likely head (and other) injuries, with the mandate and support to speak out on behalf of the players. That would no doubt grow a clearer understanding of the injuries and potential impact and reduce the number of players put at serious risk. More consistent training and better regulation across the coaching ranks from early youth (tackle) football on up would reduce risk to players, and should be further implemented. However, it would be a mistake to assume it would solve the problem completely. Training will only go so far in shifting attitudes and practices that seem to constitute the very fabric of gridiron football.

Gender, Culture, Class in American Football

The production of a successful football player is fundamentally social and is grounded in deep and long-term body training and discipline. For many players there is unbridled joy in the contact of the sport, and for others deep satisfaction in mastering control of your body for high-caliber performance. The point is not to go out and get hurt, but to strengthen your body through weightlifting, skill drills, conditioning, and practice so that you are strong enough to withstand the game's physical battery and avoid major injury. The process is also about preparing the body and bodily instinct in automatic response, facing your fear head-on and obliterating it through constant repetition so that your body takes over "in the zone" and your mind does not have time to think about whether going for that tackle will earn you a blown knee or if making that catch will mean a concussion once you are on the ground. In those moments, hesitation means either failure or injury. Unrelenting physical battery is part of the top levels of the game, and the gendered and classed culture of football holds tight one's ability to withstand that battery and play on as a mark of courage. These orientations, which today naturalize bodily violence and acclaim courageous sacrifice, are part of a much longer legacy within the sport.

The emergence of American football at the turn of the twentieth century was part of a new cult of martial masculinity in the United States, aimed at hardening an emerging generation of men as part of the nation's entry into a new position as fledgling imperialist (Greenberg 2005; Hoganson 1998). The vibrant growth of sporting culture in America was influenced by the British Victorian belief in a specifically muscular Christianity, most notably popularized by Thomas Hughes's 1857 novel *Tom Brown's School Days* (Watson, Weir, and Friend 2005). This model targeted the bodies of British citizens as sites of empire, training the future global masters in sound mind and body to be willing to sacrifice for God and country (see Putney 2001; Wilkinson 1964). Sport helped to accomplish the shift to a demonstrably muscular masculinity through games like rugby, which would be transformed into gridiron football in the United States.

The first games played in what would become the Ivy League were from the outset plagued by allegations of corruption and involved serious and catastrophic injury (Branch 2011). With growing outcry about the brutality of the game and high incidence of injury, President Theodore Roosevelt brokered a meeting between representatives from Harvard, Yale, and Princeton in 1905 (Miller 2011). In the wake of that meeting, reformers established an institutional precursor to what would eventually become the NCAA. The raw power and brutality of the sport continued, and death and disability linked to the sport eventually forced some key rule changes in the 1960s and 1970s that reduced the risk of catastrophic injury (Mueller and Colgate 2012). Still, the association between the game and battle held.

Football is often posed as an allegory to war. From the use of war metaphors in football parlance to the incorporation of military symbolism into the framework of the games, martial notions of battle, risk, sacrifice, and victory have been identified with the game (Kellett 2002; Trujillo 1995). "Militarist terms such as training camp, sudden death, veterans, aerial game, balanced attack, shootout, blitz, bomb, bullet pass, field general, flank, flare, pass, neutral zone, shotgun formation, submarine, and suicide squat suffuse football media and team language, linking and conflating sport and war" (Burstyn 1999, 180). Beyond terms, the presence of the military in football events as cosponsors or in flyovers before big games like the Super Bowl also reinforces this connection. American gender ideals construct war as the quintessential test of manhood, and in mimicking the danger for bodily harm, sports like football become "symbolically lethal" (Burstyn 1999, 175; Messner 1994). In turn, danger, risk, and injury are endemic to participation.

Facing that head-on, being willing to take the risks, and enduring the pain and injury successfully become heroic pursuits glorified by the team and fans alike (Burstyn 1999, 191).

THE TRAFFIC IN CULTURE, OR, TRANSFORMING THE WARRIOR

One of the young men in the PAAB discussions, who went on to earn a scholarship to a university with a top football program and subsequently declare for the NFL Draft, made a remark that stuck with me. Referencing instances when he tried to hide potential concussions from coaches and trainers, he said: "We're Polynesian, we're not supposed to get hurt." His offhand remark points to the ways in which Polynesian male bodies are expected to be almost invincible. Boys and men overall are exposed to more frequent injury and pain as part of their socialization (Gilligan 1996 in Burstyn 1999, 190), but racial attitudes shape the perception of Black and brown bodies as superhuman (Carrington 2010; Waytz, Hoffman, and Trawalter 2015). Crucially, these perspectives are propagated in media narratives that consistently highlight and privilege the physical toughness of these players. These cultural and physical expectations that are held by others but internalized by the young men act as a kind of currency in football.

While Polynesian strength is often represented as natural or biological, the accommodation to pain and risk is a protracted process of socialization. Some may happen through corporal punishment in the family context, but more often it is accomplished through explicit training. Some of the Samoan college players I interviewed for this project described themselves as "weak" or "afraid of getting hit" as boys just entering the sport. As part of football families, the choice to play was not theirs (at the outset); yet they shared a process of acclimating themselves to the pain and then coming to love the rough contact. In another example, one of the coaches I spoke to in Tutuila shared a story in which his father signed him up for youth football along with his cousins when they were living in the States. On the one hand, he didn't feel he had much choice (if he protested he would be branded a "sissy"), and on the other, playing organized football with his cousins was a great experience for him. In both cases (and many more shared with me) they learned to love the aspect of football where they could go out and hit or be able to withstand the hits they took, a process of conditioning to a particular form of masculinity with a high tolerance for pain and injury.

At the same time, masculine body cultures in the islands and stateside diasporic communities shape a sensibility about hard and heavy manual labor as a mark of masculinity. In Sāmoa, gendered divisions of labor tend to sort boys and men into tasks that are dirty or require physical strength and stamina, such as in gathering items for and building an umu, scraping and squeezing coconuts, or fale construction. Sporting culture is also highly physical, with rugby and football games played throughout the week on village malae or near the beach (see also Clement 2014). Stateside communities are still predominantly urban, with employment for men largely in manufacturing and labor sectors of the economy, or in service positions like security work and baggage handling. These provide an opportunity for masculine forms of labor that are valued from gender, class, and cultural perspectives.

The melding of American and indigenous Samoan institutions and associated ideologies and practices can also be seen in the articulation of the Samoan concept of toa with Western notions of "warriorhood," used in both sport and the military. *Toa* as a word or concept has a number of meanings—for example, it is the Samoan equivalent of the English word "rooster"; it also is used to describe acts of fearlessness or bravery but in a way that is formally gender-neutral. As scholar and matai Vui Dr. Toeutu Faʻaleava described (personal communication, March 2010):

A *toa* was always an individual act or event. *'O le toa mai Amoa.' 'O le toa Faleata.'* At times there were more than one, so that we would say *'o toa mai le Ituau'*, for example. The expression *'loto toa'* is an exhortation to 'let your spirit be brave.' It was not by virtue of membership in an organization such as the *aumaga*, but by having the heart and spirit of the *toa*, or being brave. It seems the circumstances or situation determines the act that is worthy of the label *'toa.'*

Confirming what other relatives have told me, he went on to explain:

Toa is gender-neutral. Nafanua [the legendary Samoan 'warrior' goddess] was a *toa*, though she was elevated to a living god by her contemporaries. The act or person that is worthy of being labeled *toa* is dependent on the circumstances, so that the concept *'toa'* is fluid, and is applied to all genders. The young girl that got up and spoke against the unfair village decision was a *toa*.

Here the distinct honor is earned by a set of orientations and behaviors that are not necessarily gender-specific.

The late University of Hawaiʻi Samoan language specialist and matai Leiataua-Lesa Fepuleaʻi Vita L. Tanielu offered a slightly different explanation, which I quote here at length (personal communication, April 2010).

'*Toa*' is one of those words that people rightfully stretch, milk, or expand in order to connect to a "power" point that they want to relay. Basically, it is of masculinity; originally from the male '*toa*' rooster verses the female '*matua-moa*' hen. On the one hand, *toa* can be traced to the '*kokoʻe or vivini*' sound signal—a high shrieking scream or yell—to tell the world of its conquest, particularly when he's winner or victor from a fight with another fellow *toa*; or when in challenge mode; or to tell the world (other *toa* nearby) to stay away from a nearby female (*matua-moa*), etc . . . It connotes a sign of fearlessness, of heroism, bravery, knightism. It ties with male masculinity, power, energy, domination, and leadership. This *toa*'s '*kokoʻe/vivini*' is akin to a (*tama*) man's '*kiusu-su*,'—a high shrieking scream or yell—when he thinks he has the power to conquer anybody or anything; one can also '*kiusu-su*' when overtaken by hilarity, anger, accomplishment, satisfaction or in response to a challenge.

The second use of toa Leiataua-Lesa described was similar to Vui's description, but with some key differences:

The other "*Toa*" refers to a hero, a brave person, normally because of a heroic feat; and mainly a man—male (*tama-loa*). As in Leatiogie (son of Feʻepo) who won a physical competition in ancient times. Recently, the Manu Samoa Rugby Team players were called '*toa*' because they performed outstandingly in the world stage and brought the small name Samoa on the map into international recognition. Manu Samoa is the name of the '*toa*' from Falealili district. Later, the Samoans named their second Rugby Team "Toa Samoa"—heroes of Samoa. Samoan history speaks of its many '*toa*,' like Manu Samoa, Tamafaiga from Manono, Leatiogie from Faleata, Tuna and Fata of Tuamasaga, etc.

. . .

Pertaining to women "*Toa*": Femininity was never tied to '*toa*-ism' simply because of our nationalism and cultural *matai* system, even though some of our ancient leaders were female (Nafanua, Salamasina, etc.). Only until the recent past (50 years ago approximately) when women's status changed tremendously—holding *matai* titles and academic success—did the notation of women's accomplishments, whether physical or mental, are referred to as '*toa*-ism.' *Toa* is then inadvertently connected to address the female members who gain great accomplishments physically as in the Olympics, or an attorney or medical doctor academically, let alone others like charity traits as Mother Theresa. Families would then bestow very high *matai* titles to these women because of the prestige and honor brought into the families by these females. Of course, I would call them *toa* as well.

When considering toa and its use as a term and concept, initially (especially in the Tutuila context) it seemed that it was a gender-neutral term that was becoming gendered male in its association with the US military. Leiataua-Lesa's explanation confirmed that the contemporary notion of toa in American Sāmoa is increasingly allied with male military service because today toa is most often used there to refer to Samoan participation in the US military—specifically as "Toa o Sāmoa." However, he also noted that over time—similar to tautua—it has become more elastic in incorporating different kinds of notable acts, including those undertaken by women as well as men. It is difficult to say if this shift is tied to deep or recent history. For example, Meleisea (1987, 52–70) notes how missionary teachings emphasized particular roles for women, primarily as wives and helpmates to their husbands. This de-emphasized their leadership roles in public spaces and likely impacted subsequent decisions about chiefly and priestly roles throughout the colonial and postcolonial period. Deep history such as can be seen with key historical figures like Salamāsina o le Tafaʻifā or the aliʻi Nafanua, who later was elevated as a goddess, suggest that political or sacred leadership was not always held by men. It is also worth noting that even through the colonial and postcolonial period women were serving in chiefly roles, including in my own extended family.

It is unclear whether *toa* as a term was gender-neutral to begin with. It may be that toa is formally gender-neutral, but is practically gendered male in that it remains fundamentally associated with what is recognized to be "male masculinity, power, energy, domination, and leadership." Like American Sāmoa where Toa o Sāmoa refers to military service members, in independent Sāmoa, "Toa o Sāmoa" has been used to describe the success of the Manu Sāmoa rugby team on the international stage, which brought national prestige and recognition. The rugby league team has also become known as Toa Sāmoa. Even though women are present in both military and sport, these are still considered to be masculine arenas.

A key strand of the contemporary understanding of toa in American Sāmoa reflects a vision of militarized masculinity because of US military enlistees being described as "Toa o Sāmoa." In this process contemporary

Indigenous masculinities are being articulated in the idiom of American military service, with different attendant practices and connotations.[6] Toa in this context is usually translated back into English as "Warriors of Sāmoa," which has a particular connotation regarding gender, sacrifice, bravery, and violence. The Merriam-Webster dictionary defines warrior as "a man engaged or experienced in warfare," and traces its etymology to fourteenth-century Middle English *wereour,* from Anglo-French *werreir, guerrier,* meaning "to wage war." The image associated with it is that of archaic standing armies or Greek soldiers engaged in battle to the death (such as can be seen in the popular film *300*). The use of "warrior" rather than "soldier" calls forth an element of savage premodernity precluded by the regimented, rationalized institutions of modern militaries. Yet in the conflation of "warrior" with "toa" in contemporary usage, the latter is not only cast as "soldier" (in real terms, as part of the US military), but is shifted from an (arguably) gender-neutral honorific for acts of bravery to take on very specific meanings associated with male sacrifice, violence, and membership in the military that are elevated to national significance.[7]

In this traffic, the Western concept of soldier-warrior becomes intertwined with the Samoan concept of toa. The legacy of war-making in precolonial Sāmoa drew on predominantly male members of the village (although Nafanua is a notable historical exception) to fight on behalf of village or district factions in their capacity as providers and protectors. In this, Samoan men took up the role of "warriors," if temporarily; they were not a "standing army" or a class apart from the larger Samoan society. The articulation of militarized masculinities and Samoan performances of masculinity have coalesced around the idea of heroism, with the concept of toa as bravery and prowess becoming linked to more explicit gendered ideas of risk and sacrifice. Below I offer one of many potential examples of how this has been taken up in the football realm.

When I was home and doing research in the fall of 2007, an album by Tokelauan singer Vaniah Toloa was wildly popular. With a combination of rich melody and skillful use of Samoan metaphor, his songs touched people deeply. One of those songs, "O 'oe o le toa," was written specifically about military service. The song honors the sacrifice made by Samoan brothers and sisters in the military, tying their exalted status to their willingness to do battle (ua sili ese lou naunau / Your worthiness exceeds them all [or your willingness (to do battle) exceeds them all]). Casting US military service as service to the Samoan nation, it exhorts the soldiers to be brave, fortified by the support of the national family (ia e loto toa [may your heart be brave] /

5.1 Toa ole Vasa. PHOTO CREDIT: AUTHOR.

o ou māmā uma nā [for they are the air that you breathe, referring to the tapuʻāiga (nation/country/family)]).

Attending weekly football games in the fall of 2007, I often heard the student spectators break into song, and this was a favorite. What I noticed though, was that one team in particular had adapted the song and its lyrics in support of its team. The Fagaʻitua Vikings styled themselves on booster T-shirts as "toa o le vasa," or "warriors of the sea." Their T-shirts adapted the song's chorus as their own kind of fight song, thus bringing the altered meaning of toa as war-making and (military) sacrifice into the context of football. Note in the lyrics the terms emphasized—warrior, country, battle, victory, swords, heart, and God.

> "*Toa Ole Vasa*"
> *O oe ole TOA*
> *E te TAU mo lou MALO*
> *Ou te TAPUAʻI e ala i le TATALO*
> *Ia lalaoa lou liu . . .*
> *Ia manuia ou FAIVA . . . E lua au PELU*

O lou FATU *ma le* ATUA

"Warrior of the Sea (Viking)"
You are a WARRIOR
You FIGHT for your COUNTRY
And in my PRAYERS, I will lift you high in BATTLE
May your head be anointed with oil . . .
And may you SUCCEED . . . With your two SWORDS
Your HEART and GOD

—inspired by song by Vaniah Toloa

"O oe o le toa"
(Tali)
O oe o le toa e te tau mo lou malo
Ou te tapuai e ala i le tatalo
Ia lalaoa lou liu
Ia manuia ou faiva
E lua au pelu o lou fatu ma le atua

"You are a warrior"[8]
(Chorus)
You are a warrior, you fight for your home country
And in my prayers, I will lift you high in battle[9]
May your head be anointed with oil
And may you succeed and be victorious[10]
Through the use of your two swords, your heart [fatu] and God
[Atua][11]

—original song and translation

This brief example provides a preliminary illustration of the circulation and articulation of Samoan concepts, images, and meanings, with American institutions of sport and military.[12]

In the United States football is, as others have pointed out, "the standard-bearer of masculinity in sport" (Butterworth 2014, 874). It has evolved to mark a working-class sensibility that extols physical toughness as a marker of valued masculinity. These motivate a performance of gender on the grid-iron that is built on risk, physical domination, fearlessness, and bodily sacrifice. The heroic masculinity demonstrated by the willingness to sacrifice (Burstyn 1999, 149), together with hypercompetitive attitudes that encourage a "win at any cost" attitude (English 2017, 188) makes for exciting sport spectacle. But it has a dark side, in its potential for "encouraging athletes to undergo and inflict physical and psychological injury" (English 2017, 187; see also Kidd 1990, 40–41).

While Samoan community sensibilities also value masculine physical toughness historically linked to roles as providers and protectors, in the contemporary moment Leiataua-Lesa pointed out that the military and sports are two of the few avenues where Samoans can acquire the title "toa" today. Aspects of valued or ideal Samoan masculinities therefore inform how expectations in athletic and other social spaces are negotiated. For example, the tamaloa lens proposed by Tipi (2013) identifies aspects of valued masculinity associated with Samoan ideals for the journey toward fulfilling expectations for adult males and their varied expression in the arena of sports: Tama mālosi, Tama loto tele, Tama onosaʻi, Tama usitaʻi, Tama poto, and Tama toa. While players may draw on them in different ways throughout their careers, particular expressions of Tama mālosi and Tama toa that articulate with hypermasculine displays of physical power and dominance are expected and valued in football (and other contact sports like rugby and boxing).

In the football context, players are under pressure to contribute to the team, "man up," and not seem "weak." Many conversations with coaches and players have confirmed that the expectation was from the coaches, the team, and individual players to perform and sacrifice your body/health if necessary. Hypermasculine norms are part of football culture more widely; however, they are articulating with selected internal norms to produce a powerful synergy that fuels success in certain sports but can be harmful to athletes' wellbeing. In our discussion one of the PAAB players shared: "Polynesians, you never want to look weak in front of them . . . Ever! We almost had a dude that died; they come over and say, 'You want a straw?' So you suck it up!" While these norms may be part of the sporting culture more widely, ideas about Samoan and Polynesian manhood as well as constructions of indigenous Polynesian masculinities compound both risk and reward for the players.

The internalization of hypermasculine stereotypes and expectations has important consequences for all players, but for Samoan and other Pacific Islander athletes, collectivist orientations may intensify the anxieties around not being able to push through, to be reliable in any context, or to let the collective down (Marsters and Tiaita-Seath 2019a, 258).[13] For example, one of the PAAB players shared about not reporting injuries, "I never would say anything [if I was hurt] . . . because I was supposed to be a leader on the team. They relied on me a lot and I don't want to let them down." Recognizing that for many Pacific athletes, identity and place is indelibly linked to others and this is often expressed in the commitment to fulfill one's [football] family expectations, it is important to be aware of how it might produce negative impacts as well. Explicit intervening discourses articulating the importance of wellbeing and resilience that support and safeguard their abilities to contribute and be of service to family and others important to them into the future may support better outcomes for Samoan and other Pacific Islander athletes (see also Marsters and Tiatia-Seath 2019b, 13).

Effective Changes or Public Relations Spin?

Many may argue that the earlier NFL and NCAA rule changes were not just about addressing safety concerns for the health and welfare of the players but were fundamentally about pacifying the public so the sport could continue in the midst of a crisis of public opinion. Whether this is also the case with recent rule changes is a matter of debate. The danger represented by repeated concussions has led the league and the NCAA to prohibit certain kinds of collisions (e.g., leading a tackle with the helmet, or tackling the quarterback or kicker after they have released the ball) in an effort to reduce those injuries. The NFL's 2013 ban on "spearing" or leading with the crown of the head, and the introduction of the NFL's game-day concussion protocol in 2009, have been the targets of discussion, as there is more pressure on the league to be seen enforcing the protocol.[14] In 2012 the NFL-backed "Heads Up Football" (HUF) tackling techniques program was introduced to much fanfare and widely promoted by USA Football. Ostensibly designed to make football safer for children and endorsed by recognizable figures in the game, it had significant reach.[15] A variety of teams adopted it and publicly advertised that their coaches were certified with the program, although it is no longer a centerpiece on USA Football's website.

The effort to reduce risk to youth players is an important start: if a player begins with youth tackle football, plays through high school, college, and has the average career length in the NFL, he has played at least ten years of football in his lifetime and potentially has sustained permanent bodily and perhaps neurological damage as a result of that participation.[16] In American Sāmoa, a youth football program was established with the assistance of USA Football, to begin training boys from a younger age (11–14) in order to develop player skills (in relation to high school recruits in places like California, Hawai'i, and Texas they are at a comparative disadvantage for having just started to play in ninth grade).[17] While it may increase their chances for recruitment, it also increases their exposure to injury by extending their participation in tackle football.

Few would question technique changes designed to make tackling safer; yet some critics viewed the Heads Up Football program "as a cynical marketing ploy—a repackaging of old terminology to reassure parents at a time the sport is confronting a widening health crisis" (Fainaru and Fainaru-Wada 2014). It came at a time when football—the US youth sport with the largest number of participants nationwide—was experiencing declining participation, as parents ask whether their children should be playing football at all. Between 2009 and 2019 tackle football participation for children ages 6–18 fell significantly, from around 2.5 million to less than 1.9 million, respectively (and these figures have not reversed in the time since).[18] A 2016 HBO Real Sports/Marist Poll of 1,298 US adults found that the "information released in recent years about the connection between playing football and long-term brain injury is influencing Americans' opinions about whether or not they would allow their child to play youth football."[19] The poll found that the information linking football to long-term brain injury made a growing proportion (44 percent) of US respondents less likely to allow their sons to play football, an increase over the 36 percent of parents reported in 2013. While the vast majority (75 percent) of parent respondents said they would still allow their child to play football, 23 percent said they would not—more than double the 10 percent reported in 2013. With overall parental concern rising, the long-term prospects of the sports depend on addressing some of the health risks.

In response to the new technique program, an independent study found that Heads Up Football showed no demonstrable effect on concussions during the study, and significantly less effect on injuries overall, than USA Football and the league had claimed."[20] While HUF did mitigate injury as compared to the leagues that did not use the tackling techniques (especially among older youth [11–15]), the major difference was whether the league was also affiliated with Pop Warner (PW).[21] In 2012 Pop Warner football implemented restrictions on player contact during practice, and in this study the combination of HUF and PW significantly reduced injury compared to leagues that had neither the new tackling techniques nor the contact restrictions during practice.[22] The study findings suggest that practice restrictions make more of a difference than the introduced tackling techniques alone, and others confirm that (not surprisingly) limiting practice and contact drills in youth football reduces the overall exposure to head impacts (Cobb et al. 2013).[23] More recently, brain researchers have recommended that contact sports should be avoided altogether before age 12 out of concern for accumulated trauma and the potential to structural damage to developing brains (Cleaver 2019); this is an important shift that should be considered more carefully in light of emerging research.

I began examining this research about six months after the conversations with the PAAB student-athletes on the bowl weekend. Their point that the game is safer now than it was when Junior Seau played, and even earlier, was based on things like the new tackling techniques promoted by USA Football, and much-heralded changes in helmet technology. Compared to the 1960s when catastrophic injury and death were regular parts of the game, it certainly is safer now (Mueller and Colgate 2012). However, until the research can demonstrate unequivocally that changes in technique and technology have made the game categorically safer rather than safer by a matter of degrees, these claims remain arguable while their marketing shapes potentially hundreds of thousands of players' understandings of risk in the game.

Talking with college student-athletes who play football over the years, they have consistently told me that everyone who plays the game knows the risks. In our talk-story session one of the PAAB players remarked:

> Well I feel like when you put those ties on you, basically signing the contract saying that you know all the risks of playing the game of football whether its concussion or torn ACL or any of that, so I feel like if you play the game of football that you should already know that . . . it is a dangerous sport but we all have to play it.

Here he maintains that players are aware of the potential risks. Most would agree that the fact that players can get hurt in tackle football is clear from the outset, and many do get hurt even in the early years. But are the kids in Pee Wee, Pop Warner, and Big Boyz leagues, and those playing high school football, and their parents aware of the range of risks over a football career including short-term injury and long-term joint damage? Do most of the players actually know what it means physiologically to have a concussion or traumatic brain injury, and the potential outcomes? Do their parents know that studies are showing increased incidence of CTE the longer one stays in the sport? I cannot say, but there is nothing I have seen that suggests they do.

Articulating risk awareness demonstrates what Furness (2016) calls "the informed soldier trope" where it is assumed that injury is inevitable and players are aware of and accept the risks involved. "Injuries, in other words, are rationalized as a 'part of the game' and thus naturalized as a burden every player must bear, ostensibly without complaints" (Furness 2016, 51).

However, veteran players have noted the difference between awareness of physical injury and those involving the brain, revealing that most do not have the capacity to accurately assess the risk head injuries represent to their long-term health (Furness 2016, 52). Even the researchers who study brain injury and sport do not know definitively what the long-term effect of playing tackle football is for different age groups, given their physical development. While brain researchers and policy makers agree that the risk of catastrophic injury is inherent to the game, they cannot yet say conclusively what kinds of contact are correlated to neurological injuries and long-term damage. This raises questions about whether youth and families coming to the game know what kinds of risk they are really taking, and whether they can make a fully informed decision about participating. Equally important, if not more so, it raises the question of whether those in positions to influence policy and practice are doing everything they can to minimize risk of injury, particularly for youth players.

Meaningful Attachments

During the Polynesian All-American Bowl weekend, in between scheduled activities, I had the chance to sit down and chat with one of the early Samoan football pioneers, Jack "The Throwin' Samoan" Thompson. We sat poolside talking about his football journey at a small motel-inn in Garden Grove, California, and as our talk-story came to an end I asked him about his thoughts on Junior Seau and whether Junior's case was a cautionary one for the youth. With a smile and a sigh, he said, "That's another two-hour conversation." While it hasn't yet materialized, it is a conversation that is fraught with emotion and bound in contradiction. What were we doing there if not supporting the next generation in their quest for football exposure, college access, upward mobility, and potential greatness?

Many of the organizers had themselves played, achieving varying degrees of success; the event coaches were part of the AIGA fraternal network whose ties spanned space and time. Core organizers George Malau'ulu (former University of Arizona quarterback and AIGA founder) and his sister Miya Malau'ulu (former Montana State head volleyball coach) and a village of volunteers and sponsors brought the game together. Gridiron Ministries, based in San Diego and led by Wesley Saleaumua and including Pastor Ray Toilolo, were in attendance. Wesley's brother Dan Saleaumua (Kansas City Chiefs, Detroit Lions, and Seattle Seahawks) was organizing on-field practices with a commanding voice and a megaphone.

The organizing team and coaches represented a variety of football levels.[24] Jack Thompson (Washington Redskins) and Ma'a Tanuvasa (Denver Broncos) were coaches of the opposing teams, while Troy Polamalu (Pittsburgh Steelers) and Jesse Sapolu (San Francisco 49ers) served as honorary captains. It was a brilliant event, infused with a spirit of brotherhood and community, and accompanied by the concerted efforts of coaches working their networks on behalf of unrecruited players. And although the bowl game was still relatively new as a venture, the event was part of a much longer genealogy of football tautua suffused with alofa. Some of the young men we spoke to over the weekend described it as "a beautiful experience" and "a blessing" to be surrounded by 'āiga/AIGA. (Based on the excitement behind the scenes, and the sense among some of what the event could look like with more resources, I was not surprised to see a much bigger, better resourced, and sponsored event emerge with the PFHOF a few years later.)

I thought about the poolside chat as I attended the inaugural events launching the Polynesian Football Hall of Fame to much fanfare and community delight in Honolulu, Hawai'i, the following week. Junior Seau was

5.2 PAAB coaches Jack Thompson, Dan Saleaumua, and Jesse Sapolu.
PHOTO CREDIT: AUTHOR.

among the inductees of this first class of football greats; he was represented by his son Tyler Seau, who was accompanied by family members in the private 'awa ceremony at the Bishop Museum.[25] Seau's children represented him with grace and composure as their father's accomplishments were recognized and honored.

The events were designed to showcase the success stories and honor the work of this class of players who had broken barriers with their journeys. They were also designed to recognize and cultivate ongoing support of the PFHOF, and discussions around risk and injury were not part of that overall messaging. No mention was made of the tragedy of Seau's passing, the circumstances that led to it, or the role of football in it. It had been a year since brain researchers confirmed that he suffered from CTE, and the family was in the midst of a pending class action lawsuit brought against the NFL on behalf of 4,500 retired players and their families.[26]

This chapter was originally drafted in the fall of 2014. Coming back to revise it in 2016–2017 and then again in 2020, I saw the induction and the difficult position for Seau's family in a more nuanced light because of developments in our own family. In the intervening years, I accompanied my father to neurology testing to try to understand the root of noticeable changes in his cognition, memory, and behavior. This was emotionally intense and eye-opening. He too received a notice of the NFL class action lawsuit, yet chose not to complete all the tests, so the results (diagnosis and potential sources) remained inconclusive even as the symptoms became increasingly difficult to manage before his passing. I imagine that our situation is not unique: How many more former players and family members are in this position? How many have little to no mental health literacy to understand mental distress, or are struggling to disentangle contributing factors? As part of the inaugural class of the PFHOF, Junior Seau's case is a difficult one to grapple with. What are the prospects for bringing this important and deeply emotional conversation into the light, and what might be gained from it?

At the end of the public Polynesian Cultural Center event for the Polynesian Football Hall of Fame, the panel was asked whether they had discussed the potential risks in playing football, risks for brain injuries and concussion, and if they could share some insight into the issue. It was Jack Thompson who answered, noting that the concussion issue is coming to the fore because of what is happening with his generation of players, or as he termed them, the "pre-93ers" in the NFL sphere.[27] He mentioned friends who had serious problems linked to concussions and the role of the NFLPA in highlighting the issue and the NFL in addressing the issue with new safety protocols, and the efforts to reach the youth level. He noted, "It just saddens me to see, certainly, my generation and the severe cases that we're having to navigate and having to bridge those waters, but I think the condition is, it's getting better, it's not where we need to—should be, but it's getting better and it's moving in the right direction." It may indeed be moving in the right direction, with more attention paid to the safety of players and managing unnecessary risk. Yet new research suggests that unless tackling is drastically reduced or eliminated completely, it will never be "safe." And the catch is, the fact that football is not safe—or rather, that it embodies risk—is precisely what maintains its popularity as a man's sport in the United States and in Pacific communities.

AN IRRECONCILABLE TENSION?

The subtle resistance to engaging questions about the long-term impact of football participation on the health of the men Samoan and other Pacific Islander communities may reflect the view that the amount of risk is negligible or unimportant ("there's risk in everything"). Many share this viewpoint, and especially those who have been through the game and survived intact. Certainly, there is some calculus balancing unknown risk against tangible and intangible benefits. But some of the hesitation may instead be linked to how deeply the conversation resonates: the recognition and acceptance of the true stakes of the game would require a reckoning we may not yet be ready to face. The phone call with my mother shows the grief attached to the loss of people like Junior Seau, valued members of our community whose lives impacted many and who went before their time. Moreover, engaging these questions exposes an irreconcilable tension: If football provides an arena not just for status and prestige, but increasingly in diaspora is woven into the fabric of the community as a field of belonging and connection, what would it mean to have to give it up?

Beyond cultural and community connections, in the context of increasing economic precarity and disappearing opportunity especially for those without formal education credentials, football offers a real and tangible pathway. We might ask whether and how declining football participation is a privilege exercised by the middle class, since middle class parents are far better positioned to navigate the culture of educational institutions to their children's benefit and elites have long fled the sport. We know that class background shapes sporting choices (Bourdieu 1978, 1988); it is worth thinking more deeply about how this factors into the (missing) conversations on football and long-term injury in Pacific communities. In some contexts, particularly for some of the players in urban areas whose stories were shared with me, the risks are not only acceptable, they pale in comparison to other risks seen on a daily basis.

While some portrayals suggesting that Samoan "culture" propels the youth into football are often simplistic or misleading, for many in the diaspora the sport has become one site for articulating cultural identity.[28] This is distinct from the islands, where the game is part of the local society but the players' racial and cultural background is not used as a signal of difference in the same way. There football is not necessarily a cultural outlet, but rather highlights more specific points of status and pride like one's family, one's school, one's village, and/or one's district. It is in the larger regional or diasporic spaces where there is stark racialized cultural difference that football becomes the locus of the nation or representative of a culture (in addition to one's family, which is always central). In the United States, Samoan and other Polynesian players and communities have and continue to forge and articulate connection in and through football, just as in Aotearoa New Zealand and Australia where rugby code participation is often a source of strength amid erasure, invisibility, or outright hostility in the wider city, state, and/or national contexts (Panapa and Phillips 2014; Teaiwa 2016; Teaiwa and Mallon 2005; Lakisa et al. 2019). Players in these highly visible contact sports are able to contest erasure and diminishment by embodying valued expressions of masculinity.

In this space of possibility, players shoulder many kinds of burdens. In addition to the physical pain associated with sustaining injury, particularly a season- or career-ending one, is the emotional cost of failure, unfulfilled expectations, and diminished personal worth. There are countless stories of student-athletes who struggle, encounter depression, or leave school altogether after sustaining a major injury.[29] In the course of my interviews there were several accounts shared with me of the incredible weight many of the players who move transnationally shoulder, laden with expectations, and facing homesickness compounded with culture shock. One former player from Tutuila told me that there were so many times when he just wanted to come home, but didn't want to be seen as a failure, knowing that not only was he representing his family but he was also paving the way for Samoan players who would come after him. So, he would go back to his dorm room, cry, and then get on with the next day. He shared what helped him to continue amid the difficulty in college: "I think my parents' influence was a motivational factor. And I had come too far; I'm thousands and thousands miles away. I mean, I'm not going back without that piece of paper."

Samoan players are often told to remember the sacrifice their families made for them, the material and emotional investments their families have made on their behalf, and to use that as motivation to sustain them through the hard times. Their ability to do so is a source of pride in cultural contexts and acts as valuable currency in football and campus settings as well. In difficult times they are exhorted to "fa'amālosi!" or stay/be strong.

Conclusion

NIU FUTURES

SHIVERING ON THE SIDELINES in the crisp, sunny Southern Hemisphere spring, we watched as the host team went up against an all-star squad from American Sāmoa in an exhibition game at Mountfort Park, Manurewa, in South Auckland. We had just recently moved to New Zealand and Sam, an old college friend and former player, invited us out. Missing the start to the North American football season and curious, we took the family and watched from the sidelines. Hosted by the Auckland league while on their malaga, American Sāmoa fielded the favored team, leveraging their successful adoption of American football to support efforts far afield from the US gridiron game. There was a small but respectable crowd for the game, and while the host team played hard, the visiting team won handily. The coach for American Sāmoa, Ethan Lake, told me after the game that because of the timing with the North American school year they had to cobble together a team from former players and those who were available to travel on short notice; they were excited the trip came together and that they were able to come to New Zealand.

In a Pacific stronghold of the Auckland supercity the largely Samoan participants had brought the game to yet a new generation.[1] It was unexpected, but also intimately familiar, indicative of the ways big and small that the Samoan diaspora remains connected. The day's events, and the ongoing project of American football made possible largely by community effort was like 'afa or sennit, a strand made stronger by the intertwining of people's lives week in and week out, year in and year out, that would be woven together with other community strands. In Sāmoa, braids of sennit (drawn from coconut fiber) have their own measure—in units of gafa, which is also the word used to refer to genealogies and descent. Drawing us all together provided warmth even on the chilly spring day. But there was something else as well: the exhibition game at the local park was much smaller than others with a delegation from American Sāmoa I had seen just a few years earlier at Honolulu's Aloha Stadium. Despite its long-standing presence in Auckland (over forty years and counting), American football is still struggling to keep its footing and grow in the wider sportscape of Aotearoa where rugby reigns supreme.[2] Pasifika players who enter college or the pros from this area of the world are few and far between.[3] Still, tended to by former players and die-hard aficionados of the game, it draws the energies of Auckland's Pacific communities in the rugby off-season. Gridiron football's relative obscurity in the wider field of New Zealand sports brings into relief the fundamental importance of sporting infrastructure and investment to provide building materials for growth and visibility, something that supports the sport's outsized dominance in the US-linked markets.

In the two major sports where Polynesian athletes are well represented or dominate—American football and the rugby codes—the top games electrify transnational communities in the islands and across the Pacific diaspora. From the celebration of Fiji rugby sevens winning the gold in the Rio Olympics in 2016 to the red wave of support for Mate Ma'a Tonga in the 2017 Rugby League World Cup, to the excitement of rooting for Harvey Langi, Isaac Seumalo, Destiny Vaeao, and Halapoulivaati Vaitai in the 2018 Super Bowl, to the fanfare of Tua Tagovailoa's NFL entry as the Miami Dolphins quarterback in 2020, these sporting contests mobilize an enormous amount of alofa, energy, affect, and capital in Pacific communities.

Although Pacific players have been part of those sport codes since the turn of the twentieth century, they have since formed a critical mass that has transformed the face of the sports since the 1980s and particularly from the 1990s forward. In addition to helping us chart community histories, the story of sport and Polynesian or Pasifika communities illuminates important aspects of globalization. Traveling both the routes of industry and capital, and the networks that connect transnational Pacific communities, sports have flourished and continue to draw significant individual and collective investment. Today few rugby contests are played without Pacific representation, and in many cases Pacific players form the backbone of union and league success. The professionalization era transformed investment and opportunity, drawing more young hopefuls into the games. Across the moana, as the professional and collegiate aspects of the football industry grew, so too did the mass of players of Samoan (and mostly Polynesian) heritage in the game. Weaving together analyses of institutional configurations and accounts of lived experience of migration, global sport expansion, and late capitalist globalization and transnational practices sheds light on both the large-scale dynamic trends and the way they are materialized in and through individual journeys and community histories.

Through the conscious and contingent cultivation of the game at all levels, and the dedicated work of those who play and coach, football has become a network of expanded routes of mobility—geographic, social, and economic. For the players of Samoan descent, and particularly those with ties to Tutuila and Manu'a, the backdrop of this movement has always been the history of US imperialism and developmentalist transformations in the islands connected to new waves of transnational movement. Developing and pursuing opportunities for accumulating gridiron capital, navigating existing and emergent representations, and forging new pathways, players continued to create new/niu futures for themselves and their families. As they did so, they generated and continue to generate massive profits, and particularly at the "amateur" levels contribute uncompensated labor for the benefit of others and the systems of which they are a part. Trying to keep pace with escalating expectations for performance, players willingly and enthusiastically train to reshape themselves as commodities toward future performance and opportunity.

Mastering new fields of (sport) labor, Pacific players and their communities also channeled passion, forged connections, and crafted new hubs of belonging. As their numbers grew, no longer were they just trying to succeed in the "white man's game," but the game that had given them openings for individual achievement also became a source of mana and a site of collective tautua. In these new narrations, players and commentators found resonances between articulated aspects of Samoan culture and the culture of football, claiming the sport as their own and crafting their own images and branding.

But the meritocratic promotion promised by sport has not always materialized, shaped by intransigent and institutionalized practices that systematically favor some over others. For example, one would expect by now to have many more Polynesian coaches at higher levels of American football, but the 2020 meeting between BYU–Provo and Navy was the first time two Division I/Football Bowl Subdivision Polynesian head coaches (Kenny Niumatalolo—Samoan, and Kalani Sitake—Tongan) faced each other on the field. Indeed, to date they are the first and only Polynesian head coaches of D-I/FBS programs. Few have been able to make coaching a career at higher levels of the collegiate game or break through to the professional game. Instead, (largely Samoan, Tongan, and Hawaiian) players trying to make coaching a career are often shuttled into precarious positions.[4] With few established pathways and personal networks still dominant, many leave the grind of long hours, high stress, relocations, and job insecurity to find spots in lower levels of the collegiate game, high school coaching, or adjacent athletic administration positions, or they leave the field altogether.

In addition to the highly contingent and precarious coaching career pathways, Polynesian players and their communities have yet to reckon with the implications of traumatic brain injury in football and long-term impacts. Established community traditions and attachments to the game will work against that reckoning, but more importantly, lack of investment in other pathways and increasingly precarious economic positioning render that reckoning a privilege many cannot afford. In the meantime, in the United States and abroad male Polynesian youth and their families will continue to look to football as a ticket to college and the pros.

If sport remains an expanded route of mobility, a valued site of labor, a significant hub for connection and belonging, and a visible venue for representation, then investing in gender parity, as well as mental health and wellbeing initiatives; adopting risk mitigation, especially for youth; and continuing to work against the inequities in education funding and college access are important ongoing and future interventions. Similarly, resisting opportunistic appropriation of Samoan culture and traits of toxic masculinity, and instead emphasizing countervailing narratives that center the service, collective responsibility, and wellbeing aspects of Samoan (and other Polynesian) masculinities can support the long-term health and continued success of Pacific communities in the islands and abroad.

Glossary

ʻāiga	Immediate or extended family; family relations
ʻalia	Twin-hulled canoes
ʻaualuma	Women's village organization
ʻaumaga	Village organization of untitled men
ʻava	A drink made from the piper methysticum plant; usually offered in ceremonial contexts to honored guests
alagāʻupu	Proverb or expression
ʻie faitaga	Formal, tailored lāvalava
ʻie lāvalava	A length of cloth or other material used to wrap one's body (usually lower half)
ʻie sina	A rare, white fine-textured mat
ʻohana	Family
ʻōlelo Hawaiʻi	Hawaiian language
aliʻi	High-ranking chief
alofa	Love or compassion
aloha	Love or compassion

cibi	A type of Fijian meke or traditional dance that was used to welcome victorious forces home; adopted by the Fijian national team as a pregame performance in response to the haka of the All Blacks
fa'afetai	Thankfulness
fa'afetai tele lava	Effusive thanks
fa'alavelave	Literally, to entangle; anything that interrupts the schedule of everyday life; often used to refer to ceremonial gathering and exchanges associated with family events such as weddings, funerals, and title investitures
fa'amatai	Hierarchy of chiefly titles; long-standing indigenous Samoan sociopolitical organization
fa'asāmoa	Often translated as "the Samoan way"; refers broadly to Samoan culture and cultural practices
fai'ai eleni	Mackerel mixed with onions and coconut milk, and then baked
faifeau	Pastor
faikakala	Colloquial of faitatala (literally, the act of making talk); gossip
faipule	Elected legislative representative
fale	Can refer to a house generally or a traditional Samoan-style house
faleaitu	Comedy; clowning
faleo'o	Small Samoan-style house
fealofani	Kindness/support; relational harmony
ha'a	Demonstrative Hawaiian bent-knee dance inspired by the Māori haka and adapted in line with lua (Hawaiian martial art) revitalization to produce a strong masculine cultural protocol
haole	Term used to refer to foreigners (now used mainly for those of white European ancestry)
kakau	Hawaiian tatau/tattoo
kihei	Garments worn during Hawaiian ceremony or protocol; often a length of printed cloth draped across the chest and tied at the left shoulder, and may include symbols referring to the wearer's knowledge or role
kirikiti	Transliteration of "cricket"; also refers to the sport as transformed by Samoans, with different rules and equipment

lāuga	Formal speech
launiu	Coconut frond
lotu	Prayer
mahalo	Thanks or gratitude
malae	Central village green
malaga	Visiting, travel, movement; also formal travel as with a designated party
mālamama	(Day)light; to understand; to be enlightened
malo	Loincloth
mālōfie	Customary tattoo for men that covers the entire area from the low waist to the knees
Kānaka maoli	Often translated as *real person* or the *real people*; refers to indigenous Hawaiians
matai	Titled chiefs; those who hold customary family titles
measina	Cultural treasures
moana	Deep sea; also used to refer to the Pacific Ocean
mosoʻoi	Ylang ylang; here refers to the tree's fragrant flowers
nifo ʻoti	War club; literal translation: teeth of death
panikeke	Round fritters
pālagi	Term used to refer to foreigners or to describe foreign origins (usually of white European ancestry)
palusami	A dish of coconut milk cooked in a package of taro leaves
pese	Song
pisupo	Tinned corned beef
pule	Power or authority
saofaʻi	Ceremonial title investiture
sāsā	A specific kind of dance with clapping, slapping, and stepping movements choreographed to produce synchronized sound
sei fulumoa	Hair adornment made of chicken feathers
siva	Can refer to dance generally or a Samoan dance specifically
tagata o le moana	Literally, people of the sea; used to refer to peoples of the Pacific
talo	Taro; a starchy root
tangata whenua	Literally, people of the land; used to refer to Māori as indigenous people of Aotearoa New Zealand

tānoa	Wooden bowl used to mix 'ava
tāupou	Usually translated as a title of a village maiden chosen to perform ceremonial duties, including mixing 'ava for honored guests
to'ona'i	Main Sunday meal
tufuga	Master artisan/practitioner
tulāfale	Talking chief
tulou lava	An expression showing deference or begging pardon
'ulā fala	Adornment traditionally worn by Samoan chiefs for ceremonial occasions, made from the fruit of the pandanus tree dyed red
'ula moso'oi	Fragrant garland necklace made from the local moso'oi flower
'ulā nifo	A necklace traditionally made from sperm whale teeth but in other parts of the Pacific made from boar's tusks, dog's teeth, coconut shell, and other materials.
'ulu	Breadfruit
umu	Food prepared in, or the shallow outdoor stone oven itself
va'a	Boat or ship
vasa	Open sea

Note: While many of the words listed might have multiple definitions, the ones provided here are closest to the meaning as used in this book. Preliminary translations have been done by the author, with reference to Milner (1996 [2001]) and Allardice (1995), with additional translation support given by Lemoa Henry Fesulua'i.

Notes

1   A note on diacritics: In some Pacific Island communities a move to adopt diacritic use has been settled (for example, in 'ōlelo Hawai'i or te reo Māori), while among Samoans it remains contested. Recognizing that this book is not only published abroad but also is likely to have an audience of Samoan language learners and non-Samoans, and following some of the arguments made by Tualaulelei, Mayer, and Hunkin (2015), I have chosen to use diacritics for Samoan words to support correct pronunciation, and to also use them for words in other languages where they would normally appear. (For example, I have used them in "Sāmoa" but not "Samoan," because the latter is an English word.) These follow Milner (1966 [2001]) and Allardice (1995), with assistance from Lemoa Henry Fesulua'i. However, given that diacritic use is contested and in order to respect decisions made by others, I have not imposed them in all cases. Noted exceptions are people's names, proper titles (programs, government agencies), or in material that has been directly quoted from another source that uses a different spelling.

2   I attended along with a group of Māori and Pacific colleagues who were visiting from Aotearoa New Zealand as part of efforts to establish an indigenous Pacific research collaboration between universities in Aotearoa and University of Hawai'i. Mahalo to the Royal Order of Kamehameha for permitting for me

to film the ʻawa ceremony and to take pictures, and to Ty P. K. Tengan for the invitation.

3 Established as a 501c3, the organization's stated purpose is to recognize and honor players, coaches, and contributors to Polynesian success in football. It awards a limited number of scholarships to graduating seniors (male or female) who played high school sports and are headed to Division II and III schools, and in 2015 it incorporated an award for the Polynesian college player of the year. The organization's website (http://www.polynesianfootballhof .org/) notes that it hosts educational programs for Polynesian youth.

4 A note on terminology: "Polynesian" has become a widely used term in the United States to differentiate ties to a specific part of the Pacific (usually Sāmoa, Tonga, and Hawaiʻi) within the wider Pacific Islander category (used in census disaggregation since 2000). Pacific Islander (or PI) is used to differentiate from Pacific, a term that includes Pacific Rim countries and heritage. Because Pacific Islanders have significantly lower population numbers relative to groups included under the banner of the Pacific Rim, "Pacific" often functions to erase Islanders/Oceania. Across the moana in Aotearoa New Zealand, Pacific or Pasifika (as an amalgamation of Pasefika/Pasifiki, transliterations of the English word *Pacific*) was adopted by the New Zealand government to categorize all Pacific peoples in the country and has become the preferred and institutionally supported term. Although Pasifika is theoretically inclusive of all Oceania, in practice the view of Pasifika tends to be near Polynesia since the largest non-Māori resident Pacific peoples are Samoan, Tongan, Fijian, Cook Islander, and Niuean because of what has historically been claimed as the New Zealand "realm." I use these different terms as relevant to the local contexts to which they refer.

5 Both are also associate professors at the University of Hawaiʻi–Mānoa. Tengan's book *Native Men Remade* (2008) thoughtfully examines and critiques the efforts to remake Hawaiian men and masculinities in and through gendered Indigenous decolonization and revitalization efforts in Hale Mua o Kūaliʻi and ʻAha Kāne.

6 On sporting movement and labor, see also Besnier (2012, 2015); Besnier, Brownell, and Carter (2018); Carter (2007, 2011, 2013); Darby (2000, 2002); Darby and Solberg (2010); Esson (2013); Kanemasu and Molnar (2012); Klein (1991, 2006, 2009); Lanfranchi and Taylor (2001); Maguire (2001); Maguire and Bale (1994); Maguire and Falcous (2011); and Poli (2010).

7 See LiPuma (1993) on culture and the specificity of French society in Bourdieu's theory of capital.

8 James and Steger describe this as "the expansion and intensification of social relations and consciousness across world-space and world-time" (2014, 425). They go on to explain: "The discursive explosion of 'globalization' in the 1990s" marked a shift in a "sensibility of global interdependence," even if there was a longer-standing global imaginary long before the term came into widespread use (2014, 422; see also Steger 2008 and Robertson 1990 and 1992).

9 In contrast to the recent proliferation of the term in academic and public discourses, global connection and movement is not a new phenomenon; it has been a world practice for centuries (see Clossey 2006; Foner 1997; Vertovec 1997). Still, there has been a marked increase in frequency and volume of these flows, in response to "time-space compression" and a "changing era of flexible accumulation" in which a variety of technological innovations have made the continuous movement of people, ideas, and commodities an entrenched practice (Harvey 1987, 1990; Mintz 1998, 128).

10 A number of models and metaphors have been suggested to begin to describe, analyze, and explain the contemporary social reality with which we are faced, including *creolization* (Hannerz 1987, 1992), *flows* (Appadurai 1990), *hybridization* (Bhaba 1994), and *articulation* (Clifford 2001). For some, the slightly unwieldy term *glocalization* captured the both/and reality of localized phenomenon nonetheless being part of a larger global context or system (Robertson 1994, 1995).

11 See also Glick-Schiller, Basch, and Szanton-Blanc (1992a; 1992b); Hannerz (1996).

12 Helen Lee (2009, 23) notes that the literature on migrants and their transnational practices has largely been dominated by analyses of remittances, particularly in the Pacific. See also Connell (2005) for an overview of the literature on Pacific remittances.

13 See Anae (1997), Lee (2003), (2004), Kallen (1982), and Small (1997); see also Antoun (2005); Malkki (1995); and Miles (2004) on the migrant experience. Sociologist Cluny Macpherson's long-term work with Samoan communities in Aotearoa New Zealand, for example, examines how Samoan migrants and successive generations transform practices of fa'asāmoa in their active maintenance of ties to home communities in the Samoan islands (e.g., Macpherson 1985, 1991, 2004; Macpherson and Macpherson 2009a, 2009b).

14 This project builds on the provocation by Marcus (1995, 1998) to follow the subject through multisited ethnography (see also Hannerz 2003). "The conceptualisation of the interrogative boundary, that is to say, the questions that impel the ethnographer, overarch geographic considerations and tie diffuse, loose, separate, mobile or distant places together in a single ethnographic field of inquiry" (Madden 2017, 52). This together with work illuminating transnational linkages and global chains, the currents and afterlives of empire, movement, and migration, and efforts to understand how localities are connected provide a conceptual framework for this project. Here I am interested in specificity of place and how individual and collective decision making shape contingent histories, as well as how relationships and infrastructure shape how, when, and why people move. In practice, the research was less like following a clearly mapped journey along defined routes and coordinates and more akin to Oceanic wayfinding, navigating short- and long-distance journeys using landmarks, currents, skyscapes, and emerging embodied knowledge.

15 For work on sport migration see Alegi (2010), Agergaard and Tiesler (2014), Besnier (2015), Elliot and Harris (2014), James (1963), Lanfranchi and Taylor (2001, 2014), and Taylor (2006), among many others; see Dewey (2008) on professionalization of rugby in the Pacific, and Grainger and Falcous (2012), and Heptonstall (2011) on rising Pacific participation in New Zealand rugby.

16 Garber, Greg. 2002. "The Dominican Republic of the NFL." ESPN: The Magazine, May 28. See also Garber, Greg. 2002. "They Might be Giants." ESPN: The Magazine, May 28; Feldman, Bruce. 2001. "Buy a Vowel?" ESPN: The Magazine, November 19; Feldman, Bruce. 2001. "Rock Star." ESPN: The Magazine, November 19; Feldman, Bruce. 2002. "Where Football Really is a Religion." ESPN: The Magazine, May 28; Miller, Ted. 2002. "American Football, Samoan Style." ESPN.com, May 28; and Syken, Bill. 2003. "Football in Paradise." Sports Illustrated, November 3.

17 Later work turned to theories of global value chains as frameworks for understanding sport migration (Klein 2011, 2012).

18 Many schools have continued with football even as the programs were costly and operated at a deficit. On the health front, while some may have anticipated that college football would be significantly impacted by the concussion crisis (discussed in chapter 5), we have seen that even a global pandemic with a highly contagious and lethal disease (COVID-19) has not stopped the popular and highly profitable machine that is college football.

19 Most successful international players have gone through the college football system; the opportunity to "code-switch" in the way that Jordan Mailata has done (from Under-20s rugby in Sydney to the Philadelphia Eagles) is extremely rare.

20 The FBS teams offer 85 scholarships per team for 127 teams, while the FCS offers 63 scholarships per team for 124 teams in the 2015–2016 season. Division II gave the equivalent of 36 scholarships per team in 2016. Overall participation in NCAA football has grown, from 40,733 players across 497 teams total in the 1981–1982 season to 45,263 players across 672 teams in the 2015–2016 season. Division I has also grown from 187 teams and 17,842 players ending the 1981 season to 251 teams and 28,830 players ending the 2015 season. Meanwhile, Division II included 173 teams and 9,796 players ending the 2015 season. See http://www.ncaapublications.com/productdownloads/PR1516.pdf.

21 Division I refers to the schools in the NCAA with most elaborate sports programs. In order to qualify for membership, schools must sponsor an equivalent minimum of at least seven sports for women and seven for men, with two team sports per gender. There are additional minimum attendance, financial aid awards, and scheduling requirements. For football, the division is split into the top range that participates in the Football Bowl Subdivision (formerly Division I-A), those that participate in smaller NCAA-run Football Championship Subdivision (formerly Division I-AA), and those that do not field football teams. See http://www.ncaa.org/about/who-we-are/membership/divisional -differences-and-history-multidivision-classification.

22 Gaines, Cork. 2016. "The Difference in How Much Money Schools Make Off of College Sports Is Jarring." *Business Insider Australia*. Gaines, Cork, and Mark Nudelman. 2017. "The Average College Football Team Makes More Money Than the Next 35 College Sports Combined." *Business Insider Australia*.

23 2016–17. Annual Report. Indianapolis, Indiana: National Federation of State High School Associations. https://www.nfhs.org/.

24 Florio, Mike. 2017. "NFL Will Reach $14 Billion in 2017 Revenue." March 6. Pro Football Talk, accessed June 19, 2018, https://profootballtalk.nbcsports.com.

25 Gough, Christina. 2020. "Total revenue of the National Football League 2001–2019." statista.com, accessed November 25, 2020. Since the 1980s, the Arena Football League was also an option for players, but the league declared bankruptcy in late 2019; the new XFL, whose 2020 launch was derailed by the COVID-19 pandemic, is said to be returning in 2023, with Dwayne "The Rock" Johnson listed as an owner. Historically the Canadian Football League has also provided a home for some players, but the contracts are far less lucrative than those in the NFL, making it a less attractive option: the 2018 salary minimum was $54,000 for the regular season.

26 The 1958 Baltimore Colts–New York Giants championship game at Yankee Stadium is often touted as the point of origin for setting professional football fortunes on the path to where they stand today. The televised excitement of "The Greatest Game Ever Played" at a moment when television was taking over American households meant the largest ever viewership of a football contest at that point—45 million people (Grano 2014, 14). An antitrust exemption in the Sports Broadcasting Bill was passed in 1961 and the next year Commissioner Pete Rozelle spearheaded the beginning of the NFL's commercial rise with a two-year television contract valued at $4.65 million that instituted an enduring national revenue-sharing model (Yost 2006, 75).

27 Building on Pierre Bourdieu, Marshall Sahlins, and Anthony Giddens's elaboration of practice theory, Sherry Ortner suggests serious games as a way to approach the "people-in-(power)-relationships-in-projects as the relatively irreducible unit of 'practice'" (1996, 13). Here football is part of the games of mobility, status, and gender that hold particular kinds of opportunities for those who play it and the communities that support them.

28 For example, the body of literature around the MiRAB model starting with Bertram and Watters (1985), or the focus on labor recruitment policies like the Recognized Seasonal Employer (RSE) scheme in Aotearoa New Zealand.

29 Recent work traces this kind of transformation; see Katerina Teaiwa's exploration of phosphate mining on Banaba (2014), Macpherson and Macpherson's discussion of the *Warm Winds of Change* (2009) in Sāmoa, Niko Besnier's analysis of modernity in Tonga (2011), and Paige West's work on the transformation of coffee as a commodity in and beyond PNG highlands (2012), for example.

30 For American Sāmoa these were implemented at the US federal and appointed local administration levels to enable further movement; for Western

Sāmoa these included scholarships for study and labor and migration schemes in Aotearoa New Zealand and Australia.

31 Without another term to recognize the liminal position of American Sāmoa as an unincorporated territory—both within and outside of US national frameworks—"transnational" most accurately expresses the physical, geographic, and cultural borders that separate the two locations.

32 Some have denounced inequality before the US Constitution, particularly around access to citizenship and rightly critiquing the racist and patronizing reasoning in the *Insular Cases*, a set of US Supreme Court rulings that undergird the jurisprudence around the unincorporated territory category. However, the case law has also been used to preserve and maintain important aspects of Samoan cultural practice including the fa'amatai and the communal land tenure system. See Hall (2001).

33 The wage rates as of September 30, 2015, for the three sectors are $5.16, $4.81, and $5.00, respectively. USDOL Wage and Rates Division, accessed March 18, 2016, http://www.dol.gov/whd/minwage/americanSamoa/retail.htm.

34 In 2015 StarKist was acquired by a South Korean conglomerate, and Van Camp has since ceased operations in the territory.

35 Data from 2000 showed that over 43 percent of the local population was born outside American Sāmoa—three-quarters of which were from independent Sāmoa and Tonga (American Sāmoa Statistical Yearbook 2009, 25); Filipinos also constitute a growing demographic working in the canneries and elsewhere.

36 This may be linked to labor force participation patterns and educational attainment: just 11 percent of Samoans had attained a bachelor's degree, and of those in the workforce 43 percent were in sales, office, or service occupations that tend to earn less, compared with 23 percent in managerial or professional occupations and 24.5 percent in manufacturing, production, or construction occupations. Moreover, these occupation patterns are strongly gendered: 66.6 percent of Samoan women were found in sales, office, or service occupations compared to 22.2 percent of men; and 39.6 of men worked in manufacturing, production, or construction jobs, compared to 0.72 percent of women; 26 percent of women were in managerial or professional occupations compared to 20 percent of men (2011–2015 ACS Selected Population Tables https://factfinder.census.gov/faces/nav/jsf/pages/index.xhtml).

37 Over half of the Native Hawaiian and Other Pacific Islander population lives in Hawai'i and California; the next largest populations reside in Washington, Texas, Florida, Utah, New York, Nevada, Oregon, and Arizona. See the US Department of Health and Human Services Office of Minority Health, "Profile: Native Hawaiians/Pacific Islanders," accessed February 20, 2021, at https://minorityhealth.hhs.gov/omh/browse.aspx?lvl=3&lvlid=65. Also see Hixson, Hepler, and Kim (2012)

38 For example, Kane (2005) reported that Native Hawaiians and other Pacific Islanders are highly overrepresented, making up 249 percent more of the army recruits than the general population.

39 These calculations were part of a collaboration between Christina Kwauk, Jesse Markham, and me at the directors' invitation.

40 Isaako Aaitui, Tait Afualo, Matt Elisara, Pita Elisara, Daniel Ekuale, William Falakiseni, Joey Iosefa, Shalom Luani, Frankie Luvu, Lene Maiava, Frederick Mauigoa, Keiki Misipeka, Shaun Nua, Aiulua Fanene, Jonathan Fanene, Domata Peko, Melila Purcell Jr., Gabe Reid, Spencer Reid, Okland Salave'a, Manuia Savea, Junior Siavi'i, Iosua Siliva, Paul Soliai, Isaac Sopoaga, Logan Tago, Kurt Taufa'asau, Matt Toeaina, Simi Toeaina, Isaiah Tuiasosopo, Kasimili Uitalia, and Destiny Vaeao are among those who attended Tutuila high schools and made it to training camp of a professional league, if not further. Scores more played college football.

41 *Labor* is used here as opposed to *work* or the Samoan counterpoint *gāluega* intentionally because conceptually it has a particular genealogy tied to capital, value, and the body.

42 In the early colonial period, American and German efforts focused on transforming Samoan patterns of labor and agricultural work to align with capitalist production and encapsulated the effort of modernizing and civilizing through inculcating new values of work (see Moses 1972; Meleisea 1987).

43 See the short documentary *Warriors Born* (Taylor 2010).

44 In many ways it builds on an exceptionalist narrative that has emerged for American Sāmoa as well; this narrative sets the islands apart from others within the constellation of US empire by showcasing Samoan culture (including the fa'amatai and the land tenure system)—and US fascination with and legal protection of it—as exceptional (Uperesa and Garriga-López 2018). In direct ways it is then shared to encompass others within it, for example, in bestowing titles upon visiting DOI officials during an 'ava ceremony. Together the exceptionalism narratives reinforce the value of territorial status and work against decolonization discussions (see Uperesa 2018).

45 For example, in 2020 Juju Smith-Schuster made headlines by buying his parents a house; in the same year Tua Tagovailoa gifted a car to his mother and bought a house in Miami.

46 See also Besnier (2014), Horton (2014), and Schieder and Presterudstuen (2014).

ONE. MALAGA

1 Missoula is located on the western edge of Montana, near the Idaho border, and the name is said to be an alteration of the Salish word for the Clark Fork River (nmisuletkʷ). Rose, Juliana. 2013. "Uncover Missoula Fails to Recognize the True History of Missoula." *YWCAofMissoula.org*, October 16. The Missoula Valley is at the convergence of five mountain ranges and several rivers, and attracted early traders, missionaries, and settlers. It was the traditional home of the Bitterroot Salish (Séliš) before the land was appropriated by the United States through the Treaty of Hell's Gate in 1855 and the Flathead Indian

Reservation was simultaneously established (see Bigart and Woodcock 1996). Fort Missoula, a military encampment, was established in 1877, the Salish were removed to Flathead Reservation in the 1870s and 1880s, and the university was founded in 1893. Briggeman, Kim. 2015. "As Missoula marks 150 years, Native tribes look back further." *Missoulian*, June 28. See also Harrington (2020). For nearly a century following, the lumber industry dominated the local economy—dangerous and backbreaking labor that Tu'ufuli joined in the off-season to earn money. In 1970 Missoula had a population of just over 58,000 people (US Census).

2　It was an extremely successful season—they broke attendance records, averaging over 24,000 spectators per game (just under half the city's population). Their semifinal game against fifth-ranked Appalachian State was the highest-rated FCS playoff cable broadcast ever, championship game or otherwise, on ESPN or ESPN2. Guffey, Dave. 2009. "Griz sets FCS viewership record." *Grizzly Football News*, December 30.

3　Presented here is a composite of many hours of shared conversation over time and in different places with both parents, most unrecorded. Key details have been confirmed or triangulated with people well placed to comment, although these did not always unfold as expected (for example, when I asked about particular details on football in Sāmoa circa 1980s in one discussion with a former sports administrator who had worked closely with my father, they jokingly said, "Why are you asking me? You should ask your dad.")

4　For a social history approach to Samoans and American football that includes nodes in California, see Rob Ruck's *Tropic of Football* (2018).

5　*Honolulu Star-Bulletin*. 1952. "Samoan Families Are Reunited as Transport Arrives," July 28.

6　Local censuses enumerated the population at 19,000 in 1950 and 20,051 in 1960. The number of people who left over the course of the decade represents approximately a third of the 1960 population (Lewthwaite et al. 1972, 138). Lewthwaite et al. (1972) estimate an actual population decline of 6,000 and cite Koenig's estimate of net migration loss of more than 5,300 people.

7　See also Ahlburg and Levin (1990) and Janes (1990). Although I focus on movement from Tutuila and Manu'a (American Sāmoa), I recognize Samoans from the other islands of Western Sāmoa also emigrated to the United States, sometimes using Tutuila as a step in migration. However, the vast majority of Western Sāmoa migration went westward—to New Zealand and Australia (see, for example, Shankman 1976 and Va'a 2001).

8　Later recruits from Hawai'i included Punahou graduates Mosi Tatupu, who played for USC and had a fourteen-year career in the NFL, and Keith Uperesa, who played for BYU and after a short stint in the NFL went on to make a career as a collegiate football coach.

9　While there are structural and social dynamics specific to Hawai'i at this time, it is beyond the scope of this chapter to detail them here.

10 See Uperesa (2014b) for a discussion of the emergence of football following American developmentalist policy and infrastructure investment in Cold War–era Sāmoa. See also Ruck (2018) for a longer social history background on the adoption of American football.

11 The role of religious institutions in promoting sport in the Pacific is an understudied area deserving further research.

12 Since piecing this history together from archival materials was difficult, I rely on a series of interviews with people who were resident on island at that time; additional details are provided by Mrs. Hawkes's accounts as told to her daughter Susan Hawkes Wheeler. This account was posted as "Football in Samoa: The BYH Connection" to the Brigham Young Academy and Brigham Young University High School web page in response to Eli Saslow's (2007) *Washington Post* article on football in American Sāmoa. http://byhigh.org /History/SportsHistory/SamoanFootball.html, accessed January 8, 2015. See also Ruck (2018, 108–113).

13 Watterson (2000, 285) demonstrates that in the decades since the 1930s booster clubs generated tens of thousands of dollars for school athletics, paid athletes for "no-show" jobs, and enabled cheating scandals that reached epidemic proportions. The nascent NCAA adopted the "full ride," or athletic scholarship, in 1957 as a method of standardizing subsidies and recruiting.

14 In addition to Fitafita roots, there were church connections supporting migration. Several family names including Ah You, Anae, Ane, Apisa, Lolotai, Manumaleuna, Paopao, Reed, Salanoa, Tatupu, Tuiasosopo, and Uperesa, among others, would become synonymous with football, in part through the achievements of this era.

15 AIGA is an acronym for All Islands Getting Along and is also the Samoan word for family or kin relations.

16 In February 2010, Domata Peko and Jonathan Fanene, local graduates, along with their Cincinnati Bengals teammate Rey Maualuga, visited the islands. The Domata Peko Foundation also donated equipment to the six local high schools and to the new American Youth Football Samoa organization (Gasu 2010b). Meanwhile, Rey Maualuga and Jonathan Fanene donated over one thousand pairs of cleats to the local high schools (Gasu 2010a). On behalf of the Bengals and the Cincinnati area, the teammates donated $40,500 to the disaster relief fund for the tsunami that hit the island on September 29, 2009. Note: This was a press release originally posted to the American Samoa Government website at http://americansamoa.gov/news/2010/gov-togiola -welcomes-home-domata-peko-rey-maualuga-and-jonathan-fanene-samoan -bengals-dona (accessed March 23, 2010) but is no longer accessible; it was reposted on the AIGA Foundation blog page February 9, 2010, at http:// aigafoundation.blogspot.co.nz/2010/02/gov-togiola-welcomes-home-domata -peko.html and accessed January 19, 2018.

17 Of those, thirty-two in the NFL were Samoan, twenty-four were Tongan, seven were Hawaiian, one was Māori and one was Torres Strait Islander. For NCAA

Division I, of the estimated 483 on 2013 rosters, 54 percent were Samoan, 30 percent were Tongan, 15 percent were Hawaiian, and less than 1 percent were of Tuvaluan and Fijian ancestry. The players are drawn from twenty-one states plus the territory of American Sāmoa, Australia, Aotearoa/New Zealand, and Tonga. These are only the estimated numbers for the highest level of college football, not including other sports or NCAA Divisions II and III, the NAIA, junior colleges, and military prep academies.

18 Particular thanks to Jesse Makani Markham for tracking this detail.

19 Sabol's innovation in the coverage of professional football was one of several kinds of experimentation with football media at the time. Keith Dunnavant notes the importance of Roone Arledge at ABC in pioneering a new and entertaining style of televised college football games, which departed from the more conservative production of NBC in the 1950s. As Dunnavant (2004, 58) explains, "For nearly a decade, television had succeeded in taking the game to the fans at home. But Arledge took the viewers to the game, giving them the best seat in the house. He made them feel it, hear it, smell it, love it. In the process, he reinvented televised college football and enhanced the sport's connection to the American public. Over the years, millions of fans gravitated to college football through the portal of the televised experience, and no man shaped the game's on-air presence more dramatically than Roone Arledge." The other network television channels were inspired by his innovations, and in 1963 CBS introduced the instant replay. "Within a short period of time, instant replay, slow-motion replay, and other permutations of the original idea enhanced the sophistication of televised football, making the broadcasts from the 1950s look like home movies from the dark ages" (2004, 62).

20 Sauer, Patrick J. 2006. "How I Did It: Steve Sabol, President, NFL Films" *Inc.* http://www.inc.com/magazine/20060201/qa-sabol.html, accessed October 30, 2009.

21 Cricket was indigenized as kirikiti starting in the late 1800s, while rugby appears to have come later, in the early 1900s; see Sacks (2017, 2019).

22 American Samoa Governor (1973, 44). The reports also indicated an active community recreation program that included rugby, basketball, volleyball, softball, and marathon running; and a Summer Fun Program that included tennis, softball, basketball, calisthenics, coconut weaving, and water safety and swimming activities for children aged 8–15.

23 Thanks to Tauanu'u Lolotai for the detail here.

24 With the reorganization of the American Samoan Rugby Union in 2010 and its admission as a full member in the International Rugby Board in 2012, there have been new efforts to link local rugby to the professional circuits of mobility, movement, and capital of the international game, configured differently from the industry of American football. In time, these new efforts may challenge the dominance of the American game on Tutuila.

25 In another nod to the intergenerational engagement in the game, all three of his sons played at Southern Oregon University; his grandson Dru, raised

in California, played for Oklahoma University before joining the Minnesota Vikings and later the New York Jets.

26 See Besnier (2014); Grainger (2006, 2010); Grainger, Falcous, and Newman (2012); Guinness and Besnier (2016); Kwauk (2014, 2016); and Horton (2012, 2014) for work on sport migrations in other parts of the Pacific.

27 Although exact employment demographics are difficult to track down for the canneries, Poblete-Cross (2010) notes that in 2009 the canneries employed 87 percent non–American Samoan labor, most from Western Sāmoa, Tonga, and the Philippines. According to the 2007 US Department of Labor Economic Report, fish canning and processing employed 45 percent of the workers surveyed (at an average of $3.60 per hour), while American Samoa government employed 34 percent (up to $7.49 per hour), and retailing, wholesaling, and warehousing employed 9 percent (US Department of Labor 2007). The updated wage rates as of September 30, 2015, for the three sectors are $5.16, $4.81, and $5.00, respectively (USDOL Wage and Rates Division, http://www.dol.gov/whd/minwage/americanSamoa/retail.htm, accessed March 18, 2016).

28 This stands in contrast to investment in infrastructure supporting transnational sport labor movement in other places, such as in baseball in the Dominican Republic (Klein 1991, 2009) and globally (Klein 2006), or soccer in Africa (Darby 2000, 2012, 2013; Darby and Akindes 2007; Darby and Solberg 2010; Esson 2013).

29 Because a school may be the only one in the area, it can draw on deep place-based and kinship loyalties. Historically, Samoana and Leone High Schools had an intense rivalry as early eastern-western representatives. More recently, Faga'itua High School has come to represent the eastern side, while Samoana draws heavily from the central Ma'opūtasi District. While this appeal to village, district, and family ties applies for several of the schools on island, it isn't always the case: Fa'asaō and Marist High Schools (once separate, now combined) offered a private parochial school option that drew students from all over the island.

30 See Okamura (2008) on ethnic inequality in Hawai'i. Haole is a descriptive local term that has become synonymous with white, and when used pejoratively often marks (cultural) foreignness and privilege or entitlement.

31 Yuen, Stacy. 2013. "Which Ethnic Group Makes the Most Money?" *Hawaii Business*, October.

32 Included are Mac Ane, Li'a Amisone, Lutero Fiso, Ed Imo, Peter Gurr, Rachel Jennings, Ethan Lake, Lino Letuli, Ace Logo, Jason Mageo, Simon Mageo, Mataese Mataese, Tumua Matu'u, Keiki Misipeka, Fata and Vanu Moe, Pati Pati Jr., Okland Salave'a, Samoa Samoa, Elia Savali, Time Sitala, Brian Smart, Meki Solomona, Suaese "Pooch" Ta'ase, Tupulua "Bone" Ta'ase, and Francis Tuitele, among many others.

33 This is a base salary that does not include signing bonuses, roster bonuses, or any incentives built into the player contract. Minimum base salaries are set on a sliding scale by accrued years a player has played in the league. Steinberg,

Leigh. 2020. "Leigh Steinberg: Explaining the NFL System of Rookie Contracts." *Touchdown Wire*, June 1.

34 Torre, Pablo O. 2009. "How (and Why) Athletes Go Broke." *Sports Illustrated*, March 23. In their 2015 National Bureau of Economic Research working paper, Carlson and colleagues found a slightly different outcome, focusing only on bankruptcies. Based on all players drafted into the NFL 1996–2003, over 15 percent had filed for bankruptcy, and their projection analyses show it could reach 40 percent of the sample as the years pass. They found that initial bankruptcy filings began soon after retirement and overall bankruptcy rates were not affected either by player's total earnings or career length.

TWO. FOOTBALL, TAUTUA, AND FAʻASĀMOA

1 This is a ceremonial role (often, but not always) performed by women, and in this context entails the ritual mixing of the ʻava.

2 The most notable exception is the Samoa Bowl, where connection between home and diaspora, and the opportunity for sons of Sāmoa abroad to return to the homeland and experience part of Samoan culture are articulated components of the event.

3 On localization/indigenization see also Appadurai (1995) on the nationalist meaning of cricket in India, James (1963) on the importance of cricket as a local game in the British West Indies under British colonialism, and Leach (1975) on the adaptation of cricket in the Trobriand Islands. Sacks (2019) provides a compelling account of the transformation of cricket into kirikiti in Sāmoa as an example of sport as a zone of contact and indigenization. Uperesa (2021) provides a survey of several different Indigenous contexts to highlight long-standing historical and emergent engagements with sport forms, with a focus on Indigenous sport for sovereignty and recognition, claiming and transforming colonial sport, and shifting gender dynamics.

4 This saying has been memorialized in the best-selling Samoan song of all time by Felise Mikaele, "Tama Samoa," which was inspired by the Manu Sāmoa's performance in the 1991 World Cup. The song lyrics are "ia pōuliuli lou tino ʻae mālamalama lau vaʻai / Tama a Samoa, seʻia tafetoto ou ala." The last segment is sometimes excluded, and it is translated here as may your path flow with blood (of your enemies). A slightly different translation is given by Salesa (2010, 344): "roughly, 'Your body may be dark/unknowing, your eyes can see/are enlightened.'" He goes on to cite the "Mavaega Feula a Feʻepo" ("A ū mai lou tua ia eʻeli ou vae ia pōuliuli lou tino a ʻia malamalama ou mata, ma ʻia tafe toto ou ala") provided in Tauiliili (2009, 47). Notably, pōuliuli and mālamama are significant terminologies, as they are also used to refer to the (pre-Christian) days of darkness and (Christian) enlightenment.

5 There are growing gridiron leagues in Aotearoa New Zealand, Australia, Japan, Tonga, and other countries, but the game remains largely an American phenomenon. This may change in the future, especially with high-profile

sport switching such as the kind Jarred Hayne accomplished in his brief move from rugby league to gridiron football and Jordan Mailata's recruitment to the NFL from Australia. Investment in the sporting infrastructure (such as New Zealand's return of a portion of sport gambling profits to each sport) may also shift the profile of the sport in those places. In independent Sāmoa there have been intermittent efforts to foster the gridiron game to channel young men to US colleges and universities. In Tonga, efforts toward a Tonga Bowl and connecting Tongan youth in the diaspora and home islands through American football have also been underway.

6   Based on a historical analysis of ethnographic works and archives related to Sāmoa, Tcherkézoff (2000) argues that the chiefly system that exists today emerged in the early twentieth century. Between 1870 and 1930, and as a result of interaction between Samoans and foreigners, the notion of title holder denoted by matai became firmly established. This appears to have been a gradual merger between the egalitarian notion of family or household head with the old notion of sacred chief (prior to that period *matai* referred to craft specialists, like the tattooist, and family heads) coupled with a general leveling of the hierarchy of titles.

7   This transformation is neither predetermined nor seamless, and can be a significant source of conflict and tension. For example, in the above-mentioned text Tcherkézoff examines three contemporary paradoxes in political ideology in independent Sāmoa (the fa'amatai and democracy; semi-universal suffrage; a three-layered system of government) and points out that relevant tensions exist between village- and national-level politics and authority as well as between those with access to salaries, the state system, and development largesse versus those without.

8   Shore (1982, 59) explains, "If asked to suggest the single most important pillar upon which their culture rested, most Samoans would probably respond without hesitation that it was their system of chiefs. In an important sense, the existence of their culture for Samoans is predicated on those institutions and practices associated with chiefs in which Samoan culture—the *fa'a-Samoa*—finds its most elegant distillation."

9   On the fa'amatai in independent Sāmoa see, for example, Freeman (1983), O'Meara (1990), Macpherson (1997), Macpherson and Macpherson (2009), Meleisea (1987, 1995), Shore (1982), Tchérkezoff (1998, 2000), Sapolu et al. (2012), Schoeffel (1981, 1987, 1995), and Va'ai (1999). In the diaspora, for Australia see Lafoa'i (2007) and Va'a (2001); for New Zealand see Hunkin (2007) and especially Cluny Macpherson's body of work on ethnicity and identity (e.g., 1985, 1991, 2004); and in the United States see Ablon (1971), Franco (1991), and McGrath (2002). On the matai system in Tutuila and Manu'a see Ember (1962), Fa'aleava (2003), Holmes (1958, 1974), Holmes and Holmes (1992), Keesing (1931; 1934), Tiffany (1971), Tiffany and Tiffany (1978), and Sēloti (2007). See also the collections edited by Huffer and So'o (2000) and So'o (2007), and Anae et al. (2017) on transnational matai.

10 Loosely translated as "love is a difficult thing."

11 Texts include Vaʻai (1999), ʻAiono (1997), Huffer and Qalo (2004), and Tui Atua (1994, 2000, 2006a, 2006b, 2007).

12 Saleimoa Vaʻai (1992, 42) points out three kinds of generic pule: *pule faʻavae* or constitutive authority vested in the founding entity of the village; *pule faʻasoa* or distributive authority exercised by matai usually in relation to family resources; and *pule faʻamalumalu* or protective authority, the domain of all in the village. See also Holmes (1958, 12) on the pule of matai as a kind of administrative authority.

13 Tautua is often translated as service but may also be used to refer to someone who serves. Drawing on Tofaeono (2000, 300), Nofoaiga (2020) notes two important meanings of tautua: "First it identifies the servant status and role of untitled men in the Samoan chiefly system. Second, it expresses the moral value of serving the family. Thus, *tautua* as the culture of service in Samoa is a family-based social and cultural status, role, value, and practice, which views the needs, rights, and roles of people in the family and community as primary" (62).

14 In his autobiography *I Gave My Heart to San Francisco*, he recounts being "stunned" by His Highness Malietoa Tanumafili II bestowing the high chief title of Seiuli on him in recognition of his accomplishments and genealogical ties (2012, 24).

15 This is often though not always the case, especially where titles are split among multiple holders and there is a tacit understanding that the title bestowal is recognizing achievement and tying the individual to the larger family group without significant expectations of monetary or in-kind contributions.

16 This appears to be more common in independent Sāmoa where titles can be split among multiple holders, as opposed to American Sāmoa where there are a finite number of titles due to the freezing of title registries by the US government in the early twentieth century.

17 Sometimes this is a prominent motivation early in their journey, but it may become more important later as they are further into adulthood and expectations have shifted.

18 Minor details have been changed to preserve anonymity.

19 It is common to suppress expression of feelings of resentment when they are not socially acceptable.

20 As Robert Franco points out, kinship relations are made and unmade through demonstrations of alofa and tautua in the form of contributions of labor or goods. "A major component of this service was productive work in such areas as cultivation, carpentry, fishing, fine mat making, and tattooing. In addition to these work activities, an individual served his ʻāiga and matai by consistently contributing resources to important ceremonial events, and by actively participating in the preparation for, and the conducting of these events. Thus, work was integral to making and maintaining kin relations in old Samoa. Without work, without working together, kinship relations would lapse, and

perhaps disappear." Thus, kinship is materialized in and through various forms of labor (Franco 1991, 21).

21 Still, "Tamasese cautions, a key point to remember is that the requirement of true service implicit in the principle of *tautua* is expected from the untitled to the titled" (Suaalii-Sauni 2007, 40).

22 The entities to which one feels called to tautua express one's sense of identity and location in relationship to others (usually families or villages), and is an index of their social locations and roles. Fa'asinomaga, usually translated as identity, signifies one's standing, connections, and obligations, and is located in place and space. Historically it was in relation to particular villages or churches, but as Nofoaiga (2020) suggests, with the vast Samoan diaspora today it is more likely to emphasize Samoan cultural aspects and "can be extended to other spaces and places" incorporating connections to "a new land, home, people, culture, language, and relationships" (65).

23 See also Schieder and Presterudstuen (2014) on changing assessments of i-taukei Fijian sport migrants abroad or Guinness and Besnier (2016, 135) on strategies of avoidance for demands by extended kin.

24 Audio clip accessed September 8, 2015, at http://www.talanei.com/pages /21675807.php.

THREE. PRODUCING THE GRIDIRON WARRIOR

1 As of 2012, *Sports Illustrated* was among the top fifteen magazines by circulation, claiming a readership of nearly 3.175 million. Sasseen, Jane, Katerina-Eva Matsa, and Amy Mitchell. 2013. *State of the News Media.* Pew Research Center. Accessed on April 18, 2015.

2 The Pacific Hall was created and curated under the direction of the most famous ethnographer of Sāmoa, Margaret Mead. The hall was created in 1970 and reinstalled in 1984, several years after her death (Harding and Martin 2016, accessed November 19, 2019, http://anthronow.com/print/anthropology -now-and-then-in-the-american-museum-of-natural-history). As of 2019 it had remained untouched by major innovations in museum practice and critiques of ethnographic representation.

3 See Gilson (1970), Kennedy (1974), and Masterman (1934).

4 For a critical discussion of the framing of American Sāmoa in this segment and more widely in US developmentalist discourses and policy, see Uperesa (2014b).

5 See Hokowhitu (2014) on the use of Māori haka and indigenous masculine culture in the branding of the New Zealand All Blacks rugby team; Tengan and Markham (2009) on the use of Hawaiian culture and imaginaries of indigenous masculinities, including the newly styled ha'a, in the rebranding of the UH Warriors football team; and Tengan (2008, 2014) on resurgent martial arts, woodcarving, and cultural ceremonies for Native Hawaiian men in the Hale Mua ("Men's House").

6 While a detailed overview of this literature is beyond the current scope, Spitulnik (1997), Mahon (2000), and Ginsburg, Abu-Lughod, and Larkin (2002) offer excellent overviews of these developments.

7 Here I draw on Edward Said's landmark treatise on representation and power in/over the East. In it, he explored the different ways the East as the Orient was constructed for Western audiences and the ways those representations were shaped by existing colonial power relations and continued to shape them to sustain power of the Occident over the Orient (1994 [1978]).

8 In completing final edits of this book I found Heather Waldroup's PhD thesis, and although her dissertation is focused on the "racialized and sexualized formation situated in the tropical islands of the eastern Pacific and drawing on historical and cultural treatments specific to these islands" (2004, 3) using Paul Gauguin and Paul Theroux's work specifically, the larger framing of Polynesianism resonates with my own analysis of the Polynesian imaginary and its use in telling the story of Samoans in American football.

9 *Polynesian Power* web promo, posted by Pacific Islanders in Communications, June 19, 2002. https://www.youtube.com/watch?v=5NZ7ec8HjxU, accessed September 8, 2006.

10 Vili the Warrior was the mascot for UH Warrior Football throughout the 2000s, and was performed by Vili Fehoko.

11 For a more developed discussion of football discipline and the production of docile bodies, see Uperesa (2018).

12 See Arvin (2015, 2019) for a critical discussion of the scientific construction of "the Polynesian race" and its proximity to Whiteness.

13 It is worth noting that in this context the lack of mixture with Whites has maintained Polynesian physical superiority, whereas historically it has been understood that this same lack of mixture maintained intellectual or cognitive inferiority (increased mixture with Whites was alleged to increase intellectual ability); see Kauanui (2008).

14 Sonny, Julian. 2014. "Inside Football Island: How Samoa Is Breeding the World's Best Football Stars," Elite Daily, April 2. http://elitedaily.com/sports/inside-football-island-samoa-breeding-worlds-best-football-stars/, accessed March 25, 2015; and "Why Polynesians Are Genetically Engineered to Be the Best Football Players in the World," Elite Daily, October 1. http://elitedaily.com/sports/polynesians-genetically-engineered-best-football-players/778724/, accessed March 25, 2015.

15 To my knowledge there is no scientific evidence to support this claim, and I am not aware of any current studies investigating this linkage between genetic material and athletic performance for Polynesians generally or Samoans specifically. There is past research that suggested shifting BMI ranges for Polynesians to take account of higher muscle and bone mass (see Rush et al. 1997 or Swinburn et al. 1999); however, other more recent publications specifically on Polynesian bones are based on outdated and spotty material, and full of

conjecture (see for example Stride 2016). Moreover, the frame expected of different positions (a lineman versus a wide receiver, for example) varies widely.

16 The population in American Sāmoa tends to be bigger than that in independent Sāmoa, and those in the diaspora larger than those raised in the islands. Scholars have linked this to the availability of carbohydrate- and animal product–rich diets. Hannah et al. (1986) reported that the twentieth century brought an increased consumption of dietary energy from imported foods, with Samoans in Hawai'i consuming the most and those in Sāmoa consuming the least, and those in American Sāmoa in between. Brewis et al. (1998) found that Samoans in New Zealand (Auckland) were significantly larger than those in independent Sāmoa. See also Bindon and Baker (1985), Galanis et al. (1999), McGarvey (1991), and Singer (2014).

17 While Samoans and other Polynesians have been moving into different positions in recent years (some very high-profile, like Heisman Trophy winner Marcus Mariota and college football national championship winner and title game MVP Tua Tagovailoa), several coaches in Sāmoa noted to me that off-island coaches overwhelmingly recruit local players for lineman positions.

18 See, for example, Beamon and Messer (2013), Carrington (2010), Hartmann (2000), Leonard (2006), and Smith (2007).

19 Racial stacking in sports refers to the influence of racial bias and stereotypes on the allocation of players to positions (for example, the view of White players as more intellectual and therefore more fitting for the quarterback position).

20 See Hokowhitu (2004) for a similar argument about colonial legacies and Māori sportsmen.

21 See, for example, the films *Coach Carter, Hoop Dreams,* and countless profiles of Black athletes.

22 See *A Community of Contrasts: Native Hawaiians & Pacific Islanders in the United States* (2014) on social indicators for Pacific Islander communities in the US context.

23 See Uperesa and Garriga-López (2017) for a discussion of these alternating representations and how they were used to attenuate sovereignty in American Sāmoa in the early twentieth century.

24 This affinity for physical aggression is explained by Richard Goodman (1990) as a response to social practices in a hierarchical society in which socially inappropriate individual feelings or emotions are forcefully contained, and the resulting feelings of anger and resentment find an outlet in more acceptable situations (such as in a peer group). The kind of aggressive performance against peers that is valued on the field is discouraged in interactions with those of higher rank or age where deference is important. In other examples, players may channel frustrations with strict family discipline into their sport play.

25 Cases like player assaults at WSU in 2016 have raised the issue of how implicit bias impacts the way young Pacific Islander men are treated in disciplinary or criminal cases involving physical violence. See Loh, Stephanie. 2017. "Review

finds no evidence of racial bias in WSU conduct board cases, including that of former Cougars DL Robert Barber." *Seattle Times*, March 1.

26 Some might expect this in settler colonial societies like New Zealand, Australia, and the United States where educational curricula show a bias toward White middle-class competencies, but in Sāmoa Christina Kwauk also found sports being increasingly narrated as a legitimate alternative to schooling success (2014). The difference is, in Sāmoa students are still expected to achieve in schooling, but sport (linked as it is to New Zealand or Australian sporting circuits, which do not require the intertwining with academics) is now seen as an escape for school-leavers. Kwauk asks whether the increasingly recognized sport route is influencing students to prematurely opt out of the schooling track. See also Irwin and Umemoto (2012, 15).

27 "Samoan Youth: Ensuring Our Success." uploaded by Vaun Raymond, May 14, 2012. https://www.youtube.com/watch?v=SAFYJnbJHZY, accessed February 10, 2018. See also player interviews featured in Morita (2013).

28 Morris, Cathy. 2016. "Challenging perceptions: Portrait of a researcher." Burke Museum. https://www.burkemuseum.org/news/challenging-perceptions -portrait-researcher, accessed February 10, 2018.

29 While views on male and female sports participation have been changing, generally this has meant that sport prowess has become a marker of ideal masculinity for boys, while for girls it can run counter to expectations for mainstream Western ideal femininity or cast them as masculinized. The kinds of sports boys and girls play are also highly gendered in some areas, with overlap in others (e.g., basketball or soccer vs. football/cheer or baseball/ softball). See also Messner (2009) and George (2005). In contrast to dominant Western gender ideologies that historically framed (White) women as helpless, damsels-in-distress, dainty, or placed on a pedestal, the different roles women play in Samoan society reflect expectations of strength, resourcefulness, service, responsibility, and integrity (see Fairbairn-Dunlop 1998; Schoeffel 1979; Shore 1981; Simanu-Klutz 2011).

30 Note that Title IX enforcement and expansion has dramatically increased high school and college opportunities for girls since 1972, but professional opportunities are still vastly unequal.

31 See also Dewey (2006), Guinness and Besnier (2014), Kanemasu and Molnar (2013), and Molnar and Kanemasu (2014) on rugby success representing empowerment for Fijian communities.

32 Dvorchak, Robert. 2006. "Steelers Victory Had Everything, Including a Bizarre Hair Tackle." *Pittsburgh Post-Gazette*.

33 The website address was: http://www.polamalusports.com (accessed on September 10, 2008). It appears to have been taken over by another entity.

34 "Meet the Biggest Man in the NFL Draft [Danny Shelton [Vlog 1]," uploaded by Grit Media March 4, 2015. https://www.youtube.com/watch?v =txjwPRm8HuY, accessed February 10, 2018.

35 In interviews Shelton has noted that his mother is Samoan, and his father is Peruvian.

36 As a student, Shelton taught a class for freshmen, was active and vocal about study-abroad opportunities for student-athletes, and contributed to museum exhibits (earning the Burke Nerd Award by the Burke Museum for his engagement during his time at UW). He connects his research with the tānoa held by the museum with his own tānoa tatau in the short video "Tattoos as a way of connecting to culture," https://www.youtube.com/watch?v=t9Daz_uhRmU, accessed November 17, 2020. Thanks to Professor Holly Barker for sharing some of the detail included here.

37 "Marcus Mariota Delivers Hearfelt Heismn Trophy Acceptance Speech," uploaded by mrrustyduck, January 19, 2017. https://www.youtube.com/watch?v=WecP61wLfnk, accessed November 17, 2021.

38 I saw the trophy in person in April 2016 thanks to Chris Young; see also Hinnen (2015) for a description.

39 "Beats Audio PowerBeats2 Wireless TV Commercial, 'Ohana' Featuring Marcus Mariota." https://www.ispot.tv/ad/7hOY/beats-audio-powerbeats2-wireless-ohana-featuring-marcus-mariota, accessed November 17, 2021.

40 Translation courtesy of Hawaiian music and culture expert Aaron Salā. Note: the audio on the commercial has some inaudible sections, so this is an approximate translation given.

41 "NFL Commercial, 'Football is Family' Featuring Marcus Mariota." https://www.ispot.tv/ad/AoCz/nfl-football-is-family-featuring-marcus-mariota, accessed July 15, 2016.

42 Much appreciation to Keith Camacho for pointing this out.

FOUR. GRIDIRON CAPITAL

1 The executive director, Doris Sullivan, has since retired and PIAA officially closed in 2016. Its place has been filled with organizations like Education 1st, based in Lāʻie, Hawaiʻi.

2 In the context of body quantification via objective assessments, body discourses and subjective assessments are key to scouting and prospect rankings (Silva, Bower, and Cipolli III 2018).

3 Historian Theresa Runstedler (2018) notes that the defunding of social programs, including after-school, enrichment, and athletics, in the 1990s opened the way for a slew of leagues, clinics, and so forth that comprised a new way of generating money not only in brokering access/recruitment but in services and sponsorships for coaches and teams.

4 Chapter 4 of Okamura (2008) discusses the underfunding of public schools in Hawaiʻi, which contributes to the state having the highest percentage of K–12 enrollment in private schools (71). For families who cannot afford to place their children in private school, sport performance is a well-known strategy for accessing those schools through scholarships starting at the intermediate school level.

5 A 2017 revision to NCAA bylaw 13 governing recruiting applies different restrictions to different program levels and sports. For example, it allows

coaches at institutional camps and clinics (both their own and those at other NCAA four-year member institutions) but not at noninstitutional, privately owned camps or clinics—a policy the PIAA protested.

6 A pseudonym.

7 Witness the number of stories carried by media outlets each year regarding coaches and parents of elementary- and high school–age children who are obsessed with winning.

8 See, for example, Tengan and Markham (2009) on the University of Hawai'i Warriors' marketing of pan-Polynesian identity.

9 Lieber, Jill. 1989. "Maximum Exposure." *Sports Illustrated*, May 1.

10 This can be seen, for example, in a variety of debates over surrogate motherhood, paid adoption, and bans on organ sales.

11 See, for example, Harvey (2006, 2007); Sassen (1990); and Wilson (2011).

12 Sociologist Lucia Trimbur's research on boxing and value generated through sport labor at a gym in Brooklyn, New York, found that boxing became an anchor for many African American male participants. In addition to providing an opportunity for making money through professionalization or coaching, it provided a time outlet for many underemployed men, access to networks, and a measure of control over their lives. For some locked out of opportunities in the postindustrial city, she argues, the labor of boxing replaced economic labor by providing an alternative source of value (building reputations, for example). Some aspect of her arguments resonate here: namely, how sport is used by some to generate value and masculine currency, with the pursuit of gridiron capital moderated by recourse to other frames of value (including community and culture). However, the window of opportunity for football (generally early to mid-adulthood) and its placement in relation to college and professional opportunities means that it is generally not a replacement for economic labor in the way boxing might be for some. While football serves as an alternative source of value in ways that may overlap with the boxers featured in Trimbur's work, particularly for those who go on to coach or volunteer, the primary thrust for players remains economic and capital convertibility within a constrained window of opportunity.

13 Players who "walk on" are non-scholarship players; typically, there is an opportunity for them to earn a scholarship by proving their value to the team, but scholarships are never guaranteed.

14 Here I am speaking specifically about the NFL and its recruiting grounds in the upper echelons of the college game, but it is recognized that youth sports generate significant value as well.

15 In a significant shift, and following state legislation changes and the US Supreme Court's findings of antitrust violation, the NCAA adopted a "uniform interim policy suspending NCAA name, image and likeness rules for all incoming and current student-athletes in all sports" across its three divisions in June 2021. The updated guidance allows students, in line with the applicable state law in which their school is located, to monetize NIL activities and use

agents if desired, and mandates reporting their activities in compliance with state law or school and conference requirements. This interim policy will stay in effect until the NCAA adopts new rules or federal legislation is passed. Hosick, Michelle Brutlag. 2021. "NCAA Adopts Interim Name, Image, and Likeness Policy."NCAA. https://www.ncaa.org/about/resources/media-center/news/ncaa-adopts-interim-name-image-and-likeness-policy (June 30), accessed 20 November 2021.

16 The item is "fetishized": the conditions of its production are hidden, including any relations of exploitation within which it was produced; it is divorced from other commodities, and embodies within it only the future possibilities of use and meaning (Marx 1990, 168–169).

17 Simplifying somewhat Karl Marx's foundational writings on commodities, he describes a process of capital accumulation whereby commodity items are produced for sale, increasingly en masse, in order to produce profit. The ability to accumulate profit on sales depends at the most basic level on the ability to charge more for a product than it costs to produce it, and thereby generate profit from labor. This, in turn, depends on workers' productivity stretching longer throughout the day to produce more than the value of their labor wages (Marx 1990, 643–654). Increasing profit margins depends on the ability to ratchet up the price of the commodity item by inflating what consumers will pay for the item (or exchange value) beyond what the basic use (use value) of the item might be. Today, the higher prestige built up around a name brand—the more valuable it is seen to be, or the more necessary a product is made out to be, the more consumers might be willing to pay for the item or establish an association with the brand.

18 They may also shape them in other ways: stereotypes surrounding family obligations as a barrier to performance or the potential for criminal behavior can shape views of Polynesian athletes generally and in NFL interviews and evaluation in the recruitment/draft process specifically (Dufur and Feinberg 2009; see also Grainger 2006).

19 This ranges from the radical difference between player, coaching, administration, and owner ranks (Kukahiko 2015; Oates and Durham 2004; see also the TIDES Racial and Gender Report Card https://www.tidesport.org/); to symbolic racism in NFL labor markets (Dufur and Feinberg 2009) and racially charged or stereotypical framing in media commentary (Mercurio and Filak 2010; Billings 2004); to widely used assessments like the Wonderlic Personnel Test that have racially disparate impacts and whose use and result interpretations have been questioned (Bosco and Allen 2011; Matthews and Lassiter 2007); to adopting policies that limit Black cultural expression in the game (Brown 2017).

20 Maguire (2005) describes the development of the sports-industrial complex as a process of "sportization" undergirded by scientific development wherein state and sports organizations funded research into enhanced sport performance. In this process, "the demands of competitive sport—the achievement of records,

and 'winning' outcomes" were paramount, squeezing out "research into human well-being, the quality of the sport experience and aesthetic values" (160). He notes that the "complex, or figuration, has several dimensions—structural, institutional, ideological, and cultural" (162). Earl Smith (2014) uses the term *athletic industrial complex* (drawing on C. Wright Mills and President Dwight Eisenhower's use of *military-industrial complex*) to examine the role of sports in the economy, and the impacts on education when colleges and universities have tried to leverage sport profits through conference realignment. Drawing on Smith, Runstedtler argues that the athletic industrial complex "is designed to produce failure and that it relies on continued race and class inequality and capitalizes on the logics and effects of neoliberalism" (2018, 166).

21 For example, see Beamon (2008), Beamon and Bell (2011), Edwards (1976, 1985), Hawkins (2010), and endless scandals involving collegiate athletics and academics. In popular media, see for example Branch, Taylor. 2011. "The Shame of College Sports." *The Atlantic*, October.

22 Big Boyz allows taller and heavier boys who would otherwise be excluded by the Pop Warner height-weight restrictions.

23 *USA Today*. 2021. "Who are the highest-paid college football coaches? These are the top five salaries." https://www.usatoday.com/story/sports/ncaaf/2021/11/08/highest-paid-college-football-coach-salaries/6319667001/, accessed November 11, 2021.

24 College Football Playoff website, "Revenue Distribution" http://www.collegefootballplayoff.com/revenue-distribution accessed on November 26, 2020.

25 Kirwan, William E., and R. Gerald Turner. 2009. "Playoffs Not the Answer to College Football's Financial Crisis." *Washington Post* (December 19), A17.

26 Among Division I programs, "In total, only 25 athletics departments' generated revenues exceeded their expenses in 2018–19—all were in autonomy five conferences—and the median surplus at those schools was $7.9 million. While 29 athletics departments reported positive generated net revenue in fiscal year 2018, the median number of schools to do so in a given fiscal year from 2005 to 2019 is 24." See http://www.ncaa.org/about/resources/research/finances-intercollegiate-athletics, accessed November 25, 2020.

27 This sentiment has been expressed directly to me by many of my college students in "revenue" sports.

28 The graduation success rate (GSR) of the program Mark hoped to join was just 47 percent for the 1999–2002 cohorts, trailing behind the Division I Football Bowl Subdivision, which posted an average graduation success rate of 67 percent for football as opposed to 79 percent for all student-athletes.

29 There are many, many coaches who care deeply about the welfare of student-athletes and dedicate their lives to their work. But here I am concerned with the difficult decisions they often have to make related to calculations of player contribution and value, particularly at the top levels of the game where they

work under tremendous pressure and with money, careers, and reputations at stake.

30 Stereotype threat refers to the risk of confirming negative stereotypes about individuals from minoritized or stigmatized groups negatively affecting their performance (see Steele and Aronsen 1995).

31 See also Carter (2013) on how sport migrants produce their own mobility by forging connections between localities and leveraging networks.

FIVE. "FAʻAMĀLOSI!"

1 Ferro, Shaunacy. 2013. "Does CTE, the Brain Disease Found in NFL Players, Really Exist?" *Popular Science*. Last Modified August 13.

2 Boston University Chronic Traumatic Encephalopathy (CTE) Center. "Frequently Asked Questions about CTE." https://www.bu.edu/cte/about /frequently-asked-questions/, accessed November 15, 2021.

3 Stern et al. (2021) write, "Future research examining the roles of cognitive reserve, genetics, and environmental factors in determining resilience to clinical manifestations and the progression of p-tau pathology will help elucidate the pathobiology of CTE."

4 With this knowledge, new research is exploring how repetitive head injuries predict later issues like depression, apathy, and cognitive impairment later in life (Montenigro et al. 2017), and whether age of exposure is significant (Stamm et al. 2015).

5 Ellison, Riki. 2012. "Junior Seau's Position Exacerbated His Condition, Former NFL Player Says." *Los Angeles Times*, May 10.

6 See Tengan (2008a) for a discussion of contemporary indigenous Hawaiian masculinities elaborated in and through US military service. See also Camacho and Monnig (2010) on the intertwining of militarization and masculinization of Chamorro men in the US military.

7 This follows a pattern pointed out by Faʻaleava (2003) in his own research on the Fitafita, or local Samoan contingent of the US Navy in Tutuila. He argued that in the first half of the twentieth century, the Fitafita was elevated to a kind of national ʻaumaga, and membership was a source of great prestige (not to mention wages and access to goods through the military post exchange). It eventually became an unwritten requirement for a matai title. The military, and other restricted opportunities in the cash economy, disproportionately favored male access to money and prestige, and in turn restricted women's ability to participate in official politics and the market economy. See also Holmes (1958, 46) on gender bias in ideas about formal education for women versus men.

8 I thank Daniel Tuiasosopo for assistance in translating and interpreting the song lyrics.

9 A more literal translation could be "I support you through prayer," but this context suggests battle is more apt.

10 *Faiva* is a word for fishing, but metaphorically can refer to plans and in this context wishing one success.

11 An exhortation to remember the two things that you will need in battle.

12 See also Diaz (2002, 2011) on the articulation of indigenous Pacific masculinities in and through American football.

13 The concept of the relational self is described usefully by Bush et al. (2009, 142): "It is a total being comprising spiritual, physical and mental elements which cannot be separated. It derives its sense of wholeness, sacredness and uniqueness from its place of belonging in family and village, genealogy, language, land environment and culture." Marsters and Tiatia-Seath (2019a, 251) note that "While many young Pacific peoples in New Zealand may lean toward more contemporary perceptions of mental wellbeing, the holistic and collectivist concept of wellbeing remains for Pacific youth." This can be usefully applied in the US context as well.

14 Stites, Adam. 2017. "How Does the NFL's Concussion Protocol Work?" www.sbnation.com. Last Modified January 8, 2017, accessed April 21, 2017. http://www.sbnation.com/nfl/2016/9/18/12940926/nfl-concussion-protocol -explained.

15 See, for example, "What is Heads Up Football?," posted on the USA Football YouTube channel in December 2013. https://www.youtube.com/watch?v =SwEN9JvZJE8, accessed November 15, 2021.

16 Cobb et al. (2013) noted an increasing trend of linear acceleration magnitude and impact frequency from youth to high school to college football as a result of increased practice/game time as well as increased size, athleticism, and aggression with higher levels of play. Meanwhile, the 2017 study collaboration between VA Boston Healthcare System and Boston University School of Medicine, noted earlier in this chapter, found that in their convenience sample of 202 brains subjects, 21 percent of high school, 91 percent of college, and 99 percent of NFL players had developed CTE (Mez et al. 2017).

17 According to the program's website, "Pop Warner Little Scholars, Inc. (PWLS) is a non-profit organization that provides youth football and cheer & dance programs across 42 states and several countries around the world" (http:// www.popwarner.com/About_Us.htm, accessed April 21, 2017). While in 2017 the site claimed 325,000 participants among their football, cheer, and dance programs, this was down from the 400,000 figure cited three years earlier. In the United States there are Pop Warner tackle football leagues starting at age 5, but the program in American Sāmoa is for 11–14-year-old youth. Begun in 2009 with four teams by parents wanting a youth football option, it claimed 1,400 participants as of 2019. Gasu, Tony. 2019. "AYFS Celebrates Tenth Anniversary to Kick Off the 2019 Football Season." *Samoa News*, January 23. https://www.samoanews.com/sports/ayfs-celebrates-10th-anniversary-kick -2019-football-season, accessed November 15, 2021.

18 Pielke, Roger. 2020. "The Decline of Football is Real and It's Accelerating." *Forbes*, January 28.

19 Poll, HBO Real Sports/Marist. November 22, 2016. *Reports About Football-Related Heat Injuries Impacting Youth Football.* Marist College Institute for Public Opinion. Poughkeepsie, New York. http://maristpoll.marist.edu/wp-content/misc/usapolls/us160915_MCC_RS/HBO%20Real%20Sports_Marist%20Poll_National%20Summary%20of%20Findings%20and%20Tables_Youth%20Football_November%202016.pdf, accessed October 2, 2019.

20 Schwarz, Alan. 2016. "N.F.L.-Backed Youth Program Says It Reduced Concussions. The Data Disagrees." *New York Times*, July 28.

21 See also Kerr et al. (2015).

22 This included restricting contact to one-third of practice time and eliminating full-speed head-on drills where the players were more than three yards away from each other at the start of the drill, see http://www.popwarner.com/Default.aspx?tabid=1476228.

23 Another study released around the same time, which followed a Michigan high school team over a season, investigated how the new rule changes limiting collision practices to twice a week after seasonal play had begun would affect head-impact exposure. The authors found it reduced impact exposure by 42 percent across all players in the season, "with practice-exposure declines occurring among linemen (46% decline); receivers, cornerbacks, and safeties (41% decline); and tight ends, running backs (including fullbacks), and linebackers (39% decline)" (Broglio et al. 2016, 511).

24 Including AIGA affiliates Isamu Falevai Jr., More Suesue, and Joey Thomas (then California high school coaches), Troy Lau (then Prodigy Athletes coach), Reno Mahe (former Philadelphia Eagles player), Jesse Markham, Tevita (Tee) 'Ofahengaue (former Arizona Cardinals player), Taeao Salima, Damien Satete (former US Naval Academy player), Manu Savea (former University of Arizona player), the late Pastor Titus Tuiasosopo, and Lenny Vandermade (former USC player and later a USC staff member), and many others.

25 The first class of inductees also included Olin Kreutz (University of Washington/Chicago Bears); Jack Thompson (Washington State University/Washington Redskins), the first Samoan quarterback to play in the NFL; Kevin Mawae (Louisiana State University/Tennessee Titans), the first president of the NFL Players Association of Pacific Islander descent, and the first to be elected twice; Kenny Niumatalolo (University of Hawai'i–Mānoa/US Naval Academy head coach), who was the first Samoan collegiate head coach at any level and first Pacific Islander head coach of an NCAA Division I football program; and Herman Wedemeyer (St. Mary's College/AAFC player), Hawai'i's first All-American football player.

26 The settlement was revised again after former players objected to the 2014 settlement. Under the terms of the 2015 ruling all retired players, not just the class that sued the league, would be covered under terms that removed the overall cap and included all NFL veterans. "The settlement provides payments of up to $5 million to players who have one of a handful of severe neurological

disorders, medical monitoring for all players to determine if they qualify for a payment and $10 million for education about concussions" (Belson 2015). However, players could opt out and attempt to reach alternative settlements with the NFL, and at least 200 players, including Junior Seau's family, did so. As of May 3, 2021, the registered class settlement members numbered 20,558, with the payable monetary award totaling over $847 million, covering almost 40 percent of initial claim packages submitted. See https://www.nflconcussionsettlement.com/.

27 He seems to be referring to those who played before 1993, when a collective bargaining agreement was struck between the NFL and the NFL Players Association implementing new free agency rules, a salary cap, and increased salary scales (Quinn 2012).

28 See also Bergin (2002), Teaiwa and Mallon (2005), Mallon (2012), and Lakisa, Adair, and Taylor (2014); see Halau'fia (2016) for a compelling discussion of sport and the Tongan diaspora with a focus on cultural identity, racialization, and mobility.

29 There is an important strand of emergent research with Pacific athletes, but in the New Zealand context. See Marsters (2017) and Marsters and Tiatia-Seath (2019a; 2019b).

CONCLUSION

1 Aukilani/Auckland is said to be the most Pacific/Polynesian city in the world; Samoans are the largest Pacific Islander group there behind Māori.

2 Metro Lions Gridiron Club is recognized to be the longest-running American football club in New Zealand. Located in Auckland, they celebrated their fortieth anniversary in 2019.

3 Jarred Hayne made a much-heralded but short-lived jump to the NFL (of Fijian descent, he made the leap from professional rugby in Australia to a stint with the San Francisco 49ers in 2015). However, Jordan Mailata (a six-foot, eight-inch-tall Samoan rugby league Under-20s player from Australia who participated in the NFL's International Pathways Program and was drafted in 2018 by the Philadelphia Eagles) has cashed in on the NFL lottery. In 2021 he signed a four-year contract extension worth $64 million (USD), $40.85 million of which is guaranteed, and with clauses that could bring the total value up to $80 million. Mailata was only the second player to ever be drafted without American high school or college football experience. Frank, Reuben. 2021. "Eagles reward Mailata with massive contract extension." NBC Sports. https://www.nbcsports.com/philadelphia/eagles/eagles-reward-jordan-mailata-massive-contract-extension, accessed November 18, 2021.

4 Including positions as graduate assistants (GAs), quality control assistants (QCs), and restricted-earnings coaches that often see long hours for low pay; see Kukahiko (2015).

Bibliography

Ablon, Joan. 1971. "Retention of Cultural Values and Differential Urban Adaptation: Samoans and American Indians in a West Coast City." *Social Forces* 49: 385–393.

Abu-Lughod, Lila, Faye D. Ginsburg, and Brian Larkin. 2002. *Media Worlds: Anthropology on New Terrain*. Berkeley: University of California Press.

Agergaard, Sine, and Nina Clara Tiesler. 2014. *Women, Soccer and Transnational Migration*. New York: Routledge.

Ahlburg, Dennis, and Michael J. Levin, eds. 1990. *The North East Passage: A Study of Pacific Islander Migration to American Samoa and the United States*. Canberra: National Centre for Development Studies, Research School of Pacific Studies, the Australian National University.

Aiono, Fanaafi. 1997. *O Le Faasinomaga*. Alafua, Samoa: Le Lamepa Press.

Alegi, Peter. 2010. *African Soccerscapes: How a Continent Changed the World's Game*. Athens, OH: Ohio University Press.

Allardice, R. W. 1985. *Simplified Dictionary of Modern Samoan*. Auckland: Polynesian Press.

American Samoa. Governor. 1952. Report to the Secretary of the Interior. Washington, DC: US Govt. Print. Off.

American Samoa. Governor. 1968. Report to the Secretary of the Interior. Washington, DC: US Govt. Print. Off.

American Samoa. Governor. 1973. Report to the Secretary of the Interior. Washington, DC: US Govt. Print. Off.

American Samoa. Governor. 1975. Report to the Secretary of the Interior. Washington, DC: US Govt. Print. Off.

Anae, Melani. 1997. "Towards a NZ-Born Samoan Identity: Some Reflections on 'Labels.'" *Pacific Health Dialog* 4 (2): 128–137.

Anae, Melani, Falaniko Tominiko, Vavao Fetui, and Ieti Lima. 2017. "Transnational Sāmoan Chiefs: Views of the Fa'amatai (Chiefly System)." *Journal of Samoan Studies* 7 (1): 38–50.

Andrews, David L., and George Ritzer. 2007. "The Grobal in the Sporting Glocal." *Global Networks* 7 (2): 135–153.

Antoun, Richard T. 2005. *Documenting Transnational Migration: Jordanian Men Working and Studying in Europe, Asia, and North America*. New York: Berghahn Books.

Appadurai, Arjun, ed. 1986. *The Social Life of Things: Commodities in Cultural Perspective*. Cambridge: Cambridge University Press.

Appadurai, Arjun. 1990. "Disjuncture and Difference in the Global Cultural Economy." *Theory, Culture and Society* 7: 295–310.

Appadurai, Arjun. 1995. "Playing with Modernity: The Decolonization of Indian Cricket." In *Consuming Modernity: Public Culture in a South Asian World*, edited by Carol Breckenridge, 23–48. Minneapolis: University of Minnesota Press.

Arvin, Maile. 2015. "The Polynesian Problem and Its Genomic Solutions." *Native American and Indigenous Studies* 2 (2): 27–56.

Basch, Linda G., Nina Glick Schiller, and Cristina Szanton Blanc. 1994. *Nations Unbound: Transnational Projects, Postcolonial Predicaments, and Deterritorialized Nation-States*. Langhorne, PA: Gordon and Breach.

Beamon, Krystal. 2008. "'Used Goods': Former African American College Student-Athletes' Perception of Exploitation by Division I Universities." *The Journal of Negro Education* 77 (4): 352–364.

Beamon, Krystal, and Patricia Bell. 2011. "A Dream Deferred: Narratives of African-American Male Former Collegiate Athletes' Transition out of Sports and into the Occupational Sector." *Journal for the Study of Sports and Athletes in Education* 5 (1): 29–44.

Beamon, Krystal, and Chris M. Messer. 2013. *The Enduring Color Line in U.S. Athletics: Framing 21st Century Social Issues*. New York: Routledge.

Bergin, Paul. 2002. "Maori Sport and Cultural Identity in Australia." *The Australian Journal of Anthropology* 13 (3): 257–269.

Bertram, I. Geoffrey, and Ray F. Watters. 1985. "The MIRAB Economy in South Pacific Microstates." *Pacific Viewpoint* 26 (3): 497–519.

Besnier, Niko. 2011. *On the Edge of the Global: Modern Anxieties in a Pacific Island Nation*. Stanford, CA: Stanford University Press.

Besnier, Niko. 2012. "The Athlete's Body and the Global Condition: Tongan Rugby Players in Japan." *American Ethnologist* 39 (3): 491–510.

Besnier, Niko. 2014. "Pacific Island Rugby: Histories, Mobilities, Comparisons." *Asia Pacific Journal of Sport and Social Science* 3 (3): 268–276. doi:10.1080/21 640599.2014.982894.

Besnier, Niko. 2015. "Sports Mobilities across Borders: Postcolonial Perspectives." *The International Journal of the History of Sport* 32 (7): 849–861.

Besnier, Niko, and Susan Brownell. 2012. "Sport, Modernity, and the Body." *Annual Review of Anthropology* 41: 443–459.

Besnier, Niko, Susan Brownell, and Thomas F. Carter. 2017. *The Anthropology of Sport: Bodies, Borders, Biopolitics.* Berkeley: University of California Press.

Bhabha, Homi K. 1994. *The Location of Culture.* New York: Routledge.

Bigart, Robert, and Clarence Woodcock. 1996. *In the Name of the Salish and Kootenai Nation: The 1855 Hell Gate Treaty and the Origin of the Flathead Indian Reservation.* Pablo, MT: Salish Kootenai College Press.

Bigler, Matthew, and Judson L. Jefferies. 2008. "'An Amazing Specimen': NFL Draft Experts' Evaluation of Black Quarterbacks." *Journal of African American Studies* 12: 120–141.

Billings, Andrew C. 2004. "Depicting the Quarterback in Black and White: A Content Analysis of College and Professional Football Broadcast Commentary." *Howard Journal of Communications* 15 (4): 201–210. doi:10.1080/10646170490521158.

Birrell, Susan. 1989. "Racial Relations Theories and Sport: Suggestions for a More Critical Analysis." *Sociology of Sport* 6: 212–217.

Bosco, Frank A., and David G. Allen. 2011. "Executive Attention as a Predictor of Employee Performance." *Academy of Management Proceedings* 8 (1), 1–6. doi:10.5465/AMBPP.2011.65869703.

Bourdieu, Pierre. 1977. *Outline of a Theory of Practice.* Vol. 16. Cambridge: Cambridge University Press.

Bourdieu, Pierre. 1978. "Sport and Social Class." *Social Science Information* 17 (6): 819–840.

Bourdieu, Pierre. 1984. *Distinction: A Social Critique of the Judgement of Taste.* Cambridge, MA: Harvard University Press.

Bourdieu, Pierre. 1986. "The Forms of Capital." In *The Sociology of Economic Life,* edited by Mark Granovetter and Richard Swedbag, 241–258. Boulder, CO: Westview Press.

Bourdieu, Pierre. 1988. "Program for a Sociology of Sport." *Sociology of Sport Journal* 5 (2): 153–161.

Boyer, Dominic. 2012. "From Media Anthropology to the Anthropology of Mediation." In *The Sage Handbook of Social Anthropology,* edited by Richard Fardon, Olivia Harris, Trevor H. J. Marchand, Mark Nuttall, Cris Shore, Veronica Strang, and Richard A. Wilson, 411–422. London: Sage.

Brewis, Alexandra A., Steve T. McGarvey, Jaylan Jones, and Boyd A. Swinburn. 1998. "Perceptions of Body Size in Pacific Islanders." *International Journal of Obesity* 22 (2): 185.

Broshek, Donna K., Tanya Kaushik, Jason R. Freeman, David Erlanger, Frank Webbe, and Jeffrey T. Barth. 2005. "Sex Differences in Outcome Following Sports-Related Concussion." *Journal of Neurosurgery* 102 (5): 856–863.

Brown, Drew D. 2017. "Ballers without Blackness: The Suppression of Black Cultural Agency in the NFL." In *Football, Culture and Power,* edited by

David J. Leonard, Kimberly B. George, and Wade Davis, in Routledge Research in Sport, Culture and Society, 44–58. London and New York: Routledge.

Bureau, US Census. 2010. *2010 Census for American Samoa.* (www.census.gov).

Bureau, US Census. 2013. American Samoa 2010 Census Detailed Crosstabulations Part 1.

Bureau, US Census. 2021. "Resident Population in Missoula County, Mt [Mtmissopop]" FRED, Federal Reserve Bank of St. Louis. https://fred.stlouisfed.org /series/MTMISSoPOP.

Burstyn, Varda. 1999. *The Rites of Men: Manhood, Politics, and the Culture of Sport.* Toronto and Buffalo, NY: University of Toronto Press.

Bush, Allister, Fa'amausili Chapman, Mercy Drummond, and Tofa Fagaloa. 2009. "Development of a Child, Adolescent and Family Mental Health Service for Pacific Young People in Aotearoa/New Zealand." *Pacific Health Dialog* 15 (1): 138–146.

Butterworth, Michael L. 2014. "The Athlete as Citizen: Judgement and Rhetorical Invention in Sport." *Sport in Society* 17 (7): 867–883. doi:10.1080/17430437.20 13.806033.

Camacho, Keith L., and Laurel A. Monnig. 2010. "Uncomfortable Fatigues: Chamorro Soldiers, Gendered Identities, and Decolonization in Guam." In *Militarized Currents: Toward a Decolonized Future in Asia and the Pacific,* edited by Setsu Shigematsu and Keith L. Camacho, 147–180. Minneapolis: University of Minnesota Press.

Campolettano, Eamon T., Steven Rowson, Stefan M. Duma, Brian Stemper, Alok Shah, Jaroslaw Harezlak, Larry D. Riggen, Jason Mihalik, Alison Brooks, Kenneth Cameron, Christopher C. Giza, Thomas McAllister, Steven P. Broglio, and Michael McCrea. 2019. "Factors Affecting Head Impact Exposure in College Football Practices: A Multi-Institutional Study." *Annals of Biomedical Engineering* 47 (10): 2086–2093. doi:10.1007/s10439-019-02309-x.

Carlson, Kyle, Joshua Kim, Annamaria Lusardi, and Colin F. Camerer. 2015. "Bankruptcy Rates among NFL Players with Short-Lived Income Spikes." *American Economic Review* 105 (5): 381–384. doi:10.1257/aer.p20151038.

Carrington, Ben. 2010. *Race, Sport and Politics: The Sporting Black Diaspora.* London: Sage.

Carter, Thomas. 2011. *In Foreign Fields: The Politics and Experiences of Transnational Sport Migration.* New York: Pluto Press.

Carter, Thomas F. 2007. "Family Networks, State Interventions and the Experience of Cuban Transnational Sport Migration." *International Review for the Sociology of Sport* 42 (4): 371–389. doi:10.1177/1012690208089832.

Carter, Thomas F. 2013. "Re-Placing Sport Migrants: Moving Beyond the Institutional Structures Informing International Sport Migration." *International Review for the Sociology of Sport* 48 (1): 66–82.

Castille, Lianne, Christy L. Collins, Natalie M. McIlvain, and R. Dawn Comstock. 2012. "The Epidemiology of New Versus Recurrent Sports Concussions among High School Athletes, 2005–2010." *British Journal of Sports Medicine* 46 (8): 603–610.

Chappell, David A. 1997. *Double Ghosts: Oceanian Voyagers on Euroamerican Ships*. Armonk, NY: M. E. Sharpe.

Chappell, David A. 2000. "The Forgotten *Mau*: Anti-Navy Protest in American Samoa, 1920–1935." *Pacific Historical Review* 69 (2): 217–260.

Clement, Julien. 2014. "Participating in the Global Competition: Denaturalizing 'Flair' in Samoan Rugby." *The Contemporary Pacific* 26 (2): 369–387.

Clossey, Luke. 2006. "Merchants, Migrants, Missionaries, and Globalization in the Early-Modern Pacific." *Journal of Global History* 1 (1): 41–58.

Coakley, Jay J. 2004. *Sports in Society: Issues & Controversies*. 8th ed. Boston: McGraw-Hill Higher Education.

Cobb, Bryan R., Jillian E. Urban, Elizabeth M. Davenport, Steven Rowson, Stefan M. Duma, Joseph A. Maldjian, Christopher T. Whitlow, Alexander K. Powers, and Joel D. Stitzel. 2013. "Head Impact Exposure in Youth Football: Elementary School Ages 9–12 years and the Effect of Practice Structure." *Annals of Biomedical Engineering* 41 (12): 2463–2473. doi:10.1007/s10439-013-0867-6.

Collins, Patricia Hill. 2006. "New Commodities, New Consumers: Selling Blackness in a Global Marketplace." *Ethnicities* 6 (3): 297–317. doi:10.1177/1468796806068322.

Connell, John. 2005. *Remittances in the Pacific: An Overview*. Manila, Philippines: Asian Development Bank.

Connell, John, and Moshe Rapaport. 2013. "Mobility to Migration." In *The Pacific Islands*, edited by Moshe Rapaport, 275–286. Honolulu: University of Hawai'i Press.

Connell, R. W. 1995. *Masculinities*. Berkeley: University of California Press.

Connell, R. W. 2012. "Globalization, Imperialism, Masculinities." In *Handbook of Studies on Men and Masculinities*, edited by Michael S. Kimmel, Jeff R. Hearn and R. W. Connell, 71–89. Thousand Oaks, CA: Sage.

Corsellis, Jan, C. J. Bruton, and Dorothy Freeman-Browne. 1973. "The Aftermath of Boxing." *Psychological Medicine* 3 (3): 270–303.

Dallmeier, Julian D., Somayeh Meysami, David A. Merrill, and Cyrus A. Raji. 2019. "Emerging Advances of in Vivo Detection of Chronic Traumatic Encephalopathy and Traumatic Brain Injury." *The British Journal of Radiology* 92 (1101): 20180925. doi:10.1259/bjr.20180925.

Daneshvar, Daniel H., David O. Riley, Christopher J. Nowinski, Ann C. McKee, Robert A. Stern, and Robert C. Cantu. 2011. "Long-Term Consequences: Effects on Normal Development Profile after Concussion." *Physical Medicine and Rehabilitation Clinics of North America* 22 (4): 683–700.

Darby, Paul. 2000. "The New Scramble for Africa: African Football Labour Migration to Europe." *The European Sports History Review* 3 (1): 217–244.

Darby, Paul. 2012. "Gains Versus Drains: Football Academies and the Export of Highly Skilled Football Labor." *The Brown Journal of World Affairs* 18 (2): 265–277. Accessed December 5, 2020. www.jstor.org/stable/24590876.

Darby, Paul. 2013. "Moving Players, Traversing Perspectives: Global Value Chains, Production Networks and Ghanaian Football Labour Migration." *Geoforum* 50: 43–53. doi:10.1016/j.geoforum.2013.06.009.

Darby, Paul, Gerard Akindes, and Matthew Kirwin. 2007. "Football Academies and the Migration of African Football Labor to Europe." *Journal of Sport and Social Issues* 31 (2): 143–161.

Darby, Paul, and Eirik Solberg. 2010. "Differing Trajectories: Football Development and Patterns of Player Migration in South Africa and Ghana." *Soccer & Society* 11 (1–2): 118–130.

Desmond, Jane. 1999. *Staging Tourism: Bodies on Display from Waikiki to Sea World*. Chicago: University of Chicago Press.

Dewey, Robert F. 2008. "Pacific Islands Rugby: Navigating the Global Professional Era." In *The Changing Face of Rugby: The Union Game and Professionalism since 1995*, edited by Greg Ryan. Newcastle, UK: Cambridge Scholars Publishing.

Dewey, Robert F., Jr. 2006. "The Historic Expression of Power and Identity in Fiji Rugby." *Dreadlocks Vaka Vuku*. Special Issue, Proceedings of the Pacific Epistemologies Conference, 2006.

Diaz, Vicente M. 2002. "'Fight Boys, 'Til the Last . . .': Islandstyle Football and the Remasculinization of Indigeneity in the Militarized American Pacific Islands." In *Pacific Diaspora: Island Peoples in the United States and across the Pacific*, edited by Paul Spickard, Joanne L. Rondilla and Debbie Hippolite Wright. Honolulu: University of Hawai'i Press.

Diaz, Vicente M. 2011. "Tackling Pacific Hegemonic Formations on the American Gridiron." *Amerasia* 37 (3): 2–25.

Diaz, Vicente M., and J. Kehaulani Kauanui. 2001. "Native Pacific Cultural Studies on the Edge." *The Contemporary Pacific* 13 (2): 315–342.

Dick, R. W. 2009. "Is There a Gender Difference in Concussion Incidence and Outcomes?" *British Journal of Sports Medicine* 43 (Suppl. 1): i46–i50.

Drummond, Katie. 2014. "Can the NFL Survive Its Concussion Crisis?" *The Verge* (January 31).

Dufur, Mikaela J., and Seth L. Feinberg. 2009. "Race and the NFL Draft: Views from the Auction Block." *Qualitative Sociology* 32 (1): 53–73.

Dunnavant, Keith. 2004. *The Fifty-Year Seduction: How Television Manipulated College Football, from the Birth of the Modern NCAA to the Creation of the BCS*. New York: St. Martin's Press.

Dyreson, Mark. 2001. "American Ideas About Race and Olympic Races from the 1890s to the 1950s: Shattering Myths or Reinforcing Scientific Racism?" *Journal of Sport History* 28 (2): 196–215.

Edmond, Rod. 1997. "U.S. Trajectories into Hawai'i and the Pacific: Imperial Mappings, Postcolonial Contestations." In *Representing the South Pacific: Colonial Discourse from Cook to Gauguin*, 57–87. Cambridge: Cambridge University Press.

Edwards, Harry. 1979. "Sport within the Veil: The Triumphs, Tragedies, and Challenges of Afro-American Involvement." *The Annals of the American Academy of Political and Social Science* 445 (1): 116–127.

Edwards, Harry. 1985. "Beyond Symptoms: Unethical Behavior in American Collegiate Sport and the Problem of the Color Line." *Journal of Sport and Social Issues* 9 (2): 3–13.

Edwards, Harry. 1988. "An End of the Golden Age of Black Participation in Sport?" *Civil Rights Journal* 3 (Fall).

Eisen, George, and David K. Wiggins, eds. 1994. *Ethnicity and Sport in North American History and Culture.* Westport, CT: Greenwood Press.

Eitzen, D. Stanley. 2009. "Upward Mobility through Sport? Myths and Realities." In *Sport in Contemporary Society: An Anthology*, edited by D. Stanley Eitzen, 249–256. Boulder, CO: Paradigm Publishers.

Elliott, Richard, and John Harris. 2014. *Football and Migration: Perspectives, Places, Players.* New York and London: Routledge.

Elliot, Richard, and Joseph Maguire. 2008. "'Thinking Outside the Box': Exploring a Conceptual Synthesis for Research in the Area of Athletic Labor Migration." *Sociology of Sport* 25 (4): 482–497.

Ember, Melvin. 1962. "Political Authority and the Structure of Kinship in Aboriginal Samoa." *American Anthropologist* 64 (5): 964–971.

Embree, Edwin R. 1934. "A New School in American Samoa." *Journal of Negro Education* 3 (1): 50–56.

English, Colleen. 2017. "Toward Sport Reform: Hegemonic Masculinity and Reconceptualizing Competition." *Journal of the Philosophy of Sport* 44 (2): 183–198.

Esson, James. 2013. "A Body and a Dream at a Vital Conjuncture: Ghanaian Youth, Uncertainty and the Allure of Football." *Geoforum* 47: 84–92.

Fa'aleava, Toeutu. 2003. "*Fitafita*: Samoan Landsmen in the United States Navy, 1900–1951." PhD dissertation, Ethnic Studies, University of California, Berkeley.

Fabian, Johannes. 1983. *Time and the Other: How Anthropology Makes Its Object.* New York: Columbia University Press.

Fainaru-Wada, Mark, and Steve Fainaru. 2013. *League of Denial.* New York: Three Rivers Press.

Fairbairn-Dunlop, Peggy. 1998. *Tamaitai Samoa: Their Stories.* Suva: Institute of Pacific Studies; Carson City, CA: KIN Publications.

Foner, Nancy. 1997. "What's New About Transnationalism? New York Immigrants Today and at the Turn of the Century." *Diaspora: A Journal of Transnational Studies* 6 (3): 355–375.

Franco, Robert W. 1991. *Samoan Perceptions of Work: Moving up and Moving Around.* New York: AMS Press.

Franks, Joel. 2000. *Crossing Sidelines, Crossing Cultures: Sport and Asian Pacific American Cultural Citizenship.* Lanham, MD: University Press of America.

Franks, Joel. 2002. *Hawaiian Sports in the Twentieth Century*. Lewiston, NY: Edwin Mellen Press.

Franks, Joel. 2009. "Pacific Islanders and American Football: Hula Hula Honeys, Throwin' Samoans, and the Rock." *International Journal of the History of Sport* 26 (16): 2397–2411.

Freeman, Derek. 1983. *Margaret Mead and Samoa: The Making and Unmaking of an Anthropological Myth*. Canberra: ANU Press.

Furness, Zack. 2016. "Reframing Concussions, Masculinity, and NFL Mythology in *League of Denial*." *Popular Communication* 14 (1): 49–57.

Galanis, Daniel J., Stephen T. McGarvey, Christine Quested, and Brenda Sio. 1999. "Dietary Intake of Modernizing Samoans: Implications for Risk of Cardiovascular Disease." *Journal of the Academy of Nutrition and Dietetics* 99 (2): 184–190.

Gasu, T. 2010a. "Bengals' Fanene and Maualuga Donate 1,000+ Pairs of Cleats to Local Football." *Samoa News* (March 6).

Gasu, T. 2010b. "Domata Peko Foundation Donates to AYFS League." *Samoa News* (February 19).

Gavett, Brandon E., Robert A. Stern, and Ann C. McKee. 2011. "Chronic Traumatic Encephalopathy: A Potential Late Effect of Sport-Related Concussive and Subconcussive Head Trauma." *Clinics in Sports Medicine* 30 (1): 179–188.

Gems, Gerald R. 2006. *The Athletic Crusade: Sport and American Cultural Imperialism*. Lincoln: University of Nebraska Press.

Gillett, R. D., Mike A. McCoy, and David G. Itano. 2002. *Status of the United States Western Pacific Tuna Purse Seine Fleet and Factors Affecting Its Future*. Honolulu: University of Hawai'i-NOAA Joint Institute for Marine and Atmospheric Research.

Gilson, Richard Phillip. 1970. *Samoa 1830 to 1900: The Politics of a Multi-Cultural Community*. Melbourne and New York: Oxford University Press.

Goodman, Richard A. 1990. "Laughter and Anger: On Samoan Aggression." In *The Samoa Reader: Anthropologists Take Stock*, edited by Hiram Caton, 135–142. Lanham, MD: University Press of America.

Graeber, David. 2001. *Toward an Anthropological Theory of Value: The False Coin of Our Own Dreams*. New York: Palgrave Macmillan.

Grainger, Andrew. 2006. "From Immigrant to Overstayer: Samoan Identity, Rugby, and Cultural Politics of Race and Nation in Aotearoa/New Zealand." *Journal of Sport and Social Issues* 30 (1): 45–61.

Grainger, Andrew. 2009. "Rugby Island Style: Paradise, Pacific People, and the Racialisation of Athletic Performance." *Junctures: The Journal for Thematic Dialogue* (12).

Grainger, Andrew. 2011. "Mercenaries and Overstayers: Talent Migration in Pacific Island Rugby." In *Sport and Migration: Borders, Boundaries and Crossings*, edited by Marc Falcous and Joseph Maguire, 129–140. London: Routledge.

Grainger, Andrew D., Mark Falcous, and Joshua I. Newman. 2012. "Postcolonial Anxieties and the Browning of New Zealand Rugby." *The Contemporary Pacific* 24 (2): 267–295.

Grano, Daniel A. 2014. "The Greatest Game Ever Played: An NFL Origin Story." In *The NFL: Critical and Cultural Perspectives*, edited by Thomas P. Oates and Zack Furness, 13–39. Philadelphia: Temple University Press.

Greenberg, Amy. 2005. *Manifest Manhood and the Antebellum American Empire.* Cambridge: Cambridge University Press.

Guinness, Daniel, and Niko Besnier. 2016. "Nation, Nationalism, and Sport: Fijian Rugby in the Local-Global Nexus." *Anthropological Quarterly*: 1109–1141.

Hall, Daniel E. 2001. "Curfews, Culture, and Custom in American Samoa: An Analytical Map for Applying the U.S. Constitution to U.S. Territories." *Asian-Pacific Law and Policy Journal* 2 (1): 69–106. www.hawaii.edu/aplpj.

Hall, Stuart. 1998. *Representation: Cultural Representation and Signifying Practices.* London: Sage.

Hanna, J. M., D. L. Pelletier, and V. J. Brown. 1986. "The Diet and Nutrition of Contemporary Samoans." In *The Changing Samoans: Behavior and Health in Transition*, edited by P. T. Baker, J. M. Hanna, and T. S. Baker, 275–296. London: Oxford University Press.

Hannerz, Ulf. 1987. "The World in Creolisation." *Africa* 57: 546–559.

Hannerz, Ulf. 1996. *Transnational Connections: Culture, People, Places.* London and New York: Routledge. http://www.columbia.edu/cgi-bin/cul/resolve ?clio5389029.

Hannerz, Ulf. 2003. "Being There . . . And There . . . And There! Reflections on Multi-Site Ethnography." *Ethnography* 4 (2): 201–216.

Harrington, Jennifer J. 2020. "Tribal Consultation Policy and Practice: A Case Study of the Confederated Salish and Kootenai Tribes and Nmisuletkʷ (The Middle Fork of the Clark Fork River) as a Tribal Trust Resource." MA thesis, Forestry, University of Montana–Missoula.

Harris, Philip M., and Nicholas A. Jones. 2005. *We the People: Pacific Islanders in the United States.* Washington, DC: US Census Bureau.

Hartmann, Douglas. 2000. "Rethinking the Relationships between Sport and Race in American Culture: Golden Ghettos and Contested Terrain." *Sociology of Sport Journal* 17 (3): 229–253.

Harvey, David. 1987. "Flexible Accumulation through Urbanization: Reflections on 'Post-Modernism' in the American City." *Antipode* 19 (3): 260–286.

Harvey, David. 1990. "Between Space and Time: Reflections on the Geographical Imagination." *Annals of the Association of American Geographers* 80 (3): 418–434.

Harvey, David. 2006. "Neo-Liberalism as Creative Destruction." *Geografiska Annaler: Series B, Human Geography* 88 (2): 145–158.

Harvey, David. 2007. *A Brief History of Neoliberalism.* New York: Oxford University Press.

Harvey, Hosea H. 2013. "Reducing Traumatic Brain Injuries in Youth Sports: Youth Sports Traumatic Brain Injury State Laws, January 2009–December 2012." *American Journal of Public Health* 103 (7): 1249–1254.

Hau'ofa, Epeli. 2008 [1994]. "Our Sea of Islands." In *We Are the Ocean: Selected Works*, 27–41. Honolulu: University of Hawai'i Press.

Hawkins, Billy. 2010. *The New Plantation: Black Athletes, College Sports, and Predominantly White NCAA Institutions*. New York: Palgrave Macmillan.

Hayes, Geoffrey, and Michael J. Levin. 1983. *A Statistical Profile of Samoans in the United States. Part I: Demography; Part II: Social and Economic Characteristics; Appendix: Language Use among Samoans. Evidence from the 1980 Census*. Washington, DC: US Department of Labor Employment and Training Administration.

Henderson, April K. 2011. "Fleeting Substantiality: The Samoan Giant in US Popular Discourse." *The Contemporary Pacific* 23: 269–302.

Heptonstall, Paul. 2011. *Welfare and Education 2011 Season Review*. Moore Park, NSW: National Rugby League.

Hoberman, John Milton. 1997. *Darwin's Athletes: How Sport Has Damaged Black America and Preserved the Myth of Race*. New York: Houghton Mifflin Harcourt.

Hoganson, Kristin L. 1998. *Fighting for American Manhood: How Gender Politics Provoked the Spanish-American and Philippine-American Wars*. New Haven, CT: Yale University Press.

Hokowhitu, Brendan. 2003. "Race Tactics: The Racialised Athletic Body." *Junctures: The Journal for Thematic Dialogue* 1: 21–34.

Hokowhitu, Brendan. 2004. "Tackling Maori Masculinity: A Colonial Genealogy of Savagery and Sport." *The Contemporary Pacific* 16 (2): 259–284.

Hokowhitu, Brendan. 2014. "Haka: Colonized Physicality, Body-Logic, and Embodied Sovereignty." In *Performing Indigeneity: Global Histories and Contemporary Experiences*, edited by Laura R. Graham and H. Glenn Penny, 273–304. Lincoln: University of Nebraska Press.

Holmes, Lowell Don. 1958. *Ta'u: Stability and Change in a Samoan Village*. Wellington, NZ: Polynesian Society.

Holmes, Lowell Don, and Ellen Rhoads Holmes. 1992. *Samoan Village: Then and Now*. 2nd ed. Case Studies in Cultural Anthropology. Fort Worth, TX: Harcourt Brace Jovanovich College Publishers.

hooks, bell. 2006. "Eating the Other: Desire and Resistance." In *Media and Cultural Studies: Keyworks*, edited by Meenakshi Gigi Durham and Douglas M. Kellner, 366–380. Malden, MA: Blackwell Publishing.

Hooper-Greenhill, Eilean. 2000. *Museums and the Interpretation of Visual Culture*. New York: Routledge.

Horton, Peter. 2012. "Pacific Islanders in Global Rugby: The Changing Currents of Sports Migration." *The International Journal of the History of Sport* 29 (17): 2388–2404.

Horton, Peter. 2014. "Pacific Islanders in Professional Rugby Football: Bodies, Minds and Cultural Continuities." *Asia Pacific Journal of Sport and Social Science* 3 (3): 222–235.

Hughson, John, and Marcus Free. 2006. "Paul Willis, Cultural Commodities, and Sport Fandom." *Sociology of Sport* 23: 72–85.

Hunkin, Galumalemana Alfred. 2007. "Fa'amatai in New Zealand: A View from Wellington." In *Changes in the Matai System: O Suiga I Le Fa'amatai*, edited by Asofou So'o, 61–71. Apia: Centre for Sāmoan Studies.

Irwin, Katherine, and Karen Umemoto. 2012. "Being Fearless and Fearsome: Colonial Legacies, Racial Constructions, and Male Adolescent Violence." *Race and Justice* 2 (1): 3–28.

James, C. L. R. 1963. *Beyond a Boundary*. London: Hutchinson.

James, Paul, and Manfred B. Steger. 2014. "A Genealogy of 'Globalization': The Career of a Concept." *Globalizations* 11 (4): 417–434.

Janes, Craig R. 1990. *Migration, Social Change and Health: A Samoan Community in Urban California*. Stanford, CA: Stanford University Press.

Johnston, Richard W. 1976. "Shake 'Em out of the Coconut Trees." *Sports Illustrated* (August 16).

Kahn, Miriam. 2011. *Tahiti Beyond the Postcard: Power, Place, and Everyday Life*. Culture, Place, and Nature. Seattle: University of Washington Press.

Kallen, Evelyn. 1982. *The Western Samoan Kinship Bridge: A Study in Migration, Social Change, and the New Ethnicity*. Leiden: E. J. Brill.

Kane, Tim. 2005. *Who Bears the Burden? Demographic Characteristics of U.S. Military Recruits before and after 9/11*. Center of Data Analysis, Heritage Foundation. Accessed December 5, 2020. https://www.heritage.org/defense/report/who-bears-the-burden-demographic-characteristics-us-military-recruits-and-after-911.

Kanemasu, Yoko, and Gyozo Molnar. 2013. "Pride of the People: Fijian Rugby Labour Migration and Collective Identity." *International Review for the Sociology of Sport* 48 (6): 720–735.

Kauanui, J. Kehaulani. 2008. *Hawaiian Blood: Colonialism and the Politics of Sovereignty and Indigeneity*. Narrating Native Histories. Durham, NC: Duke University Press.

Keesing, Felix Maxwell, and Institute of Pacific Relations. 1931. *A Memorandum on the Mandated Territory of Western Samoa and American Samoa*. Honolulu: The Institute of Pacific Relations.

Kellett, Pamm. 2002. "Football-as-War, Coach-as-General: Analogy, Metaphor and Management Implications." *Football Studies* 5 (1): 60–76.

Kempadoo, Kamala, and Jo Doezema. 1998. *Global Sex Workers: Rights, Resistance, and Redefinition*. London: Psychology Press.

Kennedy, Paul. 1974. *The Samoan Tangle: A Study in Anglo-German-American Relations, 1878–1900*. New York: Barnes and Noble.

Kerr, Zachary Y., Johna K. Register-Mihalik, Emily Kroshus, Christine M. Baugh, and Stephen W. Marshall. 2016. "Motivations Associated with

Nondisclosure of Self-Reported Concussions in Former Collegiate Athletes." *The American Journal of Sports Medicine* 44 (1): 220–225. doi:10.1177/0363546515612082.

Kerr, Zachary Y., Susan W. Yeargin, Tamara C. Valovich McLeod, James Mensch, Ross Hayden, and Thomas P. Dompier. 2015. "Comprehensive Coach Education Reduces Head Impact Exposure in American Youth Football." *Orthopaedic Journal of Sports Medicine* 3 (10). doi:10.1177/2325967115610545.

Kidd, Bruce. 1990. "The Men's Cultural Centre: Sports and the Dynamic of Women's Oppression/Men's Repression." In *Sport, Men, and the Gender Order: Critical Feminist Perspectives*, edited by Michael A. Messner and Donald F. Sabo, 31–43. Champaign, IL: Human Kinetics.

Kim, Sungwon, Daniel P. Connaughton, John Spengler, and Jong Hoon Lee. 2017. "Legislative Efforts to Reduce Concussions in Youth Sports: An Analysis of State Concussion Statutes." *Journal of Legal Aspects of Sport* 27: 162.

King, C. Richard. 2005. *Native Athletes in Sport and Society*. Lincoln: University of Nebraska Press.

Klein, Alan. 1991. *Sugarball: The American Game, the Dominican Dream*. New Haven, CT: Yale University Press.

Klein, Alan. 2006. *Growing the Game: The Globalization of Major League Baseball*. New Haven, CT: Yale University Press.

Klein, Alan. 2009. "The Transnational View of Sport and Social Development: The Case of Dominican Baseball." *Sport in Society* 12 (9): 1118–1131. doi:10.1080/17430430903137761.

Kopytoff, Igor. 1986. "The Cultural Biography of Things." In *The Social Life of Things*, edited by Arjun Appadurai, 64–91. Cambridge: Cambridge University Press.

Kukahiko, Keali'i Troy. 2015. "Racial Diversity Deficit in College Football: Fixing the Pipeline." *Journal of Critical Race Inquiry* 2 (2): 25–53.

Kukahiko, Keali'i Troy. 2017. "Pacific Islanders in College Football: Getting in, Staying in, and Moving On." PhD dissertation, Education, University of California, Los Angeles.

Kwauk, Christina Ting. 2014. "'No Longer Just a Pastime': Sport for Development in Times of Change." *The Contemporary Pacific* 26 (2): 303–323.

Kwauk, Christina Ting. 2016. "'Let them see a different path': social attitudes towards sport, education and development in Sāmoa." *Sport, Education and Society* 21 (4):644–660.

Labor, United States. Department of. May 2007. *Economic Report: The Minimum Wage in American Samoa*. Washington, DC: US Department of Labor, Employment Standards Administration, Wage and Hour Division. http://www.dol.gov/whd/AS/EconomicReport-2007.pdf.

Lafoa'i, Ioane. 2007. "Fa'amatai in Australia: Is It Fair Dinkum?" In *Changes in the Matai System: O Suiga I Le Fa'amatai*, edited by Asofou So'o, 13–26. Apia: Centre for Sāmoan Studies.

Lakhan, Shaheen E., and Annette Kirchgessner. 2012. "Chronic Traumatic Encephalopathy: The Dangers of Getting 'Dinged.'" *SpringerPlus* 1 (1): 2.

Lakisa, David, Daryl Adair, and Tracy Taylor. 2014. "Pasifika Diaspora and the Changing Face of Australian Rugby League." *The Contemporary Pacific* 26 (2): 347–367.

Lakisa, David, Katerina Teaiwa, Daryl Adair, and Tracy Taylor. 2019. "Empowering Voices from the Past: The Playing Experiences of Retired Pasifika Rugby League Athletes in Australia." *The International Journal of the History of Sport* 36 (12): 1096–1114. doi:10.1080/09523367.2019.1618835.

Lanfranchi, Pierre, and Matthew Taylor. 2001. *Moving with the Ball: The Migration of Professional Footballers.* Oxford: Berg.

Lanfranchi, Pierre, and Matthew Taylor. 2014. "Mobility, Migration and History: Football and Early Transnational Networks." In *Football and Migration,* 35–52. New York: Routledge.

Langlois, Jean A., Wesley Rutland-Brown, and Marlena M. Wald. 2006. "The Epidemiology and Impact of Traumatic Brain Injury: A Brief Overview." *The Journal of Head Trauma Rehabilitation* 21 (5): 375–378.

Lapchick, Richard, John Fox, Angelica Guiao, and Maclin Simpson. 2014. *The 2014 Racial and Gender Report Card: College Sport.* Orlando, FL: The Institution for Diversity and Ethics in Sport.

Lapchick, Richard, and Leroy Robinson. 2015. *The 2015 Racial and Gender Report Card: National Football League.* Orlando, FL: The Institution for Diversity and Ethics in Sport.

Leach, Jerry. 1975. *Trobriand Cricket: An Ingenious Response to Colonialism.* ACT, Australia: Ronin Films.

Lee, Helen. 2003. *Tongans Overseas: Between Two Shores.* Honolulu: University of Hawai'i Press.

Lee, Helen. 2004. "'Second Generation' Tongan Transnationalism: Hope for the Future?" *Asia Pacific Viewpoint* 45 (2): 235–254.

Lee, Helen. 2009. "Pacific Migration and Transnationalism: Historical Perspectives." In *Migration and Transnationalism: Pacific Perspectives,* edited by Helen Lee and Steve Tupai Francis, 7–41. Canberra: ANU Press.

Lee, Helen, and Steve Tupai Francis, eds. 2009. *Migration and Transnationalism: Pacific Perspectives.* Canberra: ANU Press.

Lee, S. K., with K. K. Kumashiro. 2005. *A Report on the State of Asian American and Pacific Islanders in Education: Beyond the "Model Minority" Stereotype.* Washington, DC: National Education Association of the United States.

Leonard, David J. 2006. "The Real Color of Money: Controlling Black Bodies in the NBA." *Journal of Sport and Social Issues* 30 (2): 158–179.

Leonard, David J. 2012. *After Artest: The NBA and the Assault on Blackness.* New York: SUNY Press.

Lewthwaite, Gordon R., Christine Mainzer, and Patrick J. Holland. 1972. "From Polynesia to California: Samoan Migration and Its Sequel." *Journal of Pacific History* 8 (1): 133–157.

Lilomaiava-Doktor, Sa'iliemanu. 2009a. "Beyond 'Migration': Samoan Population Movement (Malaga) and the Geography of Social Space (Vā)." *The Contemporary Pacific* 21 (1): 1–32.

Lilomaiava-Doktor, Sa'iliemanu. 2009b. "Samoan Transnationalism: Cultivating 'Home' and 'Reach.'" In *Migration and Transnationalism: Pacific Perspectives*, edited by Helen Morton Lee and Steve Tupai Francis. Canberra: ANU Press.

Linnekin, Jocelyn. 1991. "Structural History and Political Economy: The Contact Encounter in Hawai'i and Samoa." *History and Anthropology* 5: 205–232.

LiPuma, Edward. 1993. "Culture and the Concept of Culture in a Theory of Practice." In *Bourdieu: Critical Perspectives*, edited by Craig Calhoun, Edward LiPuma and Moishe Postone, 14–34. Chicago: University of Chicago Press.

Lutz, Catherine A., and Jane L. Collins. 1993. *Reading National Geographic*. Chicago: University of Chicago Press.

MacAloon, John J., ed. 2013. *Muscular Christianity and the Colonial and Post-Colonial World*. New York: Routledge.

Macpherson, Cluny. 1985. "Public and Private Views of Home: Will Western Samoan Migrants Return?" *Pacific Viewpoint* 26 (1): 242–262.

Macpherson, Cluny. 1991. "The Changing Contours of Samoan Ethnicity." In *Nga Take: Ethnic Relations and Racism in Aotearoa/New Zealand*, edited by Paul Spoonley, D. Pearson, and Cluny Macpherson. Palmerston North, NZ: Dunmore Press.

Macpherson, Cluny. 2004. "Transnationalism and Transformation in Samoan Society." In *Globalization and Culture Change in the Pacific Islands*, edited by Victoria S. Lockwood, 165–81. Upper Saddle River, NJ: Pearson Prentice Hall.

Macpherson, Cluny, and La'avasa Macpherson. 2009a. "Kinship and Transnationalism." In *Migration and Transnationalism: Pacific Perspectives*, edited by Helen Lee and Steve Tupai Francis. Canberra: ANU Press.

Macpherson, Cluny, and La'avasa Macpherson. 2009b. *The Warm Winds of Change: Globalisation and Contemporary Samoa*. Auckland: Auckland University Press.

Madden, Raymond. 2017. *Being Ethnographic: A Guide to the Theory and Practice of Ethnography*. London: Sage.

Maguire, Joseph. 1988. "Race and Position Assignment in English Soccer: A Preliminary Analysis of Ethnicity and Sport in Britain." *Sociology of Sport Journal* 5 (3): 257–269.

Maguire, Joseph. 1999. *Global Sport: Identities, Societies, Civilizations*. Malden, MA: Blackwell.

Maguire, Joseph. 2001. *Identities, Societies, Civilizations*. Malden, MA: Blackwell.

Maguire, Joseph. 2005. "The Sports-Industrial Complex: Sports Sciences, Social Development, and Images of Humankind." In *Power and Global Sport: Zones of Prestige, Emulation and Resistance*, edited by Joseph Maguire, 159–176. New York: Routledge.

Maguire, Joseph, and Mark Falcous. 2011. "Introduction: Borders, Boundaries, and Crossings—Sport, Migration, and Identities." In *Sport and Migration: Borders, Boundaries, and Crossings*, edited by Joseph Maguire and Mark Falcous, 1–12. New York: Taylor and Francis.

Mahon, Maureen. 2000. "The Visible Evidence of Cultural Producers." *Annual Review of Anthropology* 29 (1):467–492.

Malkki, Liisa H. 1995. *Purity and Exile: Violence, Memory, and National Cosmology Among Hutu Refugees in Tanzania.* Chicago: University of Chicago Press.

Mallon, Sean. 2012. "Conspicuous Selections: Pacific Islanders in New Zealand Sport." In *Tagata O Le Moana*, edited by Sean Mallon, Kolokesa Māhina-Tuai, and Damon Salesa, 285–303. Wellington: Te Papa Press.

Manzenreiter, Wolfram. 2007. "The Business of Sports and the Manufacturing of Global Social Inequality." *Esporte e Sociedad* 2 (6): 1–22.

Marcus, George E. 1995. "Ethnography in/of the World System: The Emergence of Multi-sited Ethnography." *Annual Review of Anthropology* 24 (1): 95–117.

Marcus, George E. 1998. *Ethnography through Thick and Thin.* Princeton, NJ: Princeton University Press.

Markham, Jesse Makani. 2008. "An Evolving Geography of Sport: The Recruitment and Mobility of Samoan College Football Players 1998–2008." MA thesis, Geography, University of Hawai'i.

Marsters, Caleb. 2017. "Young Pacific Male Athletes and Positive Mental Wellbeing." MA thesis, Public Health, University of Auckland (UoA99264930510002091). http://hdl.handle.net/2292/34248.

Marsters, Caleb, and Jemaima Tiatia-Seath. 2019a. "Young Pacific Male Athletes' Experiences of Mental Wellbeing in Elite Rugby Union and Rugby League." In *Pacific Youth: Local and Global Futures.* Canberra: ANU Press.

Marsters, Caleb, and Jemaima Tiatia-Seath. 2019b. "Young Pacific Male Rugby Players' Perceptions and Experiences of Mental Wellbeing." *Sports* 7 (4): 1–19.

Martland, Harrison S. 1928. "Punch Drunk." *Journal of the American Medical Association* 91 (15): 1103–1107.

Marx, Karl. 1990. *Capital, Volume I.* New York: Penguin Books in association with New Left Review.

Masterman, Sylvia. 1934. *The Origins of International Rivalry in Samoa, 1845–1884.* Stanford, CA: Stanford University Press.

Matthews, T. Darin, and Kerry S. Lassiter. 2007. "What Does the Wonderlic Personnel Test Measure?" *Psychological Reports* 100 (3): 707–712.

Mayeda, David T., Lisa Pasko, and Meda Chesney-Lind. 2006. "You Got to Do So Much to Actually Make It: Gender, Ethnicity, and Samoan Youth in Hawaii." *AAPI Nexus* 4 (2): 1–20.

McCrea, Michael, Thomas Hammeke, Gary Olsen, Peter Leo, and Kevin Guskiewicz. 2004. "Unreported Concussion in High School Football Players: Implications for Prevention." *Clinical Journal of Sport Medicine* 14 (1): 13–17.

McDonald, Brent, and Lena Rodriguez. 2014. "'It's Our Meal Ticket': Pacific Bodies, Labour and Mobility in Australia." *Asia Pacific Journal of Sport and Social Science* 3 (3): 236–249.

McGarvey, S. T. 1991. "Obesity in Samoans and a Perspective on Its Etiology in Polynesians." *The American Journal of Clinical Nutrition* 53 (6): 1586S–1594S. doi:10.1093/ajcn/53.6.1586S.

McGrath, Barbara Burns. 2002. "Seattle *Fa'a Samoa*." *The Contemporary Pacific* 14 (2): 307–340.

McKee, Ann C., Robert C. Cantu, Christopher J. Nowinski, E. Tessa Hedley-Whyte, Brandon E. Gavett, Andrew E. Budson, Veronica E. Santini, Hyo-Soon Lee, Caroline A. Kubilus, and Robert A. Stern. 2009. "Chronic Traumatic Encephalopathy in Athletes: Progressive Tauopathy after Repetitive Head Injury." *Journal of Neuropathology & Experimental Neurology* 68 (7): 709–735.

McKee, Ann C., Daniel H. Daneshvar, Victor E. Alvarez, and Thor D. Stein. 2014. "The Neuropathology of Sport." *Acta Neuropathologica* 127 (1): 29–51.

McKee, Ann C., Thor D. Stein, Christopher J. Nowinski, Robert A. Stern, Daniel H. Daneshvar, Victor E. Alvarez, Hyo-Soon Lee, Garth Hall, Sydney M. Wojtowicz, and Christine M. Baugh. 2013. "The Spectrum of Disease in Chronic Traumatic Encephalopathy." *Brain* 136 (1): 43–64.

Meier, Timothy B., Bradley J. Brummel, Rashmi Singh, Christopher J. Nerio, David W. Polanski, and Patrick S. F. Bellgowan. 2014. "The Underreporting of Self-Reported Symptoms Following Sports-Related Concussion." *Journal of Science and Medicine in Sport* 18 (5): 507–511. doi:10.1016/j.jsams.2014.07.008.

Meleisea, Malama. 1980. *O Tama Uli: Melanesians in Samoa*. Suva, Fiji: Institute of Pacific Studies, University of the South Pacific.

Meleisea, Malama. 1987. *The Making of Modern Samoa: Traditional Authority and Colonial Administration in the History of Western Samoa*. Suva, Fiji: Institute of Pacific Studies, University of the South Pacific.

Meleisea, Malama. 1995. "'To Whom Gods and Men Crowded': Chieftainship and Hierarchy in Ancient Samoa." In *Tonga and Samoa: Images of Gender and Polity*, edited by Judith Huntsman, 19–34. Christchurch, NZ: Macmillan Brown Centre for Pacific Studies.

Meleisea, Malama, and Penelope Schoeffel. 2015. "Land, Custom and History in Sāmoa." *Journal of Samoan Studies* 5: 23–34.

Meleisea, Malama, and Penelope Schoeffel Meleisea, eds. 1987. *Lagaga: A Short History of Western Samoa*. Suva, Fiji: Institute of Pacific Studies, University of the South Pacific.

Melnick, Merrill J., and Donald Sabo. 1994. "Sport and Social Mobility among African-American and Hispanic Athletes." In *Ethnicity and Sport in North American History and Culture*, edited by George Eisen and David K. Wiggins, 221–241. Westport, CT: Greenwood Press.

Mercurio, Eugenio, and Vincent F. Filak. 2010. "Roughing the Passer: The Framing of Black and White Quarterbacks Prior to the NFL Draft." *Howard Journal of Communications* 21 (1): 56–71. doi:10.1080/10646170903501328.

Merry, Sally Engle. 2000. *Colonizing Hawai'i: The Cultural Power of Law.* Princeton, NJ: Princeton University Press.

Messner, Michael A. 2009. *It's All for the Kids: Gender, Families, and Youth Sports.* Berkeley: University of California Press.

Mez, Jesse, Daniel H. Daneshvar, Patrick T. Kiernan, et al. 2017. "Clinicopathological Evaluation of Chronic Traumatic Encephalopathy in Players of American Football." *JAMA* 318 (4): 360–370. doi:10.1001/jama.2017.8334.

Miles, Ann. 2004. *From Cuenca to Queens: An Anthropological Story of Transnational Migration.* Austin: University of Texas Press.

Miller, John J. 2011. *The Big Scrum: How Teddy Roosevelt Saved Football.* New York: Harper Collins.

Miller, Toby, Geoffrey Lawrence, Jim McKay, and David Rowe. 1999. "Modifying the Sign: Sport and Globalization." *Social Text* 17 (3): 15–33.

Miller, Toby, Geoffrey A. Lawrence, Jim McKay, and David Rowe. 2001. *Globalization and Sport: Playing the World.* London: Sage.

Milner, G. B. 1992. *Samoan Dictionary: Samoan-English-Samoan.* New Zealand: Pasifika Press.

Mintz, Sidney W. 1998. "The Localization of Anthropological Practice: From Area Studies to Transnationalism." *Critique of Anthropology* 18 (2): 117–133.

Miyamoto, J. K. 2005. "Community Needs as Perceived by Pacific Islander School Personnel." MA thesis, California State University, Long Beach.

Molnar, Gyozo, and Yoko Kanemasu. 2014. "Playing on the Global Periphery: Social Scientific Explorations of Rugby in the Pacific Islands." *Asia Pacific Journal of Sport and Social Science* 3 (3): 175–185.

Montenigro, Philip H., Michael L. Alosco, Brett M. Martin, Daniel H. Daneshvar, Jesse Mez, Christine E. Chaisson, Christopher J. Nowinski, Rhoda Au, Ann C. McKee, and Robert C. Cantu. 2017. "Cumulative Head Impact Exposure Predicts Later-Life Depression, Apathy, Executive Dysfunction, and Cognitive Impairment in Former High School and College Football Players." *Journal of Neurotrauma* 34 (2): 328–340.

Morimoto, Lauren S. 2015. "Locals Only: Barefoot Football and the Construction of Local Identity on Kaua'i." *Amerasia Journal* 41 (2): 86–107.

Morita, Monica K. 2013. *A Study of Pacific Islander Scholarship Football Players and Their Institutional Experience in Higher Education.* Los Angeles: University of Southern California Press.

Moses, John A. 1972. "The Solf Regime in Western Samoa: Ideal and Reality." *New Zealand Journal of History* 6 (1): 42–56.

Mower, R., David L. Andrews, and Oliver J. C. Rick. 2014. "Football and 'Ghettocentric' Logics? The NFL's Essentialist Mobilization of Black Bodies." In *The NFL: Critical and Cultural Perspectives*, edited by Thomas P. Oates and Zack Furness, 119–141. Philadelphia: Temple University Press.

Mueller, Frederick O., and Bob Colgate. 2012. *Annual Survey of Football Injury Research 1931–2011*. Waco, TX and Indianapolis: American Football Coaches Association, National Collegiate Athletic Association, and the National Federation of State High School Associations.

Myers, Fred R. 2001. *The Empire of Things: Regimes of Value and Material Culture*. 1st ed. Santa Fe, NM: School of American Research Press.

Nofoaiga, Vaitusi. 2020. "Tautuaileva: A Samoan Hermeneutic to Explore Egalitarianism in the Bible." *The Journal of Sāmoan Studies* 10: 60–69.

Oates, Thomas P. 2007. "The Erotic Gaze in the NFL Draft." *Communication and Critical/Cultural Studies* 4 (1): 74–90.

Oates, Thomas P., and Meenakshi Gigi Durham. 2004. "The Mismeasure of Masculinity: The Male Body, 'Race' and Power in the Enumerative Discourses of the NFL Draft." *Patterns of Prejudice* 38 (3): 301–320. doi:10.1080/0031322042 000250475.

Okamura, Jonathan Y. 2008. *Ethnicity and Inequality in Hawai'i*. Philadelphia: Temple University Press.

Omalu, Bennet, Gary W. Small, Julian Bailes, Linda M. Ercoli, David A. Merrill, Koon-Pong Wong, Sung-Cheng Huang, Nagichettiar Satyamurthy, Jennifer L. Hammers, John Lee, Robert P. Fitzsimmons, and Jorge R. Barrio. 2018. "Postmortem Autopsy-Confirmation of Antemortem [F-18] Fddnp-Pet Scans in a Football Player with Chronic Traumatic Encephalopathy." *Neurosurgery* 82 (2): 237–246. doi:10.1093/neuros/nyx536.

Omalu, Bennet I., Steven T. DeKosky, Ronald L. Hamilton, Ryan L. Minster, M. Ilyas Kamboh, Abdulrezak M. Shakir, and Cyril H. Wecht. 2006. "Chronic Traumatic Encephalopathy in a National Football League Player: Part II." *Neurosurgery* 59 (5): 1086–1093.

Omalu, Bennet I., Steven T. DeKosky, Ryan L. Minster, M Ilyas Kamboh, Ronald L. Hamilton, and Cyril H. Wecht. 2005. "Chronic Traumatic Encephalopathy in a National Football League Player." *Neurosurgery* 57 (1): 128–134. doi:10.1227/01.neu.0000163407.92769.ed.

Omalu, Bennet I., Ronald L. Hamilton, M. Ilyas Kamboh, Steven T. DeKosky, and Julian Bailes. 2010. "Chronic Traumatic Encephalopathy (CTE) in a National Football League Player: Case Report and Emerging Medicolegal Practice Questions." *Journal of Forensic Nursing* 6 (1): 40–46.

O'Meara, J. Tim. 1990. *Samoan Planters: Tradition and Economic Development in Polynesia. Case Studies in Cultural Anthropology*. Fort Worth: Holt Rinehart and Winston.

Ortner, Sherry B. 1996. *Making Gender: The Politics and Erotics of Culture*. Boston: Beacon Press.

Panapa, Lameko, and Murray Phillips. 2014. "Ethnic Persistence: Towards Understanding the Lived Experiences of Pacific Island Athletes in the National Rugby League." *The International Journal of the History of Sport* 31 (11): 1374–1388. doi:10.1080/09523367.2014.924105.

Pelley, Scott. 2010. "Football Island." *60 Minutes*. CBS (January 17).

Pitt, David C. 1970. *Tradition and Economic Progress in Samoa; a Case Study of the Role of Traditional Social Institutions in Economic Development*. Oxford: Clarendon Press.

Poblete-Cross, Joanna. 2010. "Bridging Indigenous and Immigrant Struggles: A Case Study of American Sāmoa." *American Quarterly* 62 (3): 501–522.

Poli, Raffaele. 2010. "African Migrants in Asian and European Football: Hopes and Realities." *Sport in Society* 13 (6): 1001–1011. doi:10.1080/17430437.2010 .491269.

Pratt, Mary Louise. 1992. *Imperial Eyes: Travel Writing and Transculturation*. London: Routledge.

Putney, Clifford. 2001. *Muscular Christianity: Manhood and Sports in Protestant America, 1880–1920*. Cambridge, MA: Harvard University Press.

Quinn, Kevin G. 2012. "Getting to the 2011–2020 National Football League Collective Bargaining Agreement." *International Journal of Sport Finance* 7 (2): 141–157. *Gale Academic OneFile*. Accessed January 7, 2019. https://link.gale .com/apps/doc/A323349962/AONE?u=learn&sid=AONE&xid=a177499b.

Rhoden, William. 2006. *Forty Million Dollar Slaves: The Rise, Fall, and Redemption of the Black Athlete*. New York: Crown.

Robbins, Joel. 2013. "Beyond the Suffering Subject: Toward an Anthropology of the Good." *Journal of the Royal Anthropological Institute* 19 (3): 447–462.

Robertson, Roland. 1994. "Globalisation or Glocalisation?" *The Journal of International Communication* 1 (1): 33–52. doi:10.1080/13216597.1994.9751780.

Robertson, Roland. 1995. "Glocalization: Time-Space and Homogeneity-Heterogeneity." In *Global Modernities*, edited by Mike Featherstone, Scott Lash, and Roland Robertson, 25–54. London: Sage.

Romo, Lynsey K. 2017. "College Student-Athletes' Communicative Negotiation of Emotion Labor." *Communication & Sport* 5 (4): 492–509.

Rony, Fatimah Tobing. 1996. *The Third Eye: Race, Cinema, and Ethnographic Spectacle*. Durham, NC: Duke University Press.

Rowe, David. 2010. "Money, Myth, and the Big Match." In *Sport, Power, and Society: Institutions and Practices*, edited by Robert E. Washington and David Karen, 51–94. Boulder, CO: Westview Press.

Ruck, Rob. 2018. *Tropic of Football: The Long and Perilous Journey of Samoans to the NFL*. New York: The New Press.

Runstedtler, Theresa. 2018. "More Than Just Play: Unmasking Black Child Labor in the Athletic Industrial Complex." *Journal of Sport and Social Issues* 42 (3): 152–169.

Rush, E. C., L. D. Plank, M. S. Laulu, and S. M. Robinson. 1997. "Prediction of Percentage Body Fat from Anthropometric Measurements: Comparison of New Zealand European and Polynesian Young Women." *The American Journal of Clinical Nutrition* 66 (1): 2–7. doi:10.1093/ajcn/66.1.2.

Sabo, Donald F., and Joe Panepinto. 1990. "Football Ritual and the Social Reproduction of Masculinity." *Sport, Men, and the Gender Order: Critical Feminist Perspectives*: 115–126.

Sack, Allen, and Ellen J. Staurowsky. 1998. *College Athletes for Hire: The Evolution and Legacy of the NCAA's Amateur Myth*. Westport, CT: Praeger Publishers.

Sacks, Benjamin. 2017. "A Footnote to Sport History: Twenty Years of Cricket, Conflict and Contestation in Samoa, 1880–1900." *The International Journal of the History of Sport*: 1–18. doi:10.1080/09523367.2017.1348349.

Sacks, Benjamin. 2019. *Cricket, Kirikiti and Imperialism in Samoa, 1879–1939*. New York: Springer.

Sage, George H. 1998. *Power and Ideology in American Sport: A Critical Perspective*. Champaign, IL: Human Kinetics.

Sahlins, Marshall. 1988. "Cosmologies of Capitalism: The Trans-Pacific Sector of the World System." *Proceedings of the British Academy* LXXIV: 1–51.

Said, Edward W. 1994 [1978]. *Orientalism*. New York: Vintage Books.

Salesa, T. Damon I. 2003. "'Travel Happy' Samoa: Colonialism, Samoan Migration, and a 'Brown Pacific.'" *New Zealand Journal of History* 37 (2): 171–88.

Sapolu, Jesse. 2012. *I Gave My Heart to San Francisco*. Newport Beach, CA: Celebrity Publishing.

Sassen, Saskia. 1998. *Globalization and Its Discontents: Essays on the New Mobility of People and Money*. New York: New Press.

Schieder, Dominik, and Geir-Henning Presterudstuen. 2014. "Sport Migration and Sociocultural Transformation: The Case of Fijian Rugby Union Players in Japan." *The International Journal of the History of Sport* 31 (11): 1359–1373. doi:10.1080/09523367.2014.921907.

Schmidt, Johanna. 2016. "Being 'Like a Woman': Fa'afāfine and Samoan Masculinity." *The Asia Pacific Journal of Anthropology* 17 (3–4): 287–304. doi:10.1080/14442213.2016.1182208.

Schoeffel, Penelope. 1981, 1979. "Daughters of Sina: A Study of Gender, Status and Power in Western Samoa." PhD dissertation, Australian National University.

Schoeffel, Penelope. 1987. "Rank, Gender and Politics in Ancient Samoa: The Genealogy of Salamasina O Le Tafaifa." *The Journal of Pacific History* 22 (3–4): 174–194.

Schoeffel, Penelope. 1995. "The Samoan Concept of Feagaiga and Its Transformation." *Tonga and Samoa: Images of Gender and Polity*: 85–105.

Schoeffel, Penelope. 2014. "Representing Fa'afafine: Sex, Socialization, and Gender Identity in Samoa." In *Gender on the Edge: Transgender, Gay, and Other Pacific Islanders*, edited by Kalissa Alexeyeff and Niko Besnier. Honolulu: University of Hawai'i Press.

Schwanke, J., and University of Montana Office of University Relations. 1968. "Giant Hawaiian Ready to Go with Football Grizzlies in Spring." In *University of Montana News Releases, 1928, 1956–Present. 3379*. Missoula: University of Montana–Missoula.

Shankman, Paul. 1976. *Migration and Underdevelopment: The Case of Western Samoa*. Boulder, CO: Westview Press.

Shore, Bradd. 1981. "Sexuality and Gender in Samoa: Conceptions and Missed Conceptions." In *Sexual Meanings: The Cultural Construction of Gender and Sexuality*, edited by Sherry B. Ortner and Harriet Whitehead, 192–215. Cambridge: Cambridge University Press.

Shore, Bradd. 1982. *Sala'ilua, a Samoan Mystery*. New York: Columbia University Press.

Simanu-Klutz, Luafata. 2011. "A Malu I Fale, 'E Malu Fo'i I Fafo Samoan Women and Power: Towards an Historiography of Changes and Continuities in Power Relations in Le Nu'u O Teine of SāOluafata 1350–1998 C.E." PhD dissertation, History, University of Hawai'i–Manoa. http://hdl.handle.net/10125/101635.

Singer, Merrill. 2014. "Following the Turkey Tails: Neoliberal Globalization and the Political Ecology of Health." *Journal of Political Ecology* 21 (1): 436–451. doi:10.2458/v21i1.21145.

Small, Cathy. 2011 [1997]. *Voyages: From Tongan Villages to American Suburbs*. Ithaca, NY: Cornell University Press.

Smith, Bernard. 1985. *European Vision and the South Pacific*. 2nd ed. New Haven, CT: Yale University Press.

Smith, Earl. 2007. *Race, Sport and the American Dream*. Durham, NC: Carolina Academic Press.

Smith, Earl. 2014. "The Athletic Industrial Complex: Conference Realignment, Race, and Title Ix." In *Race in American Sports: Essays*, edited by James L. Conyers Jr., 71–83. Jefferson, NC: McFarland.

So'o, Asofou, ed. 2007. *Changes in the Matai System: 'O Suiga I Le Fa'amatai*. Apia: Centre for Samoan Studies, National University of Samoa.

Spear, Jeremy, and Robert Pennington. 2005. *Polynesian Power: Islanders in Pro Football*. Pacific Islanders in Communications.

Spitulnik, Debra. 1996. "The Social Circulation of Media Discourse and the Mediation of Communities." *Journal of Linguistic Anthropology* 6 (2): 161–187.

Stamm, Julie M., Inga K. Koerte, Marc Muehlmann, Ofer Pasternak, Alexandra P. Bourlas, Christine M. Baugh, Michelle Y. Giwerc, Anni Zhu, Michael J. Coleman, and Sylvain Bouix. 2015. "Age at First Exposure to Football Is Associated with Altered Corpus Callosum White Matter Microstructure in Former Professional Football Players." *Journal of Neurotrauma* 32 (22): 1768–1776.

Stanovsky, Derek. 2007. "Postcolonial Masculinities." In *International Encyclopedia of Men and Masculinities*, edited by Michael Flood, Judith Kegan Gardiner, Bob Pease, and Keith Pringle, 493–496. London: Routledge.

Steele, Claude M., and Joshua Aronson. 1995. "Stereotype Threat and the Intellectual Test Performance of African Americans." *Journal of Personality and Social Psychology* 69 (5): 797–811.

Steger, Manfred B. 2008. *The Rise of the Global Imaginary: Political Ideologies from the French Revolution to the Global War on Terror*. Oxford: Oxford University Press.

Stern, Robert A., Daniel H. Daneshvar, Christine M. Baugh, Daniel R. Seichepine, Philip H. Montenigro, David O. Riley, Nathan G. Fritts, Julie M.

Stamm, Clifford A. Robbins, and Lisa McHale. 2013. "Clinical Presentation of Chronic Traumatic Encephalopathy." *Neurology* 81 (13): 1122–1129. doi: 10.1212/WNL.0b013e3182a55f7f.

Stern, Robert A., David O. Riley, Daniel H. Daneshvar, Christopher J. Nowinski, Robert C. Cantu, and Ann C. McKee. 2011. "Long-Term Consequences of Repetitive Brain Trauma: Chronic Traumatic Encephalopathy." *PM&R (Physical Medicine & Rehabilitation)* 3 (10): s460–s467.

Stodolska, Monika, and Konstantinos Alexandris. 2004. "The Role of Recreational Sport in the Adaptation of First Generation Immigrants in the United States." *Journal of Leisure Research* 36 (3): 379.

Stride, Peter. 2016. "Polynesian Bones." *Journal of Advances in Medicine and Medical Research* 16 (7): 1–9.

Swinburn, B. A., S. J. Ley, H. E. Carmichael, and L. D. Plank. 1999. "Body Size and Composition in Polynesians." *International Journal of Obesity* 23 (11): 1178–1183. doi:10.1038/sj.ijo.0801053.

Syken, Bill. 2003. "Football in Paradise." *Sports Illustrated* (November 3).

Talavage, Thomas M., Eric A. Nauman, Evan L. Breedlove, Umit Yoruk, Anne E. Dye, Katherine E. Morigaki, Henry Feuer, and Larry J. Leverenz. 2014. "Functionally-Detected Cognitive Impairment in High School Football Players without Clinically-Diagnosed Concussion." *Journal of Neurotrauma* 31 (4): 327–338.

Tauiliili, Pemerika L. 2009. *Anoafale O Le Gagana Ma Le Aganuu.* Tusi Muamua = Rev. ed. Bloomington, IN: Authorhouse 2009.

Taylor, John P. 2008. "Changing Pacific Masculinities: The 'Problem' of Men." *The Australian Journal of Anthropology* 19 (2): 125–135.

Taylor, Matthew. 2006. "Global Players? Football, Migration and Globalization, c. 1930–2000." *Historical Social Research/Historische Sozialforschung*: 7–30.

Taylor, Rachel Kahn, director. 2010. *Warriors Born: American Samoans in the U.S. Military.* 23 min. http://www.rachelkahntaylor.com/warriors-born.

Tcherkézoff, Serge. 1998. "Is Aristocracy Good for Democracy? A Contemporary Debate in Western Samoa." In *Pacific Answers to Western Hegemony: Cultural Practices of Identity Construction*, edited by Jurg Wassman, 417–434. Oxford and New York: Berg.

Tcherkézoff, Serge. 2000. "Are the *Matai* 'Out of Time'? Tradition and Democracy: Contemporary Ambiguities and Historical Transformations of the Concept of Chief." In *Governance in Samoa*, edited by Elise Huffer and Asofou So'o, 113–132. Canberra, Australia and Suva, Fiji: Asia Pacific Press, Australian National University and Institute of Pacific Studies, University of the South Pacific.

Teaiwa, Katerina Martina. 2005. "Multi-sited Methodologies: 'Homework' in Australia, Fiji, and Kiribati." In *Anthropologists in the Field: Cases in Participant Observation,* edited by Lynne Hume and Jane Mulcock, 216–234. New York: Columbia University Press.

Teaiwa, Katerina Martina. 2014. *Consuming Ocean Island: Stories of People and Phosphate from Banaba*. Bloomington: Indiana University Press.

Teaiwa, Katerina Martina. 2016. "Niu Mana, Sport, Media and the Australian Diaspora." In *New Mana: Transformations of a Classic Concept in Pacific Languages and Cultures*, edited by Matt Tomlinson and Ty P. Kāwika Tengan, 107–130. Acton, Australia: ANU Press.

Teaiwa, Teresia. 1995. "Scholarship from a Lazy Native." In *Work in Flux*, edited by Emma Greenwood, Klaus Neumann, and Andrew Sartori, 58–72. Melbourne: Melbourne University Press.

Teaiwa, Teresia, and Sean Mallon. 2005. "Ambivalent Kinships? Pacific People in New Zealand." In *New Zealand Identities: Departures and Destinations*, edited by James H. Liu, Tim McCreanor, Tracey McIntosh, and Teresia Teaiwa, 207–229. Wellington, NZ: Victoria University Press.

Teaiwa, Teresia K. 2005. "Articulated Cultures: Militarism and Masculinities in Fiji During the Mid 1990s." *Fijian Studies: A Journal of Contemporary Fiji* 3 (2): 201–222.

Tengan, Ty P. Kāwika. 2005. "Unsettling Ethnography: Tales of an ʻOiwi in the Anthropological Slot." *Anthropological Forum* 15 (1): 247–256.

Tengan, Ty P. Kāwika. 2008. *Native Men Remade: Gender and Nation in Contemporary Hawaiʻi*. Durham, NC: Duke University Press.

Tengan, Ty P. Kāwika, and Jesse Makani Markham. 2009. "Performing Polynesian Masculinities in American Football: From ʻRainbows to Warriors.'" *The International Journal of the History of Sport* 26 (16): 2412–2431.

Thangaraj, Stanley I., Jr., Constancio R. Arnaldo, and Christina B. Chin. 2016. "Introduction: You Play Sports? Asian American Sporting Matters." In *Asian American Sporting Cultures*, edited by Stanley I. Thangaraj Jr., Constancio R. Arnaldo, and Christina B. Chin, 1–20. New York: NYU Press.

Thunnan, David J., Christine M. Branche, and Joseph E. Sniezek. 1998. "The Epidemiology of Sports-Related Traumatic Brain Injuries in the United States: Recent Developments." *The Journal of Head Trauma Rehabilitation* 13 (2): 1–8.

Tiffany, Sharon W., and Walter W. Tiffany. 1978. "Optation, Cognatic Descent, and Redistributions in Samoa." *Ethnology* 17 (4): 367–390. http://www.jstor.org/stable/3773189.

Tiffany, Walter W. 1971. "Political Structure and Change: A Corporate Analysis of American Samoa." PhD dissertation, University of California.

Tipi, Faʻamalua. 2013. "When the Sun Goes Down: What Helps or Hinders Pasifika Professional Rugby Players to Successfully Transition to Another Career Pathway When They Retire from Professional Rugby." MA thesis, University of Auckland. http://hdl.handle.net/2292/20826.

Tofaeono, Amaʻamalele. 2000. *Eco-Theology: Aiga—the Household Life: A Perspective from Living Myths and Traditions of Samoa*. World Mission Scripts 7. Erlangen: Erlanger Verlag für Mission Und Okumene.

Tran, Jacqueline H., Michelle Wong, Erin Kahunawaikaʻala Wright, Joe Faʻavae, Ashley Cheri, Keith L. Camacho, and Mary Anne Foo. 2010. "Understanding

a Pacific Islander Young Adult Perspectives on Access to Higher Education."
California Journal of Health Promotion 8: 23–38.

Tran, Jacqueline H., Michelle Wong, Erin Kahunawaika'ala Wright, Joe Gafata-
itua Fa'avae, Ashley Cheri, Eric Wat, Keith L. Camacho, and Mary Anne
Foo. 2009. *The Pacific Islander Health Careers Pipeline Program: Report on
Educational Barriers, Needs, and Recommendations.* Orange County, CA:
Orange County Asian and Pacific Islander Community Alliance.

Trimbur, Lucia. 2013. *Come out Swinging.* Princeton, NJ: Princeton University
Press.

Trouillot, Michel-Rolph. 1991. "Anthropology and the Savage Slot: The Poetics and
Politics of Otherness." In *Recapturing Anthropology: Working in the Present*, edited by Richard G. Fox. Santa Fe, NM: School of American Research Press.

Trujillo, Nick. 1995. "Machines, Missiles, and Men: Images of the Male Body on
ABC's Monday Night Football." *Sociology of Sport Journal* 12 (4): 403–423.

Tualaulelei, Eseta Magaui, Fepuleai Lasei John Mayer, and Galumalemana A.
Hunkin. 2015. "Diacritical Marks and the Samoan Language." *The Contemporary Pacific* 27 (1): 184–207.

Tui Atua, Tupua Tamasese Efi, ed. 2007. *Su'esu'e Manogi: In Search of Fragrance:
Tui Atua Tupua Tamasese Ta'isi and the Samoan Indigenous Reference.*
Edited by Tamasailau Sua'ali'i-Sauni. Samoa: Centre for Samoan Studies,
National University of Samoa.

Uperesa, Fa'anofo Lisaclaire. 2010a. "A Different Weight: Tension and Promise in
Indigenous Anthropology." *Pacific Studies* 33 (2/3): 280–300.

Uperesa, Fa'anofo Lisaclaire. 2010b. "Fabled Futures: Development, Gridiron
Football, and Transnational Movements in American Samoa." PhD dissertation, Anthropology, Columbia University.

Uperesa, Fa'anofo Lisaclaire. 2014a. "Fabled Futures: Migration and Mobility for
Samoans in American Football." *The Contemporary Pacific* 27 (1): 281–301.

Uperesa, Fa'anofo Lisaclaire. 2014b. "Seeking New Fields of Labor: Football and
Colonial Political Economies in American Samoa." In *Formations of U.S.
Colonialism*, edited by Alyosha Goldstein, 207–233. Durham, NC: Duke
University Press.

Uperesa, Fa'anofo Lisaclaire. 2015. "Addressing Hyper/in-Visibility: A Roundtable
on Preliminary Research with Pacific Islander Student-Athletes." *Amerasia
Journal* 41 (2): 67–85.

Uperesa, Fa'anofo Lisaclaire. 2018. "Training for Empire? Samoa and American
Gridiron Football." In *Ethnographies of U.S. Empire*, edited by Carole
McGranahan and John Collins, 129–148. Durham, NC: Duke University
Press.

Uperesa, Fa'anofo Lisaclaire. 2021. "Entangled Histories and Transformative
Futures: Indigenous Sport in the 21st Century." In *Routledge Handbook of
Critical Indigenous Studies*, edited by Brendan Hokowhitu, Aileen Moreton-
Robinson, Linda Tuhiwai-Smith, Chris Andersen and S. Larkin, 511–524.
New York: Routledge.

Uperesa, Fa'anofo Lisaclaire, and Adriana María Garriga-López. 2017. "Contested Sovereignties: Puerto Rico and American Samoa." In *Sovereign Acts: Contesting Colonialism across Indigenous Nations and Latinx America*, edited by Frances Negrón-Muntaner, 39–81. Tucson: University of Arizona Press.

Uperesa, Fa'anofo Lisaclaire, and Thomas Mountjoy. 2014. "Global Sport in the Pacific: A Brief Overview." *The Contemporary Pacific* 27 (1): 263–279.

Va'a, Felise Paulo Saigo, Te'o Unasa Leulu Felise Va'a, Fonoti Lafitai I. Fuata'i, Muagututi'a Ioana Chan Mow, and Desmond Amosa. 2012. "Aspects of Economic Development." In *Samoa's Journey 1962-2012: Aspects of History*, edited by Leasiolagi Malama Meleisea, Penelope Schoeffel Meleisea, and Ellie Meleisea. Wellington, NZ: Victoria University Press.

Va'a, Unasa Leulu Felise. 2001. *Saili Matagi: Samoan Migrants in Australia*. Suva, Fiji: Institute of Pacific Studies, National University of Samoa.

Va'ai, Saleimoa. 1999. *Samoa Faamatai and the Rule of Law*. Le Papa-I-Galagala, Western Samoa: National University of Samoa.

Vercoe, Caroline. 2004. "The Many Faces of Paradise." In *Paradise Now? Contemporary Art from the Pacific*, edited by Melissa Chiu. New York: Asia Society.

Vertovec, Steven. 1997. "Three Meanings of 'Diaspora,' Exemplified among South Asian Religions." *Diaspora: A Journal of Transnational Studies* 6 (3): 277–299.

Vogan, Travis. 2014. *Keepers of the Flame: NFL Films and the Rise of Sports Media*. Champaign: University of Illinois Press.

Wacquant, Loïc. 1995. "Pugs at Work: Bodily Capital and Bodily Labour among Professional Boxers." *Body & Society* 1 (1): 65–93.

Waldroup, Heather Leigh 2004. "Traveling Images: Representations of the South Pacific from Colonial and Postcolonial Worlds." PhD dissertation, University of California, Santa Cruz.

Wallace, Jessica, Tracey Covassin, Sally Nogle, Daniel Gould, and Jeffrey Kovan. 2017. "Knowledge of Concussion and Reporting Behaviors in High School Athletes with or without Access to an Athletic Trainer." *Journal of Athletic Training* 52 (3): 228–235.

Watson, Nick J., Stuart Weir, and Stephen Friend. 2005. "The Development of Muscular Christianity in Victorian Britain and Beyond." *Journal of Religion & Society* 7.

Watterson, John Sayle. 2000. *College Football: History, Spectacle, Controversy*. Baltimore: Johns Hopkins University Press.

Waytz, Adam, Kelly Marie Hoffman, and Sophie Trawalter. 2015. "A Superhumanization Bias in Whites' Perceptions of Blacks." *Social Psychological and Personality Science* 6 (3): 352–359. doi:10.1177/1948550614553642.

West, Candace, and Don H Zimmerman. 1987. "Doing Gender." *Gender & Society* 1 (2): 125–151.

West, Paige. 2012. *From Modern Production to Imagined Primitive: The Social World of Coffee from Papua New Guinea*. Durham, NC: Duke University Press.

Wiggins, David K. 1994. "The Notion of Double-Consciousness and the Involve-ment of Black Athletes in American Sport." In *Ethnicity and Sport in North American History and Culture*, edited by George Eisen and David K. Wig-gins, 133–155. Westport, CT: Greenwood Press.

Wilkinson, Rupert. 1964. *Gentlemanly Power—British Leadership and Public Schools Tradition*. London: Oxford University Press.

Willis, Paul. 2000. *The Ethnographic Imagination*. Malden, MA: Polity Press.

Wilson, William Julius. 2011. *When Work Disappears: The World of the New Urban Poor*. New York: Vintage.

Yost, Mark. 2006. *Tailgating, Sacks, and Salary Caps: How the NFL Became the Most Successful Sports League in History*. Chicago: Kaplan.

Zakus, Dwight, and Peter Horton. 2009. "Pasifika in Australian Rugby: Emanant Cultural, Social and Economic Issues." *Sporting Traditions* 26 (2): 67.

Index

Academic All-American, 98
African Americans, 87
Ah You, Miki "Junior," 29
AIGA Foundation, 129
All Islands Getting Along (AIGA),
    145–146
All Poly Camp, 31, 62–63, 64
alofa (love or compassion), 53–54, 59, 60
Aloha Stadium, 57
Alzheimer's, study on, 126
American: dream, 19–20; popular culture,
    38
American Community Survey, 43
American Sāmoa, 4, 5, 7, 163nn30–31;
    concussion training in, 131; continental
    U.S. relationship with, 12–13, 21; culture,
    11, 12, 18–19, 20, 38; economy in, 13–14,
    16–17, 20; Fitafita from, 27–28, 181n7;
    football development in, 29–30, 33–37,
    40–41; students, 104; transnational
    diaspora from, 11, 61; Uperesa, Tu'ufuli,
    return to, 44–45. See also fa'asāmoa;

Sāmoa (independent); Samoan players;
    Tutuila
Aotearoa New Zealand, 53–54, 151–152,
    159n2
Apia, 61
Apisa, Bob, 29, 30
Auckland, 94, 151, 152, 184n1
'aumaga (untitled men of the village), 88,
    181n7
'ava ceremony, 48–49; for Fa'a Samoa
    Initiative, 68, 69; for PFHOF, 1–3; for
    Tinoisamoa and Sopoaga, 50–51

Big Boyz, 116
Birrell, Susan, 89
Black athletes, 83; racism against, 85–86;
    U.S. racial mythography of, 88
Black masculinities, 86
bodily capital, 108–109, 132
body stereotyping, 84–85
Boston University CTE Center, 126–127
Bourdieu, Pierre, 4–5

boxing, 127, 178n12

brand, 17; of Polamalu, Troy, 97; of Polynesian Gridiron Warrior, 101; of Samoan players, 102

British Commonwealth, 51

Brown, Wally, 25

Burstyn, Varda, 115–116

Canadian Football League (CFL), 44, 163n25

canneries, 14, 39, 169n27

capital. *See specific topics*

Carter, Thomas, 7–8

Center for Disease Control (CDC), 128

Chargers, 124

cheerleaders, 36

Christianity, 12

chronic traumatic encephalopathy (CTE), 126, 127, 147, 182n16

Church of Jesus Christ of Latter-day Saints (LDS), 65

class action lawsuit, against NFL, 147, 183n26

coaches, 180n29; advice from, 62–63; of Mark, 109–110, 118, 119; NFL, 107; on Samoan players, 82; Ta'ase, Suaese "Pooch" as, 56–58; Uperesa, Tu'ufuli, as, 36, 39–40, 45, 63

coaches, Polynesian, 153–154

collectivist orientations, 182n13

college athletic scholarships, 104, 110

college football, 162nn18–19; media on, 168n19; revenue of, 116–117

College Football Playoff, 116–117

colonialism, 7–8, 153, 165n42, 165n44

commodification: of football players, 106, 107–109, 111–114, 115, 121; of labor, 107–109, 111–112, 113; limits to, 118–119; Mark resistance to, 109–111, 116–119; of Samoan players, 114, 115; of student-athletes, 116–118

commodities: fetishism of, 112–113, 179n16; Marx on, 179n17

community service, as tautua, 60

concussion crisis: CTE in, 126, 147, 182n16; *League of Denial* on, 125–126; research

on, 125–128; RHI in, 128; student-athletes on, 129–131, 144; sub-concussive events impacting, 129. *See also* traumatic brain injuries

concussions: training, 131–132; youth laws on, 128

concussions, underreporting, 130–131, 134

Congressional Horizon Award, 56

contact restrictions, football, 143

cricket, 170n3

criminal justice system, 81

cultural capital, 4

cultural commodities, 112–113, 114

cultural identity, 149

Daugherty, Duffy, 29, 43

de-fetishization, of cultural commodities, 112–113

dementia pugilistica, 127

Department for Youth and Women's Affairs, 48, 49, 67

Department of Education, 33, 41, 67

Department of Parks and Recreation, 33

Department of the Interior, 27

diacritics, 159n1

diaspora, transnational, 11, 61, 152

Director of Guidance and Counseling Services (DGCS), 65–66

Dominican Republic, 7

Eastern Washington Eagles, 25

economic capital, 4, 45

economy: in American Sāmoa, 13–14, 16–17, 20; neoliberal capitalist, 17

Edwards, Harry, 85

elder volunteers, 65–66

Elisaia, Doug, 62–63

Elite Daily, 84

Ellison, Riki, 129, 130

ESPN, 52

ethnographic imaginations, 72, 100

ethnography, 20, 161n14

exotic difference, 73–74

Fa'aleava, Vui Toeutu, 135, 181n7

fa'amālosi (stay/be strong), 150

fa'amatai (chiefly hierarchy of Samoan lands and titles), 52, 53–54, 69–70

fa'asāmoa (Samoan culture), 18, 19, 57–58, 59, 171n8; definition of, 53; evolution of, 54–55, 69–70; in Fa'a Samoa Initiative, 64–69; football relationship with, 49–50, 52

Fa'a Samoa Initiative, 48–50; academic division of, 65–66; 'ava ceremony for, 68, 69; fa'asāmoa in, 64–69; hospitality in, 66–68; local partners role in, 64–65

Fa'asinomaga (identity), 173n22

Faga'itua Vikings, 139–140

Fainaru, Steve, 125–126

Fainaru-Wada, Mark, 125–126

Fanene, Josiah, 90

Fanoga, Mike, 62–63

femininity, 36, 93; sport regarding, 176n29; toa regarding, 136–137

Festival of Pacific Arts, 62

fetishism, commodity, 112–113, 179n16

Fitafita (military enlistees who left American Sāmoa), 27–28, 181n7

Fitisemanu, Alema, 40, 60–61

Flag Day, 19

football, gridiron. *See specific topics*

football development: in American Sāmoa, 29–30, 33–37, 40–41; in continental U.S., 30; media role in, 9; in Tutuila, 31–32, 35

football-industrial complex, 115–116, 179n20

"Football In Paradise," 71, 72, 84

"Football is Family," 99

"Football Island," 72, 86–87; Lauvao in, 89; Pelley framing in, 74–75; "Sunday Samoans" visibility in, 31

Fui (Samoan player), 32, 33–34

futures, football, 5, 38, 46–47, 154

gender inequality, sport, 92–93

gifting, 67

globalization, 5, 6, 160nn8–10

Goodman, Richard, 175n24

governor's dinner, 67

graduation success rate (GSR), 180n28

gridiron capital, definition of, 109. *See also specific topics*

Gridiron Ministries, 145

haka (performance), 74–75

Hall, Stuart, 72, 76

haole terminology, 169n30

Hau'ofa, Epeli, 10

Hawai'i, 57, 83, 92, 96; kukui nut 'ula popularized in, 78–79; Mariota connection with, 99; military presence in, 28; PIAA in, 103–105; Polynesian Pipeline in, 29, 30; Samoans in, 43; University of Hawai'i in, 91, 136, 159n2, 160n5

Hayne, Jarred, 184n3

HBO Real Sports/Marist Poll, 143

Heads Up Football (HUF), 142, 143

Heisman Trophy, 15, 98–99

hooks, bell, 89–90

Hughes, Thomas, 133

Hunkin, Faleomavaega Eni, 56

hypermasculinity, 141–142

'ie lāvalava (customary clothing item in Samoan villages), 78–79, 97

Imo, Ed, 44

indigenization: of cricket, 170n3; of sport, 20, 49–50

indigenous: masculinities, 173n5; ontologies, 11; Polynesian masculinities, 75, 80

In Football We Trust, 15, 31

informed soldier trope, 144

Insular Cases, 164n32

International Federation of American Football (IFAF), 9, 41

International Pathway Program, 9

Ivy League, 133

Jack Murphy Stadium, 124

Johnson, Dwayne ("The Rock"), 51, 55–56, 80

Johnston, Richard W., 71, 72, 74, 84. *See also* "Shake 'em Out of the Coconut Trees"

Jones, June, 81, 96

June Jones Goodwill Mission, 131

kinship relations, 169n29, 172n20

kirikiti (indigenization of cricket in Sāmoa), 170n3

Kopytoff, Igor, 107–108

Kristin (mother), 25; labor of, 39; on Seau passing, 123

kukui nut 'ula (adornment popularized in Hawai'i), 78–79

KVZK-TV, 33, 34

labor, 165n41; commodification of, 107–109, 111–112, 113; of Kristin, 39; mobility through, 15, 109, 148–149, 153, 154; Polynesian masculinity regarding, 135; power, 17, 111; route, 16; Samoans patterns of, 164n36; slavery legacy in, 107–108

Lake, Ethan, 151

Lauvao, Pepine, 89

League of Denial: The NFL, Concussions, and the Battle for Truth (Fainaru-Wada and Fainaru), 125–126

League of Denial: the NFL's Concussion Crisis, 125–126

Leone Lions, 40, 41–42

Lilomaiava-Doktor, Sa'iliemanu, 11

linemen positions, 129, 175n17

Lolo (Governor), 68

Lolotai, Albert, 32

Lystedt, Zackery, 128

Lystedt Law, 128

Magalei, Jason, 36

Mageo, Simon, 39

Mailata, Jordan, 184n3

Major League Baseball, 7

malaga (visiting, travel, movement), 38

Malau'ulu, George, 145

Malau'ulu, Miya, 145

Malietoa Tanumafili II, Afioga i le Ao o le Mālō, 50–52, 172n14

Manu Samoa rugby team, 136

Mariota, Marcus, 98–100

Mark (Samoan player), commodification resistance by, 109–111, 116–119

Marx, Karl, 179n17

masculinities, 21, 35, 93, 140; Black, 86; indigenous, 173n5; muscular, 133; Samoan, 19–20, 124–125, 149; stereotypes impact of, 141–142; toa regarding, 136, 137–138, 141

masculinity, Polynesian, 21, 149; indigenous, 75, 80; labor regarding, 135; "physicality" representation of, 89; racialization and socialization of, 134

Masoli, Jeremiah, 15

matai (titled chiefs; those who hold customary family titles), 51, 52, 171n6, 172nn15–16; evolution of, 69, 70; principles of, 53–54; Sapolu becoming, 55, 56. *See also* fa'amatai

"Maximum Exposure," 107

media, 41; on college football, 168n19; meaning-making from, 76; Pacific Islander players narrative in, 95–96, 100; Polamalu, Troy, in, 96–97; Polynesian players in, 94; power mediation through, 77; Samoan "physicality" representations in, 89; Samoan players in, 71–72, 94; Shelton in, 97–98

Meleisea, Leasiolagi Malama, 54

Michigan State University (MSU), 29

middle class, 148

middle linebackers, 129, 130

migrants, 161nn12–13

migration, post–World War II, 10

migration pathways: colonialism influencing, 7–8; transnational sport, 6–8, 46, 61

Mikaele, Felise, 170n4

military, 15, 19; Fitafita in, 27–28, 181n7; football symbolism of, 133; in Hawai'i, 28; toa regarding, 137–140

Mississippi Youth Concussion Act, 128

Missoula, 25–26, 165n1

mobility, 4–5, 20, 105; for Pacific Islander players, 18; for Samoan players, 15–17, 27, 38; through sport labor, 15, 109, 148–149, 153, 154

mobility, transnational, 5; from Oceania, 10–11; Pacific Islands regarding, 6, 10

MSU. *See* Michigan State University

muscular Christianity, 133
muscular masculinities, 133

Nafanua (Samoan "warrior" goddess), 135, 137
name, image and likeness (NIL), 116
Nansen, Johnny, 62–63
narratives: Mariota mediation of, 98–100; of Pacific Islander players, 95–96, 100; on Samoan players, 100–101
National Association of Intercollegiate Athletics (NAIA), 37
National Collegiate Athletic Association (NCAA), 8–9, 25, 27, 162nn20–21, 167n17; deficits in, 117; policies of, 116, 126, 178n5, 178n15; precursor to, 133; revenue of, 180n26; rule changes in, 142
National Football League (NFL), 163n26, 167n17, 169nn33–34, 184n27; class action lawsuit against, 147, 183n26; coaches, 107; Draft, 97, 107–108; Films, 32; funnel programs into, 8–9, 116; *League of Denial* on, 125–126; Malietoa Tanumafili II reception of, 50–52; players, 45, 63–64; Polynesian players in, 31; prospects, 108, 111; revenue of, 9; rule changes in, 142; Scouting Combine, 106–107, 108; Seau in, 123–124; suicides from, 126. *See also* concussion crisis
National High School Sports-Related Injury Surveillance Study, 128
Native Hawaiian and Other Pacific Islanders (NHOPI), 14
Navy, US, 27, 28
NCAA. *See* National Collegiate Athletic Association
NCAA policies, 116, 126, 178n5, 178n15
neoliberal capitalist economy, 17
New York Giants, 107
New Zealand, Aotearoa, 53–54, 151–152
NFL. *See* National Football League
NFL Draft, 97, 107–108
NFL Films, 32
NFL players: economic capital of, 45; tautua expectations of, 63–64
NFL Players' Association, 45

NFL prospects: agency of, 108; for Mark, 111
NFL Scouting Combine, 106–107, 108

Oceania, 10–11
'ohana (family), 99
"O 'oe o le toa," 138
osi 'āiga (occasional service), 58
Othering, 77
Otherness, 89–90

Pacific-10 Conference teams, 15
Pacific communities, 152
Pacific Islander communities, 101
Pacific Islander Health Careers Pipeline Program (PIHCPP), 91
Pacific Islander players: in media narratives, 95–96, 100; mobility for, 18
Pacific Islander students, stereotypes impacting, 91–92
Pacific Islander terminology, 160n4
Pacific Islands, 6, 10
Pacific Islands Athletic Alliance (PIAA), 103–105
Pacific players, in rugby, 152–153
Pacific terminology, 160n4
Pago Pago, 27–28
Pago Park, 36, 37, 40
parents: tautua for, 59–60; youth football concern of, 143–144, 145
Pasifika terminology, 160n4
Pelley, Scott, 74–75, 84, 86–87
Pesamino, Francis, 94–95
PFHOF. *See* Polynesian Football Hall of Fame
Philadelphia Eagles, 44
physical aggression, 175n24
physical costs, 119–120, 121, 125, 132, 142–143
Polamalu, Theodora, 48, 66–68
Polamalu, Troy, 48, 66, 67, 146; 'ava ceremony for, 68, 69; in media, 96–97; in "Samoan Stereotypes" illustration, 94–95; tautua of, 68–69. *See also* Troy and Theodora Polamalu Foundation
Polamalu camp, 49

Polynesian: Network, 18, 31; Pipeline, 8, 18, 27–29, 30, 42–44; students, 103–104; terminology, 160n4; warrior trope, 73, 74; women, 92

Polynesian All-American Bowl (PAAB), 129, 144–146

Polynesian communities: Shelton connecting with, 98, 121; TBIS reckoning for, 154

Polynesian Cultural Center, 1, 3

Polynesian Football Hall of Fame (PFHOF): 'ava ceremony for, 1–3; Seau induction to, 146–147

Polynesian Gridiron Warrior, 73, 75–76, 92, 93, 114; ethnographic imagining of, 100; Pacific Islander communities branded as, 101

Polynesianism, discourse of, 77

Polynesian players: discourse on, 86; in media, 94; in NFL, 31; racialization of, 4, 83, 85–87; stereotypes of, 84–85, 179n18; TBIS reckoning for, 154

Polynesian Power, 30, 50, 55, 72; flyer for, 77–79; Jones in, 81, 96; NFL Scouting Combine in, 106–107; Samoan players commodification in, 114; Sopoaga in, 77–81, 87; Tinoisamoa in, 80–81, 87

Polynesians: athlete stereotypes of, 90; racialization of, 174n13

Pop Warner, 116, 143, 182n17

Potoa'e, Benning Tamatane, 91

poverty rate, 14

Power Five conferences, 117

practice theory, 163n27

predominantly White institutions (PWI), 120

Pro Football Hall of Fame, 2

pule (power or authority), 53–54, 172n12

"punch drunk syndrome," 127

Purcell, Lealao Melila, 44

racialization: differential, 85, 87–88, 99–100; of Polynesian masculinity, 134; of Polynesian players, 4, 83, 85–87; of Polynesians, 174n13; of Samoan players, 83, 85–88, 114; of student-athletes, 120–121

racial mythography, of Black athletes, 88

racial stacking, 175n19

racism, 43, 85–86, 179n19

recruitment, 104

repetitive head impacts (RHI), 128

revenue: of college football, 116–117; of NCAA, 180n26; of NFL, 9

risk, of football, 130, 147–149, 154

"The Rock" (Dwayne Johnson), 51, 55–56

Roosevelt, Theodore, 133

Rose Bowl, 15

Royal Order of Kamehameha (ROK), 1–2

Rozelle, Pete, 30, 32

rugby: football compared to, 7, 33, 35–36, 51, 168n24; Manu Samoa team, 136; Pacific players in, 152–153

Sabol, Steve, 32

Saelua, Fiu Johnny, 49

Said, Edward, 174n7

Saleaumua, Dan, 145, 146

Saleaumua, Wesley, 145

Sāmoa (independent), 11, 50–51, 166n7

Samoa Bowl, 41, 170n2

Samoan: communities, 94–95; dream, 19–20; girls, 92–93; masculinities, 19–20, 124–125, 149; "physicality" representations, 89

Samoana High School cheer, 37

Samoan and other Pacific Islander: athletes, 141–142; communities, 93–94

Samoana Sharks, 40, 41–42

Samoan players, 21, 122; body stereotyping of, 84–85; branding of, 102; coaches on, 82; commodification of, 114, 115; discourse on, 72–73, 86; exotic difference portrayal of, 73–74; Fui, 32, 33–34; Mark, 109–111, 116–119; in media, 71–72, 94; mobility for, 15–17, 27, 38; motivations of, 5, 9–10, 150; narratives on, 100–101; racialization of, 83, 85–88, 114; tautua for, 18

Samoans, 175n16; athlete stereotype of, 90–91; labor force patterns of, 164n36; racism against, 43

"Samoan Stereotypes," 94–95
Samoan Youth, 90
San Diego State University, 124
San Francisco 49ers, 52, 55, 113
Sapolu, Jesse, 2, 52, 55, 56, 69, 146
Satele, Tapumanaia Galu Jr., 35, 36, 37
"savage slot" stereotype, 77
scholarships, 162n20, 167n13
schools, underfunding, 177n4
scouting, 104–105
Seau, Tiaina Baul Jr. (Junior Seau), 21; as
    cautionary tale, 145; passing of, 123–124,
    126, 130, 148; PFHOF induction of,
    146–147
Seiuli (high chief title), 55, 56
"Shake 'em Out of the Coconut Trees," 30,
    71, 72, 73–74
Shelton, Danny, 97–98, 121, 177n36
60 Minutes, 31, 72, 74–75, 86–87, 89
slave trade, NFL Draft comparison to,
    107–108
social capital, 4
social programs, defunding, 177n3
Solaita, Tony, 44
Sopoaga, Isaac, 52, 82; 'ava ceremony for,
    50–51; in *Polynesian Power*, 77–81, 87
Spartans, 29
Spear, Jeremy, 80–81
Spitulnik, Deborah, 76
sport, 176n26; camps, 31, 49, 50, 57, 62–63,
    64, 105; femininity regarding, 176n29;
    gender inequality in, 92–93; indigeniza-
    tion of, 20, 49–50; as labor route, 16;
    mobility through, 15, 109, 148–149, 153,
    154; as transnational migration pathway,
    6–8, 46, 61; White persons in, 86
Sports Illustrated, 30, 71, 72, 84, 107
sports-industrial complex, 179n20
StarKist Foods, 14
stereotypes: athlete, 84–85, 90–92,
    174n15; hypermasculinity, 141–142;
    Pacific Islander students impacted by,
    91–92; Pesamino illustrating, 94–95;
    of Polynesian players, 84–85, 179n18;
    of Polynesians, 90; Samoan and other
    Pacific Islander communities impacted

by, 93–94; within Samoan communities,
    94–95; Samoan girls impacted by, 92–93;
    "savage slot," 77; of student-athletes,
    120–121; warrior, 73, 74, 101
student-athletes: burdens on, 149; com-
    modification of, 116–118; on concussion
    crisis, 129–131, 144; racialization and
    stereotyping of, 120–121; risk awareness
    and minimization by, 130
Suaalii-Sauni, Tamasailau, 53–54
suicides, former NFL players, 126
Sullivan, Doris, 103–104
"Sunday Samoans," 31
Super Bowl, 133
Syken, Bill, 71, 72

Ta'ase, Suaese "Pooch," 42, 56–58
"Tama Samoa," 170n4
Tanielu, Fepulea'i Vita L., 136
Tanuvasa, Ma'a, 2, 146
Tapasa, Solomona, 62–63
Tatupu, Mosi, 166n8
tautua (service), 18–19, 46, 54, 56, 172n13,
    173nn21–22; choice of, 63–64; evolution
    of, 55, 58–61, 69, 70
Tautua, Glendal, 90
tautua 'ai taumalele (regular service by
    someone who resides outside the vil-
    lage), 58
tautua nofo tuavae (daily service in the
    household), 58
TBIs. *See* traumatic brain injuries
Tcherkézoff, Serge, 53
Team American Sāmoa, 42
television, 34–35
Te'o, Alema, 40–41, 62–63
territorial status, U.S., 13
They Call It Pro Football, 32
Thompson, Jack ("The Throwin' Samoan"),
    145, 146, 147–148
Thompson, Papāli'itele Jack Tihati, 52
Tinoisamoa, Pisa, 52, 82; 'ava ceremony
    for, 50–51; in *Polynesian Power*,
    80–81, 87
Tisa (governors dinner host), 66–67
Title IX, 93, 176n30

toa: Faga'itua Vikings styling as, 139–140; femininity regarding, 136–137; Leiataua-Lesa on, 136; masculinities regarding, 136, 137–138, 141; meaning of, 135–138; Vui on, 135; warrior concept regarding, 138

toa o le vasa (warriors of the sea), 139

Togiola (Governor), 84

Toloa, Vaniah, 138–140

Tom Brown's School Days (Hughes), 133

To'oto'o, Maria, 65

transnational diaspora, 11, 61, 152

traumatic brain injuries (TBIS), 21, 126, 131; CTE connection with, 127; reckoning with, 154; youth concussion laws on, 128

Trimbur, Lucia, 178n12

Troy and Theodora Polamalu Foundation, 31, 48–49

Tuiasosopo, Upu, 65–66

Tui Atua, Tupua Tamasese Ta'isi Efi, 58

Tulafono, Togiola, 74

Tutuila, 15, 23, 59, 134; football development in, 31–32, 35; Pago Pago in, 27–28; professional athletes return to, 44; sport camps in, 49, 50, 62–63, 64; Ta'ase coaching in, 56–58

Ultra Performance Camp, 105

Under-19 competitions, 41, 42

underfunding, of schools, 177n4

United States, continental (U.S.): American Sāmoa relationship with, 12–13, 21; Black athletes racial mythography in, 88; football development in, 30; football players cultural identity in, 149;

imperialism, 7–8, 153, 165n42, 165n44; muscular masculinity in, 133

University of Hawai'i, 91, 136, 159n2, 160n5

University of Michigan, 126

University of Montana Grizzlies, 25

University of Montana Hall of Fame, 23–27, 46

University of Oregon, 99

University of Washington, 98

Uperesa, Keith, 65, 166n8

Uperesa, Tu'ufuli Kalapu, 38; American Sāmoa return of, 44–45; as coach, 36, 39–40, 45, 63; later life of, 45–47, 147; physical costs on, 120; Polynesian Pipeline journey of, 27–29, 30, 42–44; at University of Montanna, 23–27

U.S. *See* United States, continental

USA Football, 142

US Naval Station Tutuila, 27

U.S. West Coast Pacific Islander youth, 94–95

Vaeao, Laolagi Savali, 36, 39–40

Van Camp Seafood Company, 14

Veterans Memorial Stadium, 62, 64

village rivalries, 36, 42

Waldroup, Heather, 77, 174n8

warrior, 139; etymology of, 138; Nafanua as, 135, 137; stereotypes, 73, 74, 101. *See also* Polynesian Gridiron Warrior

Willis, Paul, 112, 113

Young, George, 107

youth football, 142–145